The London Revolution 1640-1643

Publisher's Opening Note

What you are about to read is a deeply personal work and complete expression of its author's exploration of the truth. As a result, we strongly encourage you to explore all of the details and implications of anything you discover or encounter as a result of this work.

In accordance with The Mad Duck Coalition's mission of encouraging and providing intellectual stimulation of all kinds, we cannot endorse any of the ideas presented by any individual member of our flock.

The only things we endorse are the authorial integrity of the works we publish and the quality of intellectual engagements that they produce and inspire.

Praise for *The London Revolution 1640-1643*

"Feisty, fearless and fascinating: this book spotlights London's revolutionary upheavals at the start of Britain's seventeenth-century Civil War; it shows how London's revolutionary role has been too often downplayed; and it explains its long-term significance for later generations. Michael Sturza will provoke many debates – and a good thing too!"

— Penelope J. Corfield, emeritus Prof. London University; Fellow of the Royal Historical Society (UK); and President of the International Society for Eighteenth-Century Studies

"Michael Sturza brings the London Revolution 1640-1643 to life — a welcome tonic for tough times. …one is reminded of the complexities of social change and the essential role of class struggle… 17th century England has much to teach us relevant to the 21st century. Sturza is a vital addition to the canon. An excellent reader for students and the general public alike."

— Marvin Surkin, specialist in comparative urban politics and social change and co-author of *Detroit: I Do Mind Dying*

"A passionate, Marxist analysis exploring the role of structural and socio-economic problems in radicalizing people on the eve of the English civil war. Combing high and low politics, Sturza stresses the importance of class conflict and reminds us just how revolutionary the English revolution was."

— Tim Harris, editor of *Studies in Early Modern Cultural, Political and Social History* series and *The European Legacy journal*

"A richly detailed and documented contribution! Michael Sturza not only refutes…conservative revisionist historians…but provides significant evidence of how organized and militant social forces…played a decisive role in the end of British feudalism. …Sturza demonstrates the value and efficacy of historical materialism for understanding the… dimensions of social change and revolution."

— Burton Lee Artz, director of the Center for Global Studies at Purdue University Northwest

"The London Revolution *opens critically important new ground for understanding the English Revolution as a bottom up bourgeois revolution. Sturza picks up where Christopher Hill left off."*

— Robert Ovetz, editor of *Workers' Inquiry and Global Class Struggle: Strategies, Tactics, Objectives* and author of *When Workers Shot Back: Class Conflict from 1877 to 1921*

"Michael Sturza's book is an important contribution to correcting the distortions of modern historians about the nature of the English Civil War of 1641–49. Sturza concentrates on the events and movements in England's capital, London, and delivers a compelling analysis from a Marxist perspective."

— Michael Roberts, author of *The Great Recession – a Marxist view*; *The Long Depression*; *Marx 200: a review of Marx's economics*; and co-editor of *World in Crisis*

"No-one doubts the French Revolution, but the English Revolution remains contentious. Sturza shows that, though the English was as messy as the Guillotine was precise, capitalism's rise resulted in feudalism's beheading in the tumultuous days of the 1640s."

— Steve Keen, recipient of the Revere Award from RWER, co-author of "The Incoherent Emperor: A Heterodox Critique of Neoclassical Microeconomic Theory", and author of *Debunking Economics*

"There is no more important question for historians and social theorists than determining the driving force behind modern social change. Michael Sturza's delightful and concise work, The London Revolution [1640-1643]*…shows definitively that class was the driving force setting the stage for 1689. This is gripping history, fast-paced, well-written, and solidly based in theory and evidence."*

— Joseph Varga, president of the Working Class Studies Association

"The London Revolution 1640-1643…*offers a fresh and well-documented perspective on existing scholarship, bringing its portrait of the English Revolution sharply to life. …Sturza illustrates how the protests and street battles in the early 1640s foreshadowed the Civil War… [and] how the economic struggle against feudalism in England was inseparable from the ideological struggle…."*

— Alan Wallis, reviewer for *Marx and Philosophy Review of Books*

"In a refreshingly polemical call to arms for Marxist historiography, Michael Sturza convincingly argues that mid-seventeenth century class struggle in London decisively shaped the English Revolution…[and] the great historical transformation from feudalism to capitalism."

— Andrew Hartman, author of *A War for the Soul of America: A History of the Culture Wars* and *Karl Marx in America.*

"Exceptionally well organized and presented, [The London Revolution 1640 - 1643] is a particularly well written work of exemplary scholarship."

— Midwest Book Review

Complete commentary available at thmaduco.org

The London Revolution 1640-1643

Class Struggles in 17th Century England

Michael Sturza

New York

2022 The Mad Duck Coalition ™ First Edition

THE MAD DUCK COALITION, its imprints, and colophones are trademarks of The Mad Duck Coalition, LLC.

For information about our special discounts for libraries, reviews, bookstores, and academic professionals, contact us through our form at thmaduco.org

Published in the United States under In The Weeds, an imprint of The Mad Duck Coalition, LLC, New York.

Cover art by David Provolo

Author Photo by Joseph Semien

Back cover graphic is the coat of arms of the East India Company

ISBN: 978-1-956389-03-6

Library of Congress Control Number: 2021946942

www.themadduckcoalition.org

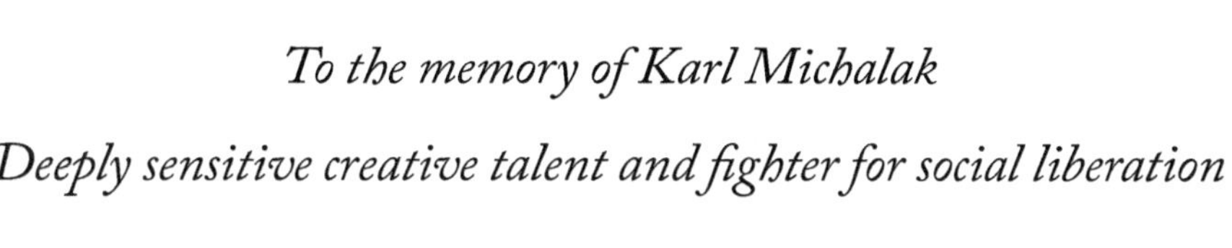

To the memory of Karl Michalak

Deeply sensitive creative talent and fighter for social liberation

Table of Contents

PREFACE

And thus I hope even British respectability will not be overshocked if I use...the term "historical materialism," to designate that view of the course of history which seeks the ultimate cause and the great moving power of all important historic events in the economic development of society, in the changes in the modes of production and exchange, in the consequent division of society into distinct classes, and in the struggles of these classes against one another.

~Frederick Engels[1]

The diminishing band who continue to write about the period have largely discarded the grand narratives of liberty and revolution. They no longer believe that two sides in the war were divided by great differences, whether social or ideological. Clear-cut interpretations of the conflict have given way to a complex and confusing story of contingency, accident, and unintended consequences.

~Keith Thomas[2]

The history of the English Revolution, Civil War, unsettled Commonwealth and degenerating Protectorate took place during the years 1640-1660. The period remains a divisive line in English history, despite less notice being taken of it in British schools and the popular press than was the case not so long ago. Just as the effects and controversies of the American Civil War are still extant, those of the English Civil War in Britain (and also Ireland) remain alive today.[3] "The past is never dead," William Faulkner famously wrote, "it's not even past." By abolishing slave labor in favor of capitalist wage labor, the defeat of the Southern plantation owners made the U.S. Civil War the last progressive bourgeois revolution to occur. Two hundred years earlier, the English Revolution destroyed the absolutist feudal political system in the British Isles. The epoch of capitalist society under the rule of the bourgeois class had begun, even if only tentatively. The issues at stake in the struggles of 1640 and after were not only whether sovereignty, that is, political power, resided in the monarch or Parliament; or whether there would be freedom of religion, how much and for whom; but whether the entire social and political system would be modified to allow for a greater possibility of better living for the masses, and the greater democracy needed to achieve it.

The Magna Carta of 1215 had led to a monarchy attenuated by a Parliament, and the 1530s Reformation of Henry VIII denuded the Church of its eternal inviolability. These rich traditions imbued the English events with

1 Introduction to *Socialism: Utopian and Scientific*, in *Karl Marx and Frederick Engels Selected Works* (New York: International Publishers, 1892, 1970), 386-387

2 "The Truth About Oliver Cromwell," *New York Review of Books* 59, no. 17 (November 8, 2012), http://www.nybooks.com/articles/archives/2012/nov/08/truth-about-oliver-cromwell Accessed June 20, 2013

3 In 2016, Her Majesty's government argued in court that foreign affairs were the royal prerogative! Stephen Castle, "Without a Constitution, 'Brexit' Is Guided by a Prerogative. But Whose?," *The New York Times*, October 16, 2016, https://www.nytimes.com/2016/10/17/world/europe/without-a-constitution-brexit-is-guided-by-a-prerogative-but-whose.html?searchResultPosition=1 Accessed April 25, 2017

a political and religious background that simultaneously encouraged and misled the aroused populace. The issues they fought over, what we today call democratic rights, would eventually be codified in the 1689 Bill of Rights, and the initial amendments to the U.S. Constitution. Their origins, however, lie here in the mid-17th century.[4]

The great French Revolution is conventionally considered the start of the modern, i.e., capitalist, age. The English Revolution, in comparison, was an even more ambiguous, partial, and contradictory affair. This complexity was captured by the socialist Oxford historian R. H. Tawney, who when asked whether the English Civil War was a bourgeois revolution replied, "Of course it was a bourgeois revolution. The problem is the bourgeoisie was on both sides."[5] Unlike France in 1789, during the 1640s in England there were no scenes in Parliament declaring feudalism abolished wholesale, no Terror unleashed against the aristocracy, no land redistributed to the peasantry. And while Oliver Cromwell was as iron-willed and decisive as Robespierre in pursuit of the military defeat of the king, he was a most inconsistent revolutionary in its aftermath.

Thus the prominent issues of the period, and the way they were resolved at the time, continue to give rise to fierce partisan debate. Many historians, beginning with the royalist Earl of Clarendon, have been unhappy with the way matters turned out, or, with a jaundiced eye on current political conflicts, wished to deny the revolutionary nature of the changes that occurred.[6] Particularly over the last fifty years, as the post-WWII order has been slowly crumbling, the topic once again became extraordinarily contentious among historians, necessarily reflecting the political leanings of the contenders. As one rightwing Revisionist historian put it, "We are all at heart either Royalists or Roundheads."[7] By the early 1980s, Revisionist historians had virtually drowned out the Marxist class analysis.

What many historians (both pro and con) regarded as the Marxist view of English events was predominant in British academia during the mid-20th century. Its prevalence was largely due to the efforts of the English historian

4 In 2015, the spate of articles in the popular press insisting on the irrelevancy of Magna Carta at its 800th anniversary only further demonstrated how at least a major section of the bourgeois class had freed itself from any moral compunctions regarding the welfare and rights of the people at large, so much so that it spit on a primary source of its own history. See e.g., Tom Ginsburg, "Stop Revering Magna Carta," *The New York Times*, June 14, 2015, https://www.nytimes.com/2015/06/15/opinion/stop-revering-magna-carta.html?searchResultPosition=1 Accessed June 15, 2015. Cf. Ferdinand Mount, "Back to Runnymede," *London Review of Books* 37, no. 8 (23 April 2015), https://www.lrb.co.uk/the-paper/v37/n08/ferdinand-mount/back-to-runnymede Accessed 1 July 2016 for a more mainstream, Tory view.

5 Christopher Hill, "Conclusion," in *Change and Continuity in 17th-Century England* (New Haven: Yale University Press, 1974, 1991), 281; R. C. Richardson, *The Debate on the English Revolution* (Manchester: Manchester University Press, 1998), 124

6 Edward Hyde, Earl of Clarendon, an advisor to both Charles I and II, wrote the first history of the Revolution and Civil War.

7 Richardson, *The Debate on the English Revolution*, 239, quoting Kevin Sharpe, who "…sided relentlessly with the people in power." David Cressy, "The Blindness of Charles I," *Huntington Library Quarterly* 78, no. 4 (Winter 2015): 640, 653, https://www.jstor.org/stable/10.1525/hlq.2015.78.4.637 Accessed February 13, 2019

Christopher Hill. His very short first book, *The English Revolution 1640*,[8] provides a concise analysis that completely rejects and replaces the portrayals of his predecessors, whether royalist, Tory or Whig (liberal).[9] To one degree or another, bourgeois historiography told a Civil War story of politicized religious fanatics who first aided and then usurped Parliament's fight for democracy, murdered the king, and established an aberrant theocratic state.[10] Hill presented the Revolution and Civil War as a conflict between *social classes.* Underlying his oeuvre was the basic Marxist tenet that the ideas and outlook of individuals were firstly impacted by their economic position, and he identified the petty bourgeois rural yeomen and urban artisans as the social basis of Parliament's New Model Army.[11] All attempts to study this period must begin with Hill's work.

A member of the Communist Party from 1935-1957, Hill was prolific, turning out numerous essays and reviews in addition to major interpretive studies, most of which are still in print or available. Much of his work concentrated on the more radical and democratic aspects and individuals of the general Puritan movement. In particular, he revived interest in the "far left," i.e., most radical, separatist religious sects, especially the early communist Gerrard Winstanley, leader of the Diggers.[12] His most thorough exposition of such groups is *The World Turned Upside Down.*[13] If he bent the stick too far in his imputation of revolutionary potential to such forces this was a small price to pay for demonstrating their influence on 17th-century society and later political thought. Hill also used the cultural history of the period to illuminate it in a broader context. His book *The Century of Revolution 1603-1714*,[14] spanning the entire Stuart era, remains the best introduction to the topic, although in one or two places it strays from the earlier analysis of *The English Revolution 1640,* to take account of some conservative historical claims current at the time.

While *The Century of Revolution* unavoidably treats many events in brief, more unsatisfactory is Hill's scant mention of the initial revolution in London described here.[15] This singular omission is also true of his similar work, published a few years later, *Reformation to Industrial Revolution 1530-*

8 Christopher Hill, *The English Revolution 1640* (London: Lawrence & Wishart, 1940, 1985). Also available at Marxists Internet Archive, https://www.marxists.org/archive/hill-christopher/english-revolution/index.htm Accessed 15 May 2016

9 Hill wrote it just before he went to serve in WWII, in case he did not return.

10 This view began as official Restoration state policy with the 1660 Act of Indemnity and Oblivion. "The conflict and the Commonwealth were to be seen as an aberration, an eclipse…" Jesse Childs, "Reduced to Ashes and Rubbage," *London Review of Books* 41, no. 1 (3 January 2019), https://www.lrb.co.uk/the-paper/v41/n01/jessie-childs/reduced-to-ashes-and-rubbage Accessed 18 January 2019

11 Hill, *1640*, 59, 62, 63

12 The Diggers, or True Levellers, were poor people who attempted to plant crops on common or unused land. They were easily and cruelly attacked and dispersed.

13 Christopher Hill, *The World Turned Upside Down: Radical Ideas During the English Revolution* (London: Penguin Books, 1980)

14 Christopher Hill, *The Century of Revolution 1603-1714* (New York: W.W. Norton, 1961, 1980)

15 Hill, *Century*, 102-103

1780,[16] an even wider-ranging, somewhat more leisurely introductory social history centered around the Civil War period. Both of these are basic texts, invaluable for their high-level and comprehensive view of the era, but notably lacking in material on the 1640-1643 mass movement in London.

It is necessary to bear in mind that Hill's politics had been formed in a party loyal to Moscow at a time when it was moving in an overtly reformist direction under Stalin (known as the "popular front" period).[17] Thus he saw Danton, rather than Robespierre, as Cromwell's later historical analog,[18] and he regarded the Russian Revolutions of 1905 and February 1917 as bourgeois rather than workers' revolutions, despite the presence of councils (*soviets* in Russian) formed by workers and soldiers.[19] It is never easy to learn that the political tool for one's aims and ideals has been found wanting. Without an understanding of why and how the 1917 Bolshevik Revolution degenerated, not a few ex-Communists arrived at a cynical view of "the god that failed." Hill was very far from these, but he did make a certain peace with bourgeois academia. His post-1957 writings, erudite and valuable, lack his earlier militant edge, while remaining informed by his political past.

Of greatest consequence was the view Hill and Tawney held in the 1940s and '50s conflating a misconstrued "progressive gentry," with the bourgeois revolutionary leadership.[20]

> Professor R. H. Tawney and others have analyzed the cleavage *within the landed class*, between what Marxists would call "feudal" and "bourgeois" elements, which developed in the decades before 1640 and *which underlay the divisions in the civil war*.[21] [Emphasis added]

Tawney's purposeful but flawed 1941 essay, "The Rise of the Gentry, 1558-1640"[22] kicked off a major, but inconclusive, academic controversy over the gentry that lasted into the early 1960s. Hill's view of a progressive gentry, distinguished from its "feudal elements," often cited Tawney's work, but was schematic to begin with. On the one hand, the basis for this distinc-

16 Christopher Hill, *Reformation to Industrial Revolution* (London: Penguin Books, 1967, 1992)

17 The "popular front" (aka "people's front") was (and sometimes still is) a collaboration between capitalist and reformist workers parties for electoral purposes, running on a common, watered-down, i.e., non-revolutionary, program acceptable to the bourgeois elements in it.

18 Christopher Hill, "Political Animal," *New York Review of Books* 24, no. 10 (June 9, 1977), http://www.nybooks.com/articles/archives/1977/jun/09/political-animal/ Accessed September 15, 2013

19 Christopher Hill, "The English Civil War Interpreted by Marx and Engels," *Science & Society* 12, no. 1 (Winter 1948): 135, http://www.jstor.org/stable/40399879 Accessed 20 November 2016

20 Hill, *1640*, 29, 35, 38, 54, 59; *Century*, 87; Christopher Hill, "Lord Clarendon and the Puritan Revolution," in *Puritanism and Revolution* (London: Pimlico, 1958, 2001), 192. This was despite Hill's own earlier statements: "But the House of Commons did not make the revolution: its members were subject to pressure from outside, from the people of London, the yeoman and artisans of the home counties." *1640*, 52; "The House of Commons elected in the autumn of 1640 was not a revolutionary assembly. Elected on the traditional propertied franchise, the M.P.s were a cross-section of the ruling class." *Oliver Cromwell 1658-1958* (London: The Historical Association, 1958), 12. Reprinted in *The Collected Essays of Christopher Hill* Vol. 3 (Amherst: University of Massachusetts Press, 1981, 1986)

21 Christopher Hill, "Historians on the Rise of British Capitalism," *Science & Society* 14, no. 4 (Fall 1950): 308, http://www.jstor.org/stable/40400023 Accessed 15 December 2016

22 *The Economic History Review* 11, no. 1 (1941), http://www.jstor.org/stable/2590708 Accessed 20 November 2016

tion within the gentry was unwarranted — land in the 17th century was no longer governed by feudal economic relations, however much feudal rank and patriarchal attitudes continued. On the other, it collapsed any disparities between two *different* classes, the gentry and the rapidly developing bourgeois, or capitalist, class that were acting in concert. This collapse flowed from Tawney's assertion that "The landowner living on the profits and rents of commercial farming, and the merchant or banker…represented, not two classes, but one. Judged by the source of their incomes, both were equally *bourgeois*."[23] Although commercial leasing of farms by the upper class was far from unknown at the beginning of the seventeenth century, copyhold tenantry was still preponderant, and a source of wide conflict.

Pressed by anti-Marxists, Hill began to retreat from the notion that a section of the gentry had led the revolution.[24] But he appears to have been unable to present any good alternative to it, despite Valerie Pearl's seminal account of the London revolutionary bourgeois leadership in her 1961 study.[25] Forced to acknowledge the untenability of his position,[26] the muddied argument left Hill open to attacks pointing to an alleged lack of clear-cut class divisions in the anti-absolutist struggle.[27] By 1974, and again in 1980, he attempted to answer his critics by one-sidedly stressing the revolution as an objective fact or unconscious process.

> …the phrase [bourgeois revolution] in Marxist usage does *not* mean a revolution made by or consciously willed by the bourgeoisie. … The English revolution, like all revolutions, was caused by the breakdown of the old society… The hypothesis is that this outcome, and the Revolution itself, were made possible by…the structures, fractures, and pressures of the society, rather than the wishes of leaders, which dictated the outbreak of revolution and shaped the state which emerged from it. … Once the old constraints had broken down, or been broken, the shape of the new order was determined in the long run by the needs of a society in which large numbers of unideological men minded their own business.[28] [Emphasis in original]

23 Tawney, "Rise of the Gentry," 18 [Emphasis in original]; Hill, *Century*, 87

24 Christopher Hill, "Recent Interpretations of the Civil War," *History* 41, nos. 141, 143 (February, October, 1956): 70-71, https://www.jstor.org/stable/24402908 Accessed 25 April, 2020. Reprinted in *Puritanism and Revolution* (London: Pimlico, 1958, 2001)

25 Valerie Pearl, *London and the Outbreak of the Puritan Revolution* (London: Oxford University Press, 1961). Hill's avoidance of the London events is especially odd given that Pearl's book, published the same year as Hill's *The Century of Revolution* and listed in its bibliography, was based on her Ph.D. thesis reportedly supervised by Hill. Her thesis is cited in *Oliver Cromwell 1658-1958*, 13 fn. 9. The reprint in *The Collected Essays of Christopher Hill* Vol. 3 cites Pearl's book instead.

26 Christopher Hill, "Parliament and People in 17th-Century England," *Past & Present*, no. 92 (August, 1981): 101, 118, http://www.jstor.org/stable/650751 Accessed 26 November 2016. Revised and reprinted in *The Collected Essays of Christopher Hill* Vol. 3. See the section in Chapter 7 below "The English gentry, an anomalous class."

27 See J. H. Hexter, "Storm Over the Gentry" (1958), and "Personal Retrospect and Postscript" (1961), in *Reappraisals in History* (Chicago: University of Chicago Press, 1979), 117-162, 255-258; Robert Brenner, *Merchants and Revolution: Commercial Change, Political Conflict, and London's Overseas Traders, 1550-1653* (London: Verso, 2003), 640-641; Henry Heller, *The Birth of Capitalism: A 21st Century Perspective* (London: Pluto Press, 2011), 119, https://www.jstor.org/stable/j.ctt183p671.8 Accessed 16 December 2018

28 Christopher Hill, "A Bourgeois Revolution?," in *Three British Revolutions: 1641, 1688, 1776*, ed. J.G.A. Pocock (Princeton: Princeton University Press, 1980), 110-112, https://www.jstor.org/stable/j.ctt7zvts5.7 Accessed 25 April 2020. Reprinted in *The Collected Essays of Christopher Hill* Vol.

His opponents further seized on this as a blow to Marxist theory, as indeed it was.[29] It is flesh and blood human beings who make history, and revolutions, at least successful ones, don't occur without a leadership.

So who *did* lead the revolution in London? Puritan clergy played a considerable role, and well-off middle layers of the guild memberships were drawn into it by events, but the key answer comes from Robert Brenner's convincing work on the free-trading Atlantic merchants in his study *Merchants and Revolution*.[30] This book was not published until 1993, although a 50-page article by Brenner on the topic was published twenty years before in Hill's own journal.[31] While Hill was clearly aware of the importance of this new group of English merchants to the post-Civil War regimes,[32] he appears never to have commented on their leading political role during the 1630s and early 1640s.[33] He did recommend Brenner's book, along with those of others, in the preface to a reissued edition of his essays,[34] but if he reviewed or wrote about it in the last decade of his life I am unaware of it. Even in retreat he could elegantly refute conservative critics at times, but he was a poor polemicist, too polite and too often advancing weak or vague arguments. Nevertheless, he supplied a comprehensive explication of the period that in fact very largely holds up. His great credit was in pointing out and stubbornly adhering to the enormous advances made as a result of the revolutionary decades, and his identification of ordinary people from the lower classes brought into active political life. More than anyone else he astutely asserted, not least through repeated analyses of Puritan ideology, the understanding of the mid-17th century events as a *social* revolution, in place of a religious or "Puritan" revolution.

During the 1940s and 1950s Hill had to contend with conservative historians, particularly Hugh Trevor-Roper.[35] Beginning in the 1970s, however,

3 (Amherst: University of Massachusetts Press, 1980, 1986); Hill, "Conclusion," 279. See also David Underdown, "Puritanism, Revolution, and Christopher Hill," *The History Teacher* 22, no. 1 (November 1988): 69-71, http://www.jstor.org/stable/493099 Accessed 22 November 2017

29 See in particular the slippery article by the liberal Lawrence Stone, "The Bourgeois Revolution of Seventeenth-Century England Revisited," *Past & Present*, no. 109 (November 1985), http://www.jstor.org/stable/650609 Accessed 10 August 2015

30 On the Atlantic merchants see Chapter 8 below. Hill himself had mentioned a distinction between "big trading bourgeoisie" and "free-trade bourgeoisie". *1640*, 59

31 Robert Brenner, "The Civil War Politics of London's Merchant Community," *Past & Present*, no. 58 (February 1973), http://www.jstor.org/stable/650257 Accessed 19 November 2016. For the magazine's history see Christopher Hill, R. H. Hilton, and E. J. Hobsbawm, "Past and Present. Origins and Early Years," *Past & Present*, no. 100 (August 1983), http://www.jstor.org/stable/650618 Accessed 10 August 2015

32 Hill, *Reformation*, 156-157

33 The closest reference Hill seems to have made about the Atlantic merchants prior to the Civil War is a comment in passing: "A break-through came with a combination of religious dissidents (Puritan and Catholic) as settlers [in North America] with sympathetic merchants who were prepared to forego immediate profit…" Christopher Hill, "Plain Sailing," *New York Review of Books* 21, no. 18 (November 14, 1974), http://www.nybooks.com/articles/archives/1974/nov/14/plain-sailing/ Accessed September 15, 2013

34 Christopher Hill, "Preface to the Revised Edition," *A Nation of Change and Novelty* (London: Bookmarks, 1993), 11

35 Who once denigrated the Civil War period as "an untidy interruption." Robert Ashton, "The Civil War and the Class Struggle," in *The English Civil War and After 1642-1658*, ed. R. H. Parry (Berkeley: University of California Press, 1970), 93

a more deliberate backlash began. Geoffrey Elton had provided an inverted paradigm in 1965,[36] but it was Conrad Russell (son of Bertrand by his third wife and later 5th Earl Russell) who first attracted wide attention. Like Elton, he attacked what was alleged to be the prevailing Marxist orthodoxy of a "high road to civil war,"[37] i.e., that it was inevitable. "Before we explain why the English Revolution happened, we should ask again whether it ever did happen," Russell wrote in 1974.[38] To pose the question this way was to take aim at, not just an interpretation, but the complex of facts themselves.

> Much of Russell's broad account…rests on the claims that virtually all Englishmen believed in 'the rule of law' and that no profound differences of political principle divided them before the Civil War. … For Russell and Elton, virtually everyone held that the country was a limited monarchy. Since there was practically no dissension on this question, the war could not have been about it.[39]

Russell's challenge was soon taken up by an increasingly reactionary group of younger historians self-consciously calling themselves Revisionists. With the elections of Margaret Thatcher and Ronald Reagan and the political wrench toward conservatism in 1980, this tendency gathered steam, heaping scorn and calumny upon any work even hinting at a class analysis, or indeed any analysis at all. "Revisionism was a revolt against materialist or determinist histories and historiographies…" wrote an English participant much later, "…a rejection of the social history of politics but also a rejection of the relevance of social change."[40]

36 Geoffrey Elton, "A High Road to Civil War?" reprinted in *Studies in Tudor and Stuart Politics and Government: Papers and Reviews 1946-1972* Vol. 1 (Cambridge: Cambridge University Press, 1974); Robert Zaller, "The Concept of Opposition in Early Stuart England," *Albion* 12, no. 3 (Autumn 1980): 220-223, https://www.jstor.org/stable/4049254 Accessed 25 February 2019

37 Conrad Russell, "Parliamentary History in Perspective 1604-1629," *History* 61, no. 201 (1976): 2-3, http://www.jstor.org/stable/24409552 Accessed 26 December 2016; Robert Zaller, "What Does the English Revolution Mean? Recent Historiographical Interpretations of Mid-Seventeenth Century England," *Albion* 18, no. 4 (Winter 1986): 618-620, https://www.jstor.org/stable/4050133 Accessed 11 November 2018. Zaller, "The Concept of Opposition," 223-228

38 Conrad Russell, "Was there an English Revolution?: The Rump Parliament, 1648-1653," *The Times Higher Education Supplement*, 8 March 1974, quoted in J. C. Richardson, *The Debate on the English Revolution* (London: Methuen & Co., 1977), 146

39 Johann Sommerville, "English and European Political Ideas in the Early Seventeenth Century: Revisionism and the Case of Absolutism," *Journal of British Studies* 35, no. 2 (April 1996): 170, https://www.jstor.org/stable/175798 Accessed 13 May 2019; Peter Lake, "From Revisionist to Royalist History; or, Was Charles I the First Whig Historian," *Huntington Library Quarterly* 78, no. 4 (Winter 2015): 676 fn. 63, https://www.jstor.org/stable/10.1525/hlq.2015.78.4.657 Accessed December 20, 2019; Mark E. Kennedy, "Legislation, Foreign Policy, and the 'Proper Business' of the Parliament of 1624," *Albion* 23, no. 1 (Spring 1991): 41-42, https://www.jstor.org/stable/4050541, Accessed 1 August 2019

40 John Morrill, "Revisionism's Wounded Legacies," *Huntington Library Quarterly* 78, no. 4 (Winter 2015): 577, 583, https://www.jstor.org/stable/10.1525/hlq.2015.78.4.577 Accessed February 13, 2019; John Walter, "Kissing Cousins? Social History/Political History before and after the Revisionist Moment," *Huntington Library Quarterly* 78, no. 4 (Winter 2015): 703, https://www.jstor.org/stable/10.1525/hlq.2015.78.4.703 Accessed June 6, 2019; John Sanderson, "Conrad Russell's Ideas," *History of Political Thought* 14, no. 1 (Spring 1993): 85, https://www.jstor.org/stable/26214422 Accessed 31 December 2018; Anthony Milton, "Arminians, Laudians, Anglicans, and Revisionists: Back to Which Drawing Board?" *Huntington Library Quarterly* 78, no. 4 (Winter 2015): 729, https://www.jstor.org/stable/10.1525/hlq.2015.78.4.723 Accessed February 13, 2019; Brenner, *Merchants and Revolution*, 644-647. See also Derek Hirst, "Of Labels and Situations: Revisionisms and Early Stuart Studies," *Huntington Library Quarterly* 78, no. 4 (Winter 2015): 596-598, https://www.jstor.org/stable/10.1525/hlq.2015.78.4.595 Accessed April 2, 2019

Attempts to summarize trends or generate theory were denounced as illegitimate inventions, divorced from and imposed on facts in hindsight.[41] Events occurred only by accident or coincidence, or at most because of free-standing choices made by high-ranking individuals: "'the people who count,' to use Mark Kishlansky's phrase."[42] Such a focus by reactionaries like Kishlansky was a deliberate attempt to eliminate class conflict. Any exception to general trends could be used to invalidate social analysis, and of course one could always be found. With so much turmoil in widely different parts of the country during that time only localized studies had any reliability or legitimacy, they claimed.[43] Within the field,

> ...revisionism became more than an interpretation of a particular time and place in history; it laid claim to a way of doing history. And it is as a methodological agenda rather than as a particular version of events that revisionism has enjoyed the greatest influence.[44]

As such it was primarily a pragmatic effort to find some way to counter the Marxist philosophy of history. E. H. Carr described the view that, "Knowledge is knowledge for some purpose. The validity of the knowledge depends on the validity of the purpose,"[45] and the Revisionists' purpose was perfectly clear. Their virulent repudiation of revolutionary history led to, as John Morrill admitted, a colleague once congratulating him for "'explaining why no civil war broke out in England in 1642.'"[46]

One method Revisionists attempted was to invert historical reality:

> ...Parliament was not gaining in importance but was actually becoming less important; the court was not politically insignificant compared with Parliament but was actually more significant than Parliament; the Crown's opponents were not innovators but were actually conservatives; and so on.[47]

As David Underdown noted, some Revisionists heavily stressed an alleged consensus within the ruling class:

41 This spurious argument was anticipated in a furious 1975 attack on Hill by Hexter. See William G. Palmer, "The Burden of Proof: J.H. Hexter and Christopher Hill," *Journal of British Studies* 19, no. 1 (Autumn 1979), https://www.jstor.org/stable/175685 Accessed 19 April 2020

42 Tim Harris, "Revisiting the Causes of the English Civil War," *Huntington Library Quarterly* 78, no. 4 (Winter 2015): 618, https://www.jstor.org/stable/10.1525/hlq.2015.78.4.615 Accessed December 31, 2018

43 Thomas Cogswell, "Coping with Revisionism in Early Stuart History," *The Journal of Modern History* 62, no. 3 (September 1990): 546, https://www.jstor.org/stable/1881176 Accessed 25 April 2019

44 Cynthia Herrup, "Revisionism — What's in a Name?," *Journal of British Studies* 35, no. 2 (April 1996): 137, http://www.jstor.org/stable/175796 Accessed 27 November 2016; Hill, "Parliament and People in 17th-Century England," 101; John Kenyon, "Revisionism and Post-Revisionism in Early Stuart History," *The Journal of Modern History* 64, no. 4 (December 1992): 692, http://www.jstor.org/stable/2124903 Accessed November 27, 2016

45 Edward Hallett Carr, *What Is History?* (New York: Vintage Books, 1961), 31

46 Mary Fulbrook, "The English Revolution and the Revisionist Revolt," *Social History* 7, no. 3 (October 1982): 252, https://www.jstor.org/stable/4285188 Accessed 30 July 2019; Hirst, "Revisionisms and Early Stuart Studies," 595

47 Milton, "Back to Which Drawing Board?" 724

> By marginalizing the parliamentary texts and defining the Court as the only public arena worthy of study, the earlier revisionists were able to depict a political nation that until 1640 was almost universally deferential and harmonious, and then suddenly exploded in rebellion. We might perhaps call this the big bang theory of the Civil War.[48]

With their heads in the sand, many Revisionists argued there was no relationship between the Parliaments of 1604-1629 and 1640,[49] disparaging any attempt to offer a synthetic account. "Is it right to assume, as always seems to be assumed, that a long-term, overall explanation is necessarily called for?"[50] Behind Peter Laslett's innocent-sounding question lies a sneer and a falsehood: that all history is merely a matter of events that happen to happen. "Conflict is a common enough form of social interaction," he maintained, "there is nothing special about the things that bring it about." [51] Perry Anderson rightly ascribed this to the "one-damn-thing-after-another view of the past."[52] The eminent historian of English agriculture, Joan Thirsk, could have been writing in answer to this sophistical assertion in a 1977 review:

> Economies, small or large, compete with one another, make demands on each other, and thereby drive each other to adopt new economic expedients having their own distinctive social repercussions. This constitutes the dynamic process of economic and social change. And the historian's herculean task is to trace and describe ever more exactly this perpetually spiraling movement, which carries distinctive regional economies forward along fresh paths, partly at their own choice, partly under the force of circumstances created outside them.[53]

The "herculean task" of local or regional studies can produce rewarding results, but they cannot by themselves answer the question of what caused the English Civil War; nor did early Revisionists try to.

> ...revisionism directly challenges the assumptions of the traditional schools in all of its key arguments: a rejection of teleological history; a refusal to accept uncritically the role of ideas and ideology as carriers of political principle (focusing instead on personality, faction, patronage, and high politics); a denial of long-term causation rooted in social or economic

48 David Underdown, *A Freeborn People: Politics and the Nation in Seventeenth-Century England* (Oxford: Clarendon Press, 1996), 6

49 Charles I called no parliaments between 1629 and 1640. See the section in Chapter 7 below "Personal Rule of the 1630s."

50 Peter Laslett, Forward to Hexter, *Reappraisals in History,* ix

51 Laslett, Forward, *Reappraisals in History*, x

52 Perry Anderson, "Maurice Thomson's War," *London Review of Books* 15, no. 21 (4 November 1993), https://www.lrb.co.uk/the-paper/v15/n21/perry-anderson/maurice-thomson-s-war Accessed 4 March 2019. See also David Underdown, "Merchants and Revolution: Commercial Change, Political Conflict, and London's Overseas Traders, 1550-1653 by Robert Brenner," *Albion* 26, no. 2 (Summer 1994), http://www.jstor.org/stable/4052332 Accessed 22 November 2017; Brian Manning, "The English Revolution and the Transition from Feudalism to Capitalism," *International Socialist Review* 2, no. 63 (Summer 1994), Marxists Internet Archive, https://www.marxists.org/history/etol/writers/manning/1994/xx/engrev.htm Accessed 1 June 2016

53 Joan Thirsk, "Economic and Social Development on a European-World Scale," *American Journal of Sociology* 82, no. 5 (March 1977): 1099, https://www.jstor.org/stable/2777816 Accessed October 12, 2018

> change. The revisionist view of seventeenth-century England sees a world where...order, unity, and consensus were the dominant political values...[54]

To support their atomization of history Revisionists attempted to substitute various constructs to blame for the Revolution: bad decisions by the king; the court's conflicts with some of the nobles; either the unimportance of the House of Commons (!) or its alleged unanimity; the local interests and/or opportunist appetites of MPs; or, later, religious enthusiasm,[55] thereby imitating the Whig narrative of a "Puritan revolution." Whatever kernels of truth existed here or there, these feeble or exaggerated explanations uniformly excluded any view of revolution, eliminating the possibility of any coherent progress whether in political or economic history.

> Any attempt to replace the model of a consensually unified, early modern world-view with one containing meaningful differences, even self-conscious opposition, will soon draw a revisionist charge of *anachronism*: forcing modern categories onto a premodern society. Revisionists rigorously police contemporary historical writing for interloping modern phenomena, social models, and schemes of analysis. ... This prerogative rigor regarding terminology and concepts aims not to keep the empirical discussion of historical change from starting off on the wrong foot, but to throttle it in its crib.[56] [Emphasis in original]

An example of the narrowness of the Revisionist outlook was described in a 2012 review:

> "Politics" is absent from [poet John] Milton's deeply political oeuvre because, for [Blair] Worden, politics is synonymous with the constitution. For Worden, it is only when Milton began writing explicitly about constitutional matters...that he became a political writer.[57]

A particular travesty in their campaign of vilification is their common amalgamation of the Whig and Marxist viewpoints, seeing the latter as only a more militant or more superficial version of the former, a conflation that became all too generally accepted.[58] That both Whigs and Marxists posit certain teleological views of history does not make them the same. Quite the contrary, there is an epic gulf between the condescending bourgeois nationalism of Whigs, with their mystical talk of "national character" and "spirit

54 S. K. Baskerville, "Puritans, Revisionists, and the English Revolution," *Huntington Library Quarterly* 61, no. 2 (1998): 151, https://www.jstor.org/stable/3817796 Accessed November 11, 2018

55 Theodore K. Rabb, "The Role of the Commons," *Past and Present*, no. 92 (August 1981): 59-60, https://www.jstor.org/stable/650749 Accessed 7 February 2019; Nicholas Tyacke, "Revolutionary Puritanism in Anglo-American Perspective," *Huntington Library Quarterly* 78, no. 4 (Winter 2015): 746, https://www.jstor.org/stable/10.1525/hlq.2015.78.4.745 Access May 30, 2019

56 James Holstun, *Ehud's Dagger: Class Struggle in the English Revolution* (London: Verso, 2002), 21

57 Phil Withington, "Past v. Present," *London Review of Books* 34, no. 9 (10 May 2012), https://www.lrb.co.uk/the-paper/v34/n09/phil-withington/past-v.-present Accessed August 9, 2013. This is an insightful critique of essays by Blair Worden, Trevor-Roper's protégé and literary executor.

58 "Was marxism ever anything more than whig history with statistics?" Glenn Burgess, "On Revisionism: An Analysis of Early Stuart Historiography in the 1970s and 1980s," *The Historical Journal* 33, no. 3 (September 1990): 609-610, https://www.jstor.org/stable/2639733 Accessed 22 November 2018; "the long reign of Whig historiography and its Marxist variant..." Zaller, "The Concept of Opposition," 220; Cogswell, "Coping with Revisionism," 545

of the times," versus the historical materialist, egalitarian internationalism of Marxism. "…the word materialism grates upon the ears of the immense majority of British readers. 'Agnosticism' might be tolerated, but materialism is utterly inadmissible,"[59] Engels wrote at the end of the 19th century. The liberal historian Lawrence Stone neither claimed nor was ever considered to be a Marxist, but Revisionists attacked him because he "adapted" Marx in his defense of a revolutionary view. Their inflated claims to have thus refuted Marxism were at best self-delusion.[60]

Revisionist historians certainly argued among themselves, but the tendency as a whole was only able to exist and become predominant due to the harsh rightwing program of strikebreaking and union-busting by Thatcher and Reagan, and the consequent body blow to the working class caused by de-industrialization, implemented by each country's ruling capitalists. In their desire to support this reactionary program, Revisionism rushed to extend conservative ideology into history itself. (A similar academic trend developed in France attacking the class analysis of the French Revolution.)[61] The collapse of the Stalinist bureaucracy in the USSR in 1991 set off an orgy of triumphalism by the imperialist powers, making it appear that Marxism and communism had "failed." In fact, despite its qualitative bureaucratic deformation, the Soviet Union had remained a fortress against the unrestrained imperialist mayhem that occurred after its fall. At the same time, though the heirs of Stalin in Moscow falsely claimed the mantle of the Russian Revolution, the obvious noncapitalist operation of the economy and society, along with, for example, the dissemination of the works of Marx and Lenin, left an imprint for all the struggling, exploited and oppressed laboring peoples of the world to look to. Cromwell's Protectorate played a similar role, for a shorter time, with regard to royalism.

The Revisionists had their effect, however, and they are not the only ones who seek to undersell the revolutionary nature of the period. With few exceptions, mainstream historians of all persuasions today regard the Marxist paradigm as disproven and unuseful.[62] This is largely based on the erroneous idea that Marxism constitutes "economic determinism," a purely objectivist accusation, which is treated as little more than a secular version of Calvin's predestinarianism.[63] Had it actually been so, the revolutionary classes would

59 Engels, Introduction to *Socialism: Utopian and Scientific,* 381

60 Morrill, "Revisionism's Wounded Legacies," 578-579, 582-583; Burgess, "On Revisionism," 612

61 See Eric Hobsbawm, *Echoes of the Marseillaise* (New Brunswick: Rutgers University Press, 1990); Bryan D. Palmer, "The Eclipse of Materialism: Marxism and the Writing of Social History in the 1980s," *Socialist Register* 26 (1990): 121, https://socialistregister.com/index.php/srv/article/view/5577 Accessed 14 November 2020

62 "But really, the important lessons had been learned by all, and at least down to the present, class war and the strangled triumph of liberal democracy are off the mainstream agenda." Morrill, "Revisionism's Wounded Legacies," 592. "…the 1640s witnessed a bourgeois revolution; while it is of course possible to make such an argument…sharp criticism of this mode… has led to its near total disappearance from recent history." Cogswell, "Coping with Revisionism," 541. "…the long out of fashion notion that the English Revolution was a bourgeois revolution." Buchanan Sharp, "The Place of the People in the English Revolution," *Theory and Society* 14, no. 1 (January 1985): 104, https://www.jstor.org/stable/657400 Accessed 16 June 2019

63 Morrill, "Revisionism's Wounded Legacies," 582

presumably never have suffered any defeats. "It should be noted that it was the Puritan ministers who did most to popularized (sic) teleology by insisting that their 'cause' was precisely what revisionist scholars deny it was: predestined."[64]

The Revisionist charge that Marxism reduced events solely to economics, and ignored purely political factors, is almost funny applied to the most consequential, and most feared, *political* movement in two different centuries. If there was reductionism at work, it was the Revisionists who were busy at it. No serious person could imagine giving credence to such a truncated, mechanical and linear method, and neither did Marx and Engels. Once the shibboleth of determinism is disposed of the enormous contributions of the 20th century leftwing historians come into focus.

The Marxist understanding of the English Revolution and Civil War as the result of a *class* conflict that overthrew the feudal political system and brought the bourgeoisie to power is correct.

> Men make their own history, but they do not make it just as they please; they do not make it under circumstances chosen by themselves, but under circumstances directly encountered, given and transmitted from the past.[65]

Those circumstances are firstly dictated by the technical level of a given society. They are the context that all economic and social interactions, of any kind, take place in, and no individual, organization, party, movement or class can escape from it. We may wonder at the advances of modern science, but those advances are also the limitations that modern society operates within.

> History does have a materialist base for Marxists but this does not mean that extra-economic or non-material forces can be ignored. In fact, the Marxist approach compels one to analyze social forms as totalities and to integrate economic with non-economic factors.[66]

This contradicts the normal bourgeois method of examining historical phenomena in isolation from each other. For Marx and Marxists, social classes are defined by their role in the economic production of goods. They are historically evolved structures one is born into, and may or may not (more often not) be able to transcend, depending on the obstacles and opportunities in a particular society.[67] The types of goods a society produces, who labors (or doesn't) to produce them, under what conditions and for whose benefit, must be the prerequisite questions for any historian. All other social, cultural, and ideological trends must be carefully analyzed in this light, otherwise history becomes a disembodied, idealist construction. "The intellectual historian

64 Baskerville, "Puritans, Revisionists, and the English Revolution," 157

65 Karl Marx, *The Eighteenth Brumaire of Louis Bonaparte,* in *Karl Marx and Frederick Engels Selected Works* (New York: International Publishers, 1852, 1970), 97

66 Jon S. Cohen, "The Achievements of Economic History: The Marxist School," *The Journal of Economic History* 38, no. 1 (March 1978): 31, https://www.jstor.org/stable/2119314 Accessed 16 June 2019

67 This abbreviated description should not be taken to mean all classes in society are equally stable, carry the same weight, or remain internally unchanging over time.

may (at his risk) pay no attention to economics, the economic historian to Shakespeare, but the social historian who neglects either will not get far." The understanding of the foundational aspect of economics was quite common among Continental European historians prior to WWII.[68]

That the bourgeois revolution occurred as it did in 17th century England was not foreordained; it could have developed differently (just as it did in France). But since it *did* develop as it did, tracing the historically specific, long-term process offers the best method to understand it. The snobbish focus of Revisionists on social consensus is merely a smokescreen. Whether open or not, there are always frictions and antagonisms in a class-divided society, even within classes. Their argument is a self-evidently conservative bias to reinforce the political status quo. In actuality, people simply make the best lives they can within the social system under which they live. It is therefore not the ordinary day-to–day workings of a society that are the most momentous, necessary as it is to understand these, but the exceptional, unordinary events that disturb its tranquility, often in complicated ways. Revolutions occur when the social class that rules society is overthrown by a lower class, permanently realigning the economic and legal systems to suit the requirements of the new ruling class. Such turnovers are progressive when they facilitate, sooner or later, an unmistakably higher level of economic production, and a corresponding expansion of political freedom. The Revisionists' opposition *on principle* to the idea of history as a process voids this essential aspect, substituting a very static, laboriously atomized view that directs their work; one that is simply unable to explain how or why societies change over time.

The purpose of the current work is to resurrect the events of the early to mid-17th century in England, centered in and around London, and examine the development of the factors that constituted those events a revolution. In the process how the young English class of bourgeois entrepreneurs grew, and came to replace the feudal monarchy and aristocracy in power, will be shown. Much as Marx sketched out,[69] one of the unique factors in England's case, enabling the bourgeoisie's advance, was an *alliance* between its vanguard elements, and a section of the aristocracy whose interests paralleled its own. The London mass movement and its bourgeois leadership

> carried out a revolution in London itself. The municipal revolt of 1641–1642 involved no mere replacement of "ins" by "outs." The citizen militants shattered the old oligarchic constitution; in the process, they achieved at least a partial transformation in the social foundations of political power in the City.[70]

68 Eric Hobsbawm, "From Social History to the History of Society," *Daedalus* 100, no. 1 (Winter 1971): 21-22, 25, https://www.jstor.org/stable/20023989 Accessed 4 April 2020. Reprinted in *On History* (New York: The New Press, 1997)

69 Karl Marx, "A Review of Guizot's Book 'Why Has the English Revolution Been Successful?,'" in *Marx and Engels On Britain* (Moscow: Foreign Languages Publishing House, 1850, 1962), 347. A different translation, with the title "England's 17th Century Revolution," is at Marxists Internet Archive, https://www.marxists.org/archive/marx/works/1850/02/english-revolution.htm Accessed 4 April 2017.

70 Brenner, *Merchants and Revolution*, 373

In revolutionary politics, it is the relationship of forces, most decisively class forces, that is ultimately determinative. "The test of any such analysis is not whether or no it sounds convincing, but whether it helps to interpret the facts and solve some of the problems which confront the historian..."[71] The social class analysis meets the criteria of scientific hypotheses: it cogently accounts for the known facts in the simplest way possible. This does not imply that there are no other contributing (or detracting) factors, that leading individuals have no importance, or that there is nothing more to be discovered or said. The clash of unfolding events offers a sufficient number of contradictions to unravel, and it is in these events that the subjective factor of history comes to the fore. (In Part Two of *The Century of Revolution*, covering 1640-1660, Christopher Hill reversed the order of his chapters, putting "Politics and the Constitution" ahead of "Economics.") What economic class analysis provides is a *fundamental* explanation of historical dynamics on which to build, a guide to evaluation, which is exactly what the Revisionists (and conservatives before and since) are at such pains to attack and discredit in their hurry to fragment events, and write mass action (and even Parliamentary action!) out of history.

To establish the thesis I have relied mainly on Marxian or leftwing historians whose contributions, all too often, have been largely ignored, dismissed, or distorted by bourgeois detractors who would prefer to forget or explain away the revolutionary origins of their own class history.[72] Critically read, these left historians go a long way toward solving the puzzle that was the English Revolution. From their work I have attempted to build a coherent account, reinforced where applicable by a wider selection of writers, few of whom would likely be sympathetic to my viewpoint. It behooves me to acknowledge the overwhelming amount of material that exists on this subject, not always accessible or affordable by a non-academic such as myself. Much of it would doubtless help flesh out and refine what is essentially an elaborated outline.

My own argument rests on 1) the *contradictory* social position of the reforming gentry in the House of Commons, and 2) the critically important component of the revolutionary London Puritan leadership provided by the free-trading bourgeois Atlantic merchants. The first argument redresses a flaw in the writings of Christopher Hill, described above, of which prodigious advantage was taken by his opponents; the second refutes those modern day historians who claimed, as a result of this weakness, that the bourgeois class was either "missing" from the Marxist description of the English revolution, or was uniformly conservative.[73]

71 R. H. Hilton, "Capitalism — What's in a Name?," *Past & Present*, no. 1 (February 1952): 36, http://www.jstor.org/stable/649987 Accessed 7 December 2016. Reprinted in *The Transition from Feudalism to Capitalism* (London: Verso, 1978)

72 "Manning had been working on *The English People and the English Revolution, 1640–1649* for twenty years, but its appearance in 1976 meant that it was swept away by the flood tide of Revisionism." Morrill, "Revisionism's Wounded Legacies," 584

73 See J. H. Hexter, "A New Framework for Social History," in *Reappraisals in History* (Chicago: The University of Chicago Press,1979), 16; Zaller, "The Concept of Opposition," 213-214

Certainly in America, and perhaps also Britain today, an educated and/or politically aware audience is unlikely to be familiar with even the major events of this time, fascinating and original as they are.[74] (See the high-level time line in the Appendix for reference.) Whereas the vast majority of historical writing concentrates on the House of Commons, this book seeks to provide the most detail in regard to the actions of the masses, and the political changes that occurred in London in 1641-1642, surely the least well-known aspects of the revolution. "...most histories tended to treat such [popular] interventions as incidental to the real history of the period..."[75] It was the radically Puritan petty bourgeois artisan craftworkers, shopkeepers, early manufacturers, domestic traders, and mariners who provided the horsepower of the revolution, and not the moderate gentry. As with all "history from below," the "common people" tend to be the least documented[76] and written about,[77] but it is the participation of these sectors as a body, more or less consciously led, and in support of a program incompatible with feudal social relations, that indeed constitute these events a revolution. However, in the lead-up to and early conduct of the Revolution and Civil War, a section of the reformist gentry in the House of Commons inarguably played a very considerable role, for better and worse, *in tandem* with the petty-bourgeois popular movement in London. Their activities therefore cannot in any way be ignored. In this fact resides the partial nature and short-term failure of the revolution in these decades, and the hybrid result of the revolution in 1688.

A truly useful understanding of the English Revolution is impossible without regard to the history which led to it. The much debated issue over many decades, in and out of the Marxist movement, of the transition from feudalism to capitalism in England would ideally be the place to start. That extensive topic, however, is properly outside my scope, and would require a separate study of its own.[78] So let us initially just observe that

74 "The peak year for the study of history in Britain at A-level was 1976, when 149,000 students took History or Economic History. The number fell by roughly two-thirds over the next twenty years." Dave Renton, "Marxists and historical writing in Britain," Making History - Institute for Historical Research, 2008, https://archives.history.ac.uk/makinghistory/resources/articles/marxist_history.html Accessed 29 October 2019

75 John Walter, "The English People and the English Revolution Revisited," *History Workshop Journal*, no. 61 (Spring 2006): 171, https://www.jstor.org/stable/25472843 Accessed June 15, 2019

76 To the singular far-sightedness of one George Thomason, Puritan bookseller and member of the Stationers Company, we owe a collection of 22,000 pamphlets and other materials from all sides published during the period 1640-1661, now in the British Library.

77 It is an indictment of bourgeois historiography as a whole that "The power and significance of this Committee [of Safety] in the early months of 1642 has never been commented on by historians." Pearl, *London and the Outbreak*, 146. Twenty years earlier an American historian wrote, "One political problem after another remains insoluble because of our ignorance of what actually went on in the councils of the City." J. H. Hexter, *The Reign of King Pym* (Cambridge: Harvard University Press, 1941, 1968), 95-96 fn. 76.

78 For a summary introduction to the historiography of the debate in the Marxist movement that began in the 1940s, see Heller, *The Birth of Capitalism*, 23-50. *The Transition from Feudalism to Capitalism* (London: Verso, 1978) contains the original contributions to the 1940s-50s debate among Marxist academics, plus reprinted essays including: Hilton, "Capitalism — What's in a Name?"; John Merrington, "Town and Country in the Transition to Capitalism," *New Left Review*, no. 93, (September/October, 1975), https://www.proquest.com/docview/1301995994/fulltextPDF/BB8F766F4E4741DCPQ/1? Accessed 23 September 2020. Among others on the topic see: E. J. Hobsbawm, "The General Crisis of the European Economy in the 17th Century" and "The Crisis of the Seventeenth Century — II," *Past & Present*, no. 5, 6 (May, November 1954), https://www.jstor.org/

> ...gradually from the fifteenth to the seventeenth centuries a change began to come over the structure of this agricultural community. The food and wool from the village began to sell far afield: the spinsters and the husbandmen were turned into commodity-producers for a national market.[79]

One feature beyond debate is the sudden rise in economic activity that occurs in the second half of the 16th century. After a brief review of some earlier formative events in England's history, it is here that our story must really begin.

stable/649822, https://www.jstor.org/stable/649814 Accessed 4 April 2020. Reprinted as "The Crisis of the Seventeenth Century" in *Crisis in Europe 1560-1660*, ed. Trevor Aston (New York: Anchor Books, 1967); Robert Brenner, "Dobb on the transition from feudalism to capitalism," *Cambridge Journal of Economics* 2, no. 2 (June 1978), http://www.jstor.org/stable/23596403 Accessed 8 October 2015.

79 Hill, *1640,* 21

NOTES ON NOMENCLATURE

The term "gentry" as used in England is somewhat vague, and used either broadly or narrowly by different historians at different times.[1] Here I use the term to refer solely to the knights and squires (aka "the squireocracy"), who owned land in the countryside and ran local affairs, populated the House of Commons, and were the junior partners in the ruling class. This differentiates them from the nobility, mainly dukes and earls, who as peers of the realm traditionally held hereditary seats in the House of Lords.

Similarly, the term "aristocracy," which at least in America is usually synonymous with nobility, is sometimes used by academics to include the "commoners" of the gentry, and here I use it in this latter collective sense of the entire ruling class, along with the terms "landlords" or "landowners."

Note also that in this period the term "gentleman," which meant someone who did no physical labor, applied to all of the foregoing, but did not always imply direct land ownership. Younger sons of the gentry or nobility who inherited no land were nonetheless considered gentlemen, which gave them the legal right, for example, to wear a sword. (Women of course didn't own land, unless they were widows with no male relatives to take it away from them, and even then the crown could, and often did, impose itself on them.) Younger sons retained their status until such time as, failing to make, marry, or inherit their own fortunes, or be provided for by their families, they found a niche for themselves in another social group (such as lawyer, clergy, doctor, merchant, mercenary, mariner, master craftsman or colonist).[2] Rich merchants, on the other hand, might be treated as gentlemen by the lower classes, but not the higher, although some bought themselves country estates in the hopes of becoming respectable and accepted as such.

1 See the discussion in P. R. Coss, "The Formation of the English Gentry," *Past & Present*, no. 147 (May 1995), https://www.jstor.org/stable/651039 Accessed 24 January 2019

2 Richard Grassby, "Social Mobility and Business Enterprise in Seventeenth-century England," in *Puritans and Revolutionaries*, eds. Donald Pennington and Keith Thomas (Oxford: Oxford University Press, 1978), 372-375. See also Joan Thirsk, "Younger Sons in the 17th Century," *History* 54, no. 182 (October 1969), https://www.jstor.org/stable/24407104 Accessed 31 October 2018

1) INTRODUCTION

Cromwell is Robespierre and Napoleon rolled into one; the Presbyterians, Independents and Levellers correspond to the Gironde, the Montagnards and the Hébertists and Babeuvists; in both cases the political outcome is rather pitiable, and the whole parallel, which could be elaborated in much greater detail incidentally also proves that a religious and an irreligious revolution, as long as they remain political, will in the final analysis amount to the same thing.

~Frederick Engels[1]

The central political issue in 17th century England was the struggle against monarchical absolutism. The Stuart dynasty's attempts to consolidate its absolute rule over a changed and changing society, and its failure to do so, unlike the monarchies of Spain and France, reflected specific economic, historic, political and geographic factors of England. Government-fostered domestic manufacture and commercial capitalism measurably expanded in the second half of the 16th century, intensifying the contradictions with the rigid hierarchy of the feudal system. The overall rise in economic activity gave force to the Puritan movement in the Church of England. Puritan demands for religious reform against anything that smacked of Catholicism were an only partially disguised argument for a more rational and democratic society. By the early 17th century, the conflicts caused by a capitalist economy held within the bounds of feudal social and political relations were on open display for all to see.

While Puritanism was a trans-class movement, it appealed most widely, and in its most radical forms, to the large stratum of London's "middling people," petty-bourgeois craftworkers, shopkeepers and domestic traders. They formed a popular democratic movement which both supported and pressured the reform-minded gentry in the House of Commons. Their organization was supported and led in good part by pro-free trade Puritan merchants. These new or Atlantic merchants had only recently made their fortunes in Virginia during the late 1620s and 1630s, and were in the main more religiously and politically radical than most other Puritans at the time.

As London overwhelmingly dominated the country economically and politically it was the key to revolution in the country at large. Thus the developed south and east were strongly for Parliament, whereas the far less industrial parts of the country, which were also the less solidly Protestant and Puritan parts, in the north and west of England and Wales supported the king.[2] During the Civil War, both sides fully understood that the retaking

1 "The Condition of England, Part I The Eighteenth Century," Marx and Engels, *Collected Works* Vol. 3 (London: Lawrence & Wishart, 1844 , 1975), Marxists Internet Archive, https://marxists.architexturez.net/archive/marx/works/1844/condition-england/ch01.htm Accessed 28 July 2019

2 Hill, *Century*, 103-104; Samuel R. Gardiner, *History of the Great Civil War* Vol. I 1642-1644 (London: Longmans, Green, and Co., 1886), 23, Internet Archive, https://archive.org/details/in.ernet.dli.2015.505225/mode/1up?view=theater Accessed 5 August 2019

of London by royalist forces would put an end, not only to the war, but to Parliament's political program, and perhaps to Parliament itself.

Significant outposts of parliamentarianism in the more remote areas existed, however, in the manufacturing towns and their environs, most of which depended on the cloth and clothing trade.[3] In addition, a great deal of support for Parliament came from large and small yeomen (freeholders) who owned and worked their own land, and were therefore their own masters,[4] along with the larger portion of the peasantry who held their land by copyhold ("tenure by copy of the court roll according to the custom of the manor").[5] But the rights of copyholders to the land they worked were under threat from "improving" aristocrats, those who were seeking to enhance their livelihoods through coercive methods such as enclosure.[6] The many thousands thrown off the land were mostly forced to become impoverished wage-workers.

In the century beginning with Oliver Cromwell's Protectorate (1653-1658) and Charles II's Restoration in 1660,

> Many copyholders and small freeholders either lost claims to their land or sold out. This was the period during which large landowners, capitalist tenants, and agricultural laborers became the dominant figures in agriculture and the small, independent farmers shrank in importance.[7]

Similarly, in the cities and towns

> ...when expanding markets and improved methods of production gave rise to a more complicated type of industry, the small master craftsman was gradually displaced by the capitalist trader and manufacturer on the one hand, and by the mere journeyman on the other.[8]

In the pre-Civil War decades, however, these trends were just beginning to take hold. Here we are concerned with a more embryonic state of society, when the process of capitalist development was only beginning to cause substantial dislocation to, and conflict with, the feudal state power, itself mirrored and interpenetrated with the established state church.

The revolutionary break came in London in the weeks before and after Christmas 1641. During this time, "The alliance of the parliamentary Puritans...enjoyed the overwhelming support of the middle and lower ranks of the London citizens, men by no means to be dismissed as a mere 'rabble'

3 Hill, *Century*, 103-104; Austin Woolrych, "The English Revolution: an introduction," in *The English Revolution 1600-1660*, ed. E. W. Ives (London: Edward Arnold, 1968), 22

4 Brian Manning, *Aristocrats, Plebeians and Revolution in England* (London: Pluto Press, 1996), 67-68

5 R. H. Hilton, *The Decline of Serfdom in Medieval England* (London: Macmillan, 1970), 48

6 Hill, *1640*, 25 fn. 1; *Century*, 13; Hilton, *The Decline of Serfdom*, 58-59. See the section in Chapter 7 below "Social consequences of growth in the capitalist economy."

7 Cohen, "The Marxist School," 49-50

8 Margaret James, *Social Problems and Policy During the Puritan Revolution 1640-1660* (New York: Barnes and Noble, 1966), 193

or 'mob'..."[9] The respectable, petty-bourgeois middling people, were the bedrock supporters of the revolution.

By the end of 1643, however, the revolutionary tide in the city had ebbed; the reasons are analyzed in Chapter 15. But by then it was too late. The question of power had been posed point blank, the feudal system had already been dealt a near-fatal blow. The House of Commons and the London government were committed to preserving their gains (and themselves), and war was the preeminent concern of both.

9 Pearl, *London and the Outbreak*, 279

2) HISTORICAL BACKGROUND (Pre-1500)

Of course, the struggle of the Long Parliament with the autocracy of Charles I, and Cromwell's severe dictatorship, were prepared by the previous history of England. But this simply means that revolutions cannot be made when you want them, but are an organic product of the conditions of social evolution...

~Leon Trotsky[1]

Prior to 1500, three pivotal events in English history helped to transform English society and prepare the way for the success of the 17th-century revolution. The first was the early unification of England. Six hundred years before Ferdinand and Isabella completed the reconquest of Spain, Alfred the Great created a single Saxon kingdom through his military victories at Ashdown (871) and Edington (878) over the Danish Vikings, who continued to occupy the east of England.

Alfred's peace settlement laid the basis, through later battles and royal intermarriage, for the union of Saxon and Danish territories, prior to the Norman invasion in 1066. Having won the day-long Battle of Hastings, William the Bastard obtained the entire country in one fell swoop, making his bloody imposition of a French-speaking ruling class that much simpler. The early establishment of central government united England to a degree then unknown in the countries of Western Europe, where multiple territories and jurisdictions significantly hindered their development.

The struggle between the Anglo-Norman nobility and the all-powerful and abusive monarchy took a forceful turn early in favor of the former with the Great Charter of the Barons' Rebellion in 1215. Magna Carta is rightly remembered for its enunciation of some important democratic rights, established in law, however limited their applicability or reinterpretation by posterity.[2] Earlier charters had come to naught, but what made Magna Carta different was the famous "security" clause (Article 61) which, for the first time, provided for a council of barons to "advise" the king and enforce the Charter's provisions.[3] This put a significant brake on the monarchy's power; any transgression would presumably run up against the brick wall of the united nobility.[4] Magna Carta "made it the duty of the senior nobles to discipline a king who ruled in his own interest and not those of the *communem utilitatem regni*" ("common utility of

1 "Mr. Baldwin and 'Gradualness,'" in *Leon Trotsky on Britain* (New York: Monad Press, 1925, 1973), 45

2 See Charles Rembar, *The Law of the Land: The Evolution of Our Legal System* (New York: Touchstone, 1981), 167-171

3 "Magna Carta 1215," Yale Law School, http://avalon.law.yale.edu/medieval/magframe.asp Accessed 1 June 2017; "The Articles of the Barons," British Library, https://www.bl.uk/collection-items/the-articles-of-the-barons Accessed 17 September 2018; "A Brief History of Magna Carta," House of Lords, UK Parliament, 8-9, 14, researchbriefings.files.parliament.uk/documents/LLN-2015-001/LLN-2015-001.pdf Accessed 7 May 2015

4 Rachel Foxley, "'More precious in your esteem than it deserveth?' Magna Carta and seventeenth-century politics," in *Magna Carta: History, Context and Influence*, ed. Lawrence Goldman (London: University of London Press, 2018), 68, https://www.jstor.org/stable/j.ctv5136sc.12 Accessed 1 December 2018.

the realm").[5] This security clause was eliminated in later revisions, but repeated clashes of rival noble and royal factions kept the idea alive.

By the end of the 13th century (after further bloody conflicts), an operational structure for Parliament had been worked out.[6] Representatives of gentry and town burgesses were eventually included, at first episodically. But beginning in 1341 they met separately as junior partners in a second, lower House of Commons.[7] Thus, Parliament became "an assemblage of the ruling elite, the national synod of the gentry."[8] Parliament was not originally intended to be a legislative, but a judicial body to hear petitions, to debate and advise the king on "good" laws for him to make. This rather quickly became an established requirement of Parliamentary approval for new statutes. Later monarchs gave formal acknowledgment of Parliament's control over finances: no tax could be imposed without the landowners' consent (most especially on the landowners themselves). This clumsy arrangement tied King, Lords, and Commons together in an uneasy, unequal and unstable power-sharing relationship. It thereby provided a chink in the royal armor, giving initial leverage to the early 1600s radicals who, working together in and out of the House of Commons, were able to use it to their advantage.

No such *modus vivendi* was permanently reached on the Continent. As modern nations emerged with the recovery of commodity production and the extension of international trade, absolutism became successfully established in Spain and France. A powerful centralized government was needed to defend the emerging nations' borders from foreign enemies, and to subdue the commercial bourgeoisie, whose growing wealth threatened the rigid social order of the feudal system itself. The rise of autocratic power also negated the political rights of the nobility, while preserving their economic privileges against peasant revolts and pressures for better terms.[9]

To these ends the monarchs established a standing army and a centralized state bureaucracy,[10] which they used to extend their military rule or influence over much of the rest of Europe and the Americas. The result was retrograde stagnation, with a feudal political system that severely inhibited economic progress. (In the 17th century, Spain's population fell 18%.)[11] England, however, had no foreign borders (except the small one with Scotland, traditionally policed by the powerful northern lords). The twin notions of a

5 David Rollison, "The Specter of the Commonalty: Class Struggle and the Commonweal in England before the Atlantic World," *The William and Mary Quarterly* 63, no. 2 (April 2006): 233, 245, https://www.jstor.org/stable/3877352 Accessed 31 December 2018

6 "A Brief History of Magna Carta," 16-17

7 Rollison, "The Specter of the Commonalty," 225-226; "Rise of the Commons," UK Parliament, http://www.parliament.uk/about/living-heritage/evolutionofparliament/originsofparliament/birthofparliament/overview/riseofcommons/ Accessed 3 July 2016

8 Zaller, "The Concept of Opposition," 229

9 Perry Anderson, *Lineages of the Absolutist State* (London: Verso, 1974), 19-20, 22-24; Christopher Hill, "Land in the English Revolution," *Science & Society* 13, no. 1 (Winter 1948/1949): 24, http://www.jstor.org/stable/40399929 Accessed 15 December 2016

10 Anderson, *Absolutist State*, 52-53, 65-66, 86-87, 95-96, 100-102

11 Anderson, *Absolutist State*, 82

standing royal army and an interfering central bureaucracy were anathema to the English aristocracy, who reasonably feared they would be used against themselves. The early unification of England meant they felt no imperative to make concessions to the monarchy, and they used their power in the state to prevent such developments.[12] This ensured the aristocrats' own free dominance in their localities, making the government dependent on local Justices of the Peace (JPs), invariably landowners and employers themselves, to enforce the law. The central government also relied on informers, "an unpopular and bribable class."[13]

His majesty had any number of ways of controlling Parliament, which could not sit unless the king called it. He could veto its acts, and prorogue or dismiss it at will. The Good Parliament of 1376 passed several acts to curtail corruption in the government, after which the magistrates returned to their localities while the government simply carried on as before.[14]

Parliament, however, could place limits on the king. Foreign affairs were wholly the prerogative of the monarch, but Parliament had to authorize funds for any army.[15] This did not much inhibit the crown as it could normally count on the support of the nobles especially when it came to waging war (usually in France.) This changed when money replaced land in importance, and conquering territory or plundering was no longer necessary to gain wealth. After that, Parliament's power to authorize funds became a major detriment to the monarchy.

The third event of moment, and one most under-appreciated, was the Peasants' Revolt in 1381. Despite being short-lived, this uprising was as significant as the later Peasants' War in early 16th century Germany. It covered virtually the whole of southern and eastern England, reaching as far north as southern Yorkshire.[16] Despite its historical name, early artisans made up a large proportion of the peasant army, the poor of London supported it, and in some places lower clergymen or better-off yeomen provided leadership.[17]

In the decades before the Revolt, plague had so reduced the population that peasants often refused to provide services unless they were paid;[18] the labor shortage thus undermined their feudal economic relationship with the landholders. The Revolt began in Essex and Kent, where it seems to have been well organized. As the peasantry would do again in 1642, they destroyed manor records of station, taxes, tithes — the personal information of the

12 Anderson, *Absolutist State*, 121 fn. 11, 122-123, 125, 127

13 Hill, *Century*, 23; *Reformation*, 31

14 George M. Trevelyan, *England in the Age of Wycliffe 1368-1520* (New York: Harper Torchbooks, 1899, 1963), 30-31

15 Conrad Russell, "Parliament and the King's Finances," in *The Origins of the English Civil War*, ed. Conrad Russell (Basingstoke, Hampshire: Macmillan Education, 1973), 91-92

16 Trevelyan, *England in the Age of Wycliffe*, 254-255 (map)

17 Rodney Hilton, *Bond Men Made Free* (Abingdon, Oxfordshire: Routledge, 1973, 2003), 154, 158-160, 173-174, 181-185; Rollison, "The Specter of the Commonalty," 234-235

18 Trevelyan, *England in the Age of Wycliffe*, 193

age.[19] Having gained entrance to London, the first thing the rebel army did was proceed to the houses of the most hated government officials and, without looting them, burn them down. This conscious discipline did not last, but it shows that this was no mere mob. At every prison they came to they freed the inmates.[20] The militants' demand for freedom hastened the subsequent demise of villeinage (serfdom), freeing the villeins from bondage to the land; they now had the legal right to move if they so chose. The assertion that no connection existed between these two developments is preposterous.

> The continuation of local revolts for at least a couple of decades after 1381 is well known and this in itself is evidence of the continued self-assertiveness of the English lower classes. The upper class was clearly very apprehensive about popular sedition... In spite of the strengthening of labour legislation in the statute of Cambridge of 1388, wages went up; and in spite of the threats to intensify the conditions of villeinage these were, in fact, considerably relaxed.[21]

As villeinage died out, a new arrangement conditioned by the peasant class struggle led to material improvements in the peasants' well-being through copyhold: a quantity of land leased for a low money rent. Peasants were mostly no longer required to provide labor service to the lord, and could now sell any surplus they were able to produce. The lease was often for life, and their descendants had the right to inherit the copyhold upon payment of a substantial fine (fee). Thus, copyhold was a form of "customary tenure... without the taint of servility..."[22] This transformed the landlord-peasant relationship from one based on medieval *obligation*, to one based purely on *payment* (rent), in essence a capitalist contractual relationship. Tenants were now given written title to the land. It gave the copyholder a substantial claim on the holding, a necessary prerequisite to opening the way for market relations to further develop.[23] Consequently, by 1640, generations of the same family might, in theory, have occupied a farm for as much as two centuries.

The production of wool, England's first and longest-lasting export, also began around 1400, facilitating aristocratic acquiescence by providing them an alternative source of income.[24] "The commutation of peasant labour services...was part of the process of withdrawal by the bigger landlords from agricultural practice."[25] Copyhold was a compromise, an intermediate form of capitalist social relations at a time before a capitalist economy had become

19 Mark O'Brien, *When Adam Delved and Eve Span: A History of the Peasants' Revolt of 1381* (London: Bookmarks Publications, 2016), 45-46

20 O'Brien, *When Adam Delved*, 60, 62, 64

21 Hilton, *Bond Men Made Free,* 206; Rollison, "The Specter of the Commonalty," 236-238.

22 Hilton, *The Decline of Serfdom*, 44

23 Karl Marx, *Capital* Vol. 3 (New York: International Publishers, 1975), 807; Rodney Hilton, "Feudalism and the Origins of Capitalism," *History Workshop*, no. 1 (Spring 1976): 20-21, http://www.jstor.com/stable/4288032 Accessed 3 July 2020. Reprinted as "Introduction," in *The Transition from Feudalism to Capitalism.*

24 Hill, "Land in the English Revolution," 23

25 Rodney Hilton, "The Content and Sources of English Agrarian History before 1500," *The Agricultural History Review* 3, no. 1 (1955), 14-15, https://www.jstor.org/stable/40272749 Accessed 13 April 2020

general. Copyhold stopped short of making the peasants freemen; they still had to pay a nominal rent on land they did not own outright. But a qualitative advance had taken place in their relationship to the lord. The protections they achieved had been won through struggle; for just this reason however it was a legal gray area and insecure status.[26]

The early decline of serfdom and labor service removed a major obstacle to the development of capitalist market relations in the countryside of England. This situation contrasted markedly with other European countries. Despite occasional peasant *jacqueries* on the Continent, absolutism and the *seigneurial* system were on the whole able to maintain feudal relations in the countryside. The implementation of copyhold in England was uneven, and terms varied, but its spread continued during the late fourteenth and fifteenth centuries, making it the normal custom.[27]

At a certain point, when landlords needed to increase production of food and wool, copyholders' rights (low rents, right of inheritance) came to place intolerable limits on market agriculture's forward advance.[28] This led to new conflicts as landlords attempted to overcome the limitations of copyhold in their own favor by attacking tenants' rights, and throwing them off the land. As the price of wool rose in the late 15th century, a wave of land conversions from crop production to raising sheep was carried out by aristocrats for the more remunerative export of wool to Flanders. This caused government worries about what they called "depopulation" (unemployment and homelessness) and food supply. The conversion process often involved enclosure of land for larger flocks and greater efficiency.[29] The enclosures cut off access to commons, land where small peasants historically pastured their few animals on which they depended to live, or sometimes flooded them with an excess number of sheep.[30] (Commons were also a source of fuel and building material.)[31] Either way, small peasants were forced to abandon their farms. While some might eke out a living on "waste" (unused) or forest lands where these were available further out in the country,[32] most were forced to become wage workers if they were not to starve.

26 Hill, *Reformation,* 54-55; Marx, *Capital* Vol.3, 798-799

27 Mark Bailey, "The transformation of customary tenures in southern England, *c.*1350 to *c.*1500," *The Agricultural History Review* 62, no. 2 (2014): 220, http://www.jstor.com/stable/43697978 Accessed 11 August 2020; Hilton, *The Decline of Serfdom*, 48-51

28 Hill, *1640,* 35; *Century*, 127; Hilton, *The Decline of Serfdom*, 58-59

29 Karl Marx, *Capital* Vol. 1 (New York: International Publishers, 1973), 718-720. "It was a commonplace of the age that English commerce was overwhelmingly dependent upon the Low Countries and that economically London was a satellite of Antwerp." F. J. Fisher, "Commercial Trends and Policy in Sixteenth-Century England," *The Economic History Review* 10, no. 2 (November 1940): 97, http://www.jstor.org/stable/2590787 Accessed 24 February 2017

30 Joan Thirsk, *Tudor Enclosures* (London: The Historical Association, 1959), 13-14

31 Brian Manning, *The English People and the English Revolution* (London: Penguin Books, 1978), 133, 134; Marx, *Capital* Vol. 1, 717; Hill, *Reformation,* 70

32 Brian Manning, *1649: The Crisis of the English Revolution* (London: Bookmarks, 1992), 77, 99; Thirsk, *Tudor Enclosures*, 7-8

3) THE SIXTEENTH CENTURY

But chivalry's day is over. One day soon moss will grow in the tilt yard. The days of the moneylender have arrived, and the days of the swaggering privateer; banker sits down with banker, and kings are their waiting boys.

~Thomas Cromwell in *Bring Up the Bodies*[1]

Early political developments

The end of serfdom and the establishment of the wool trade to the Low Countries in the early 15th century was followed by the episodic but ferocious civil War of the Roses. It was fought between noble houses for the throne of England during the latter half of the 15th century and greatly weakened all sides. Preceded by the peasant Rebellion of 1450,[2] it had the effect of creating "a legitimacy crisis that left no kind of lordship, religious or secular, unchallenged and unchallengeable" by the lower classes.[3]

The upstart Henry Tudor (Henry VII) who defeated Richard III in 1485 and, so the story goes, picked up his crown from the dust of the battlefield, was thus able to seize the throne. Henry began to curb manifestations of aristocratic independence in favor of the central state. Following a Yorkist insurrection in 1487, he established the prerogative court of Star Chamber as an expeditious judicial weapon against the nobility to consolidate his rule. As would be expected, aristocrats were usually able to escape justice in the common courts.[4] Both he and his second son, Henry VIII, ruthlessly disposed of other potential claimants to the throne, along with any other opposition.

Father and son were alarmed by the large and growing underclass of former peasants, now landless and workless, forced to become "beggers, robbers, vagabonds" due to enclosures. Neither agriculture nor artisan manufacture could possibly absorb them all. Especially under Henry VIII, but also Edward VI and Elizabeth, the most vicious legislation and bloody punishments were enacted to suppress them.[5] Thousands of these unfortunates were whipped, branded or hung.[6]

The falloff of the old nobility opened up room for the gentry to advance.[7] Henry VIII renewed the nobility by conferring titles on his supporters, but also sought to control and make use of the new money men. He made Thomas Cromwell, banker and lawyer, his chief minister in 1532. Cromwell

1 Hilary Mantel, (New York: Henry Holt & Co., 2012), 141-142

2 Rollison, "The Specter of the Commonalty," 240-241

3 Rollison, "The Specter of the Commonalty," 239-240

4 Anderson, *Absolutist State*, 119

5 Marx, *Capital* Vol. 1, 734-736; Hill, *1640*, 29

6 Marx, *Capital* Vol. 1, 736 fn. 1

7 Christopher Hill, "The Social and Economic Consequences of the Henrician Reformation," in *Puritanism and Revolution* (London: Pimlico, 1958, 2001), 32

favored Protestantism and "ran considerable political risks to make sure that the Bible in English translation was published and circulated in England."[8] He simultaneously reinforced the monarchy and Parliament's role in government by having the House of Commons endorse Henry's Reformation. This helped to tie the gentry more closely to the government, uniting the landed ruling class. Thus England was torn away from Rome, ending the outflow of wealth from the one to the other, and subordinating the church to the state, "parishes to squires." Henry's government spent much of the savings on shipbuilding and armaments.[9]

Cromwell ended the teaching of canon law at universities.[10] By closing down the monasteries and seizing their lands, to the benefit of the royal treasury and the pauperization of their tenants,[11] he attacked a key base of the old nobles' patronage power and incomes. This one stroke cut in half the number of clerics who sat in the House of Lords.[12] Henry VIII's sale, or gifts, of a large number of estates from the confiscated monasteries increased the aristocracy's wealth and numbers.[13] The Reformation land settlement "created a vested interest in Protestantism" in the ruling class,[14] that was to subsequently vex Queen Mary Tudor. Parliament also approved a revision in the order of succession from the Catholic Mary to Elizabeth, and, later, back again. Henry renewed the charter of the Merchant Adventurers company, preserving their monopoly among English merchants on woolen cloth exports to the Low Countries and northern Germany, thereby keeping them tied to the monarchy and the feudal order.

Economic growth under Elizabeth

Competition in English trade from mainly German merchants of the Hanseatic League went back some three hundred years, but these foreigners were largely cut out early in Elizabeth's long reign (1558-1603), helping to stabilize cloth exports.[15] During the earlier short reign of Elizabeth's underage half-brother Edward VI, energetic Protestantism and economic expansion in the realm had gone hand-in–hand. The first Protestant Book of Common Prayer in English was created by Archbishop

8 Christopher Hill, "The New History of England," *New York Review of Books* 25, no. 5 (April 6, 1978), http://www.nybooks.com/articles/archives/1978/apr/06/the-new-history-of-england/ Accessed September 15, 2013. Reprinted in *The History Teacher* 12, no. 1 (November 1978), http://www.jstor.org/stable/491350 Accessed 15 December 2016

9 Hill, *Reformation*, 35; "Henrician Reformation," 30-31, 39.

10 Christopher Hill, *Society and Puritanism in Pre-Revolutionary England* (New York: St. Martin's Press, 1958, 1997), 256

11 Joan Thirsk, *Economic Policy and Projects: The Development of a Consumer Society in Early Modern England* (Oxford: Clarendon Press, 1978, 1988), 159; Hill, "Land in the English Revolution," 27; Marx, *Capital* Vol. 1, 721, 722 fn. 1

12 Hill, *Reformation*, 47

13 Hill, "Land in the English Revolution," 23-24; Anderson, *Absolutist State*, 124-125

14 Hill, "Henrician Reformation," 41. "Charles II told the Pope in 1670 that many landowners were restrained from declaring themselves in favour of Catholicism solely by fears for their property." 43

15 Brenner, *Merchants and Revolution*, 6-7, 56-58; Fisher, "Commercial Trends and Policy," 97, 108-109

Thomas Cranmer in 1549 under Edward.[16] At the same time, systematic encouragement of manufacturing began.[17] Commonwealthmen were financiers and politicians who supported developing domestic industry through what were called projects. They sought to cut the country's reliance on expensive imports, provide employment to the numerous poor, and make improvements such as draining swamps. Successful projects provided their investors with substantial profits; thus their claim to do well by doing good.[18]

This policy was interrupted by the boy king's death, and Mary Tudor's ascension to the throne. When reinstated by Elizabeth's government, the policy benefited from the religious wars on the Continent, which drove many Protestant artisans, especially from France and Holland, to seek refuge in England beginning in the 1560s. These foreigners, invited by town officials seeking to foster various kinds of products and processes, brought skills and new techniques with them. Some failed, but many fulfilled the Commonwealthmen's hopes: increased domestic trade; greater money circulation; less reliance on imports; and in some cases even development of an export trade to the Continent[19] (though textiles always remained by far the largest commodity shipped abroad before the Civil War.)[20] It was not a linear process; the overall expansion brought plenty of worrying economic imbalances.[21] But the overall result was "the integration of English towns into a single national unit, to an extent which was not paralleled on the Continent."[22] The consequent social dislocations, however, forced the government to intervene to regulate trade, and economic life more generally.

Rural domestic manufacture (the "putting-out" system) was primarily a feature of pastoral areas in England, where the principal activity was raising livestock. In arboreal areas, cereal farming was more labor intensive leaving little time for by-employment, making families mostly dependent on their crop. Only those with larger farms, more varied produce, capital for improvements and/or the ability to hire additional workers, were able to prosper. At the end of Elizabeth's reign, anything less than 10-20 acres of arable land was "insufficient to provide subsistence for a family."[23] Those in pastoral areas who raised livestock, however, were able to diversify by

16 Diarmaid MacCulloch, "Mumpsimus, Sumpsimus," *London Review of Books* 34, no. 10 (24 May 2012), https://www.lrb.co.uk/the-paper/v34/n10/diarmaid-macculloch/mumpsimus-sumpsimus Accessed 28 March 2014

17 Lawrence Stone, *The Crisis of the Aristocracy, 1558-1641*, Abridged Edition (Oxford: Oxford University Press, 1971), 175; Thirsk, *Economic Policy and Projects,* 12-13. Government involvement in the promotion of industrial goods, notably iron, went back to Henry VIII. Thirsk, 24-26

18 Thirsk, *Economic Policy and Projects,* 18. For the ideological background of the commonwealthmen see Rollison, "The Specter of the Commonalty," 246-249

19 Thirsk, *Economic Policy and Projects,* 14-22, 33, 43-44

20 Rosemary Weinstein, "London at the Outbreak of the Civil War," in *London and the Civil War,* ed. Stephen Porter (New York: St. Martin's Press, 1996), 33

21 Fisher, "Commercial Trends and Policy," 110-112

22 Hill, *Reformation,* 25

23 Derek Hirst, *The Representative of the People? Voters and Voting in England Under the Early Stuarts* (Cambridge: Cambridge University Press, 1975), 31

weaving cloth on looms in their own homes and selling it to a local trader on a regular basis. Having a foot in each segment of the economy provided peasant workers with greater income security, enabling them to maintain themselves on smaller holdings.[24] Other trades were pursued by such artisan-farmers as well.[25] "'Urban and rural interests were thus to a large extent identical.'"[26] During the time of the early Stuarts, however, "a great deal of cloth production took place in centralised workshops in which a master weaver had three or more looms, sometimes as many as ten, and employed for wages half a dozen to a dozen men."[27] This augured the end of manufacturing in the home, turning independent weavers into wage workers.

Between 1560 and 1630, numerous manufactured products for home consumption came onto the domestic market in England. Often these originated as by-employment on farms, sometimes produced by women and children. They included the making of knit stockings, buttons, pins and nails, salt, starch, soap, knives and tools, tobacco pipes, pots and ovens, ribbons and lace, woven linens, as well as alum mining, brewing, and distilling of *aqua vitae*. New crops included rape, flax and hemp, woad, madder and weld (used in cloth dyeing), tobacco, flowers and vegetables. These new goods were in addition to the established industries of wool cloth; the mining of coal, iron and lead; and the raising of corn, dairy and meat. The growth and spread of these new products brought money to the lower classes, and capitalist relations "into dark, neglected corners of the kingdom."[28]

Household production was

> supported by a network of credit, consisting of small loans and debts raised by small producers among their neighbors and kinsmen in village and town. ... Most of the consumer occupations, in short, were started on a shoe-string. ... Each household enterprise subsisted on a precarious base...but it was the multitude of household undertakings that ensured the survival of the occupation. Only after many decades of domestic enterprise did larger, more capital-intensive undertakings emerge from among the more successful operators.[29]

As small, casually produced consumer goods proliferated in the countryside, industry was proceeding in the vicinity of some towns.

> During the last sixty years of the sixteenth century the first paper and gunpowder mills, the first cannon foundries, the first alum and copperas

24 Joan Thirsk, "Seventeenth-Century Agriculture and Social Change," in *Land, Church, and the People*, ed. Joan Thirsk (Reading, Berkshire: The British Agricultural History Society, 1970). Reprinted in *Seventeenth Century England: Society in an Age of Revolution*, ed. Paul S. Seaver (New York: New Viewpoints, 1976), 75-76, 80-81, 91-92, 97-98; Manning, *English People*, 229-230

25 Manning, *1649*, 73

26 Manning, *English People*, 230

27 Manning, *1649*, 75

28 Thirsk, *Economic Policy and Projects*, 2-3, 6-7

29 Thirsk, *Economic Policy and Projects*, 170-171, 172-173

> [iron sulphate] factories, the first sugar refineries, and the first considerable saltpetre works were all introduced into the country from abroad. … The important thing about the "new" Elizabethan industries was that in all of them plant was set up involving investments far beyond the sums which groups of master-craftsmen could muster, even if these artisans were men of some small substance. While in London, Sheffield, or any provincial town, the typical workshop of the smith, the cutler, or the weaver could be equipped with its forge or grinding wheel or loom and other necessary tools for a few pounds, the establishments erected in these new industries cost hundreds, and in many cases thousands, of pounds. A further heavy outlay had to be made on materials and labour, because the process of production frequently required a long time, and it was many months before any return could be expected from sales.[30]

Mining, for example, was heavily and expensively modernized by ventilation tunnels and pumps, allowing for deeper digging and much greater output.

> While the annual output of a coal mine before the middle of the sixteenth century had rarely exceeded a few hundred tons…collieries producing from 10,000 to 25,000 tons of coal…and employing scores and sometimes hundreds of miners, became common before 1640…[31]

In the years before the civil war, 450,000 tons of coal would be extracted annually in Newcastle alone.[32]

The slow growth of town manufacture served the interests of the ruling landowners, who were not infrequently investors, as well as the merchants who governed the larger towns on behalf of the aristocrats. But by the late Elizabethan age, with both foreign and domestic Catholic enemies subdued, the nascent manufacturing bourgeoisie no longer needed the protection of the crown. The micromanagement of feudal supervision inhibited the free range of business, so eventually "industry escaped from the restrictions of the towns into the countryside where it permeated agrarian relationships."[33] Taxes, living and production costs, and especially wages, were lower in more remote areas; early manufacturers could "escape" guild regulation and interfering town authorities by moving to the suburbs or small towns. This became particularly important as the textile export industry declined in the latter part of the century.[34] That early manufacturers were able to do so presupposed an available pool of "free" labor (i.e., the landless poor).

30 J. U. Nef, "The Progress of Technology and the Growth of Large-Scale Industry in Great Britain, 1540-1640," *The Economic History Review* 5, no. 1 (October 1934): 5-6, http://www.jstor.org/stable/2589915 Accessed 6 February 2017

31 Nef, "The Progress of Technology and the Growth of Large-Scale Industry in Great Britain," 10-11

32 Barry Coward, "London and the English Civil War," *The Historian,* no. 99 (Autumn 2008): 10, https://search.proquest.com/docview/274985556/fulltextPDF/B3512A7ED25C41C4PQ/2?accountid=35635 Accessed 30 August 2020

33 Brian Manning, "The Nobles, the People, and the Constitution," *Past & Present,* no. 9 (April 1956): 49, http://www.jstor.org/stable/650042 Accessed 10 August 2015. Reprinted in *Crisis In Europe 1560-1660,* ed. Trevor Aston (New York: Anchor Books, 1967). Original includes "some preliminary matter" not reprinted in the book. Pearl, *London and the Outbreak,* 15-16; Hill, *Reformation,* 90

34 Brenner, *Merchants and Revolution,* 36-37

Later political and religious developments

Under Elizabeth, the Trained Bands, an annual mustering of able-bodied men to be drilled and instructed in each parish, were instituted with modern equipment, replacing the outmoded and degenerated local militia.[35] In London and the towns, they were usually captained by members of the livery companies (guilds). The Bands' primary purpose was to help protect the nation in the event of (Spanish) invasion, but they could also be used for domestic purposes if the need arose.[36] For this reason, "meaner" men and servants were excluded except in time of war.[37] Their officers were local notables, either officeholders (such as the sheriff) or better-off men of the community, although the local gentleman was the usual titular leader. Caches of weapons were also established around the country, kept under lock and key, for use in an emergency.

Elizabeth's Protestant reign was dogged by the Catholic minority that still existed in England, and the open hostility of its spiritual head the See of Rome. This forced her to tolerate a greater plurality in the Church than she liked, until the defeat of the Spanish Armada in 1588 freed her from the need for Puritan political support.[38] Within the same year she established the court of High Commission as a religious analogue to the Star Chamber. The Act of Uniformity was passed, mandating Sunday attendance at one's local church on penalty of fines which the poor, at least, could not afford. This struck mainly at Catholic recusants, who refused on principle to attend the episcopal church, but also at Puritans, even if they were not separatists, as many objected attending the services of conservative ministers. The prerogative courts could act on their own or usurp the common courts' decisions. This high-handed juridical power was directed by the state. Its vicious punishments, steep costs, and frequent excommunications for trivial offenses, which carried legal and economic consequences,[39] would become regular features, and a major target for Puritan opponents into the 17th century.

The Elizabethan period also saw foreign trade dramatically expand to Russia, Morocco, Venice, Turkey, Persia, and the East Indies carried out by overlapping groups of monopoly merchants not associated with the Merchant Adventurers. The new trade was based on imports of silks and spices, currants and wines, while cloth exports to these areas initially remained negligible.[40] (Only late in the century with the production of dyed cloths, and especially "New Draperies," clothing made of lighter materials, did cloth and

35 Lawson Chase Nagel, "The Militia of London, 1641-1649" (PhD diss., King's College, London, September 1982), 9-10, https://kclpure.kcl.ac.uk/portal/files/2927314/403590.pdf Accessed 4 November 2016

36 The first occasion in London was in 1601 against the rebel Earl of Essex. Nagel, "The Militia of London," 15

37 Hill, *World*, 19; *Reformation*, 60

38 Leo F. Solt, "Revolutionary Calvinist Parties in England under Elizabeth I and Charles I," *Church History* 27, no. 3 (September 1958): 236, https://www.jstor.org/stable/3161388 Accessed 16 June 2020

39 Hill, *Society*, 307, 310-311, 313-314, 321

40 Brenner, *Merchants and Revolution*, 11

clothing exports to the Mediterranean become substantial.) Luxury imports had formerly been carried by Spanish, Portuguese or Dutch shipping, and reexported to England from those countries. But the intermittent disruptions to the English import trade from Continental ports by the vagaries of political diplomacy, and the lucrative returns to be had, impelled new groups of English merchants to go directly to the sources. This was facilitated by the long-term decline of Spain and Portugal as commercial powers, as well as the growing demand for imported items in England, and the highly profitable re-export of these specialized goods from London to other parts of Europe.[41]

The royal charters of the overseas trading groups, such as the Levant Company and the East India Company, granted their members monopolies in two ways. One granted the company the exclusive right to trade with a given country or area of the world. The other limited investors in the companies to "mere merchants," i.e., those who did not pursue any other occupation as well. This was a key clause in every government charter sought by merchant partnerships. The exclusion was squarely aimed at the middling class of shopkeepers, small producers, domestic traders and ship captains, many of whom made good livings, had accumulated some capital, and wanted to share in the high profits afforded by overseas commerce. They were potentially in a position to compete with and undersell the monopoly merchants, thus eliminating the middlemen's profits. The more successful members of this class would eventually become the future bourgeoisie in full-blown capitalist society, but at this point in time social differentiation was only beginning to occur.[42] The hostility caused by the conflict of the economic interests of the wholesale monopoly magnates on the one hand, and of the artisans and retailers on the other, was the major fault line within the growing capitalist business class.[43]

Thus before the end of the 16th century, England was an *economically* capitalist country,[44] despite the large majority of the population still engaged in agriculture.[45] The early penetration of monetary trade in rural areas; spread of manufacture; early industrialization; growth of the domestic market; diversification of agriculture; and expansion of foreign trade; all backed by bourgeois and aristocratic finance and investment, contributed to, and were symptoms of, an elemental change at the base of early modern society.

41 Brenner, *Merchants and Revolution*, 5, 12; Anderson, *Absolutist State*, 72-73, 77. See also J. H. Elliott, "The Decline of Spain," *Past & Present*, no. 20 (November 1961), https://www.jstor.org/stable/650136 Accessed 20 February 2021. Reprinted in *Crisis In Europe 1560-1660*, ed. Trevor Aston (New York: Anchor Books, 1967)

42 Brenner, *Merchants and Revolution*, 57, 83-84; Manning, *Aristocrats, Plebeians*, 8-9

43 Brenner, *Merchants and Revolution*, 684-685; Manning, *Aristocrats, Plebeians*, 66

44 Marx, *Capital* Vol. 1, 715-716; *Capital* Vol. 3, 332-333

45 Many modern-day historians cite the prevalence of those occupied in agriculture as proof of the feudal nature of English society in this early period. What matters is not the absolute numbers engaged in one form of work or another, but the form of *social relations* under which they labored.

4) THE PURITANS

The English social crisis in the seventeenth century unites within it the traits of the German Reformation of the sixteenth century and those of the French Revolution of the eighteenth-century. In the person of Cromwell, Luther clasps hands with Robespierre.

~Leon Trotsky[1]

General history

Puritanism, a minority tendency in the episcopal Church of England, began to develop during the Protestant reign of Edward VI, Henry VIII's underage son. Unlike on the Continent, where Luther, Zwingli, and Calvin had large followings, Henry's Reformation in England was a top-down affair by the government, "an act of state," which subordinated the Church to the lay authorities, many of whom would come to support Puritan ministers.[2] At the same time, there was a considerable amount of anti-Church sentiment, religious and secular. The lower classes had inherited ideas from John Wycliffe (1320-1384) and the Lollards (an early 15th century religious reform movement);[3] and much of the aristocracy and merchant classes were happy to expropriate the Church's lands and wealth. Confession, penance, absolution and indulgences were abolished, but in most other respects Church practices changed little under Henry. Services were still conducted in Latin, fasting at Lent was still enforced, and Protestant martyrs who denied the Real Presence of Christ in the bread and wine (transubstantiation) were still burnt at the stake as heretics. Only now, Catholics who denied the king was head of the Church were executed for treason as well.[4]

> The religion of the early sixteenth century had presented man with a church, a hierarchy, a clergy, a ritual, a dogma which came from God to him as a requirement. Man was to accept it for what it was, and to obey it in what it demanded. ...all class relations supposedly originated in their reflection of the heavenly hierarchy. ... To question, to desire change, was to commit the sin of Lucifer and to receive the doom of Sisyphus.[5]

Ritual in the church corresponded to ritual in the state with the same stultifying effects to which Puritans objected.[6] Elizabeth's religious settlement was still a largely conservative compromise between Catholic ostentation, superstition and hierarchy, and Protestant simplicity, rationality and individualism. Puritans who wanted the Church reformation to go further

1 "Two Traditions: The Great Rebellion and Chartism," in *Leon Trotsky on Britain* (New York: Monad Press, 1925, 1973), 116

2 Hill, "Henrician Reformation," 30-31, 41

3 Trevelyan, *England in the Age of Wycliffe*, 348-350

4 Jasper Ridley, *Bloody Mary's Martyrs* (London: Constable & Robinson, 2002), 20, 25; Hill, *Society*, 314-315

5 L. J. Trinterud, "William Haller, Historian of Puritanism," *Journal of British Studies* 5, no. 2 (May 1966): 48, http://www.jstor.org/stable/175316 Accessed 7 January 2017

6 Baskerville, "Puritans, Revisionists, and the English Revolution," 168

attempted to "set up 'a discipline in a discipline, presbytery in episcopacy.'"[7] Their

> accommodation to the official religious policy was external and essentially civic — which indeed, as Elizabeth said, was the full extent of the legal requirement. … The Queen cared not what men thought about doctrine on the Church. Men's consciences, she said, were their own. She cared only for what they did.[8]

Nonetheless, in 1577, she went over the heads of her Privy Council and archbishop to suppress "prophesyings" — public discussion classes among clergy attended by laymen.[9] The English Protestant Book of Common Prayer "remained the most elaborate liturgy of any Reformed [Calvinist] Church in Europe."[10] It had been adapted from the book of Catholic mass by Thomas Cranmer, Archbishop under Henry VIII and Edward VI,[11] (later burned at the stake by Mary Tudor). While Catholics were now forced to worship in private, the Church of England still retained much of its inheritance from Rome. It was still ruled by a religious hierarchy under the bishops, complete with a judicial church structure which inflicted penalties for sinful living and noncompliance.

> Ecclesiastical courts enforced church attendance, Sabbath observance, the payment of tithes and sexual morality. … Sabbath-breaking was a common offense. People skipped church, and shopkeepers and alehouse-keepers were cited for doing business on Sunday… There are many presentments for misbehaviour in church: drunkenness, brawling, gossiping, vomiting, scoffing at the minister, pissing in another man's hat… Sex offences were common: fornication, adultery, bastard children, cross-dressing, lewd talk.[12]

For Puritans, a "'watered-down Protestantism'" was no better than a "'watered-down Catholicism.'"[13] They were ever mindful of the dangers posed by the Catholic monarchies of Spain and France, and behind them the Anti-Christ sitting in the Vatican; they therefore pressed for a thoroughgoing reform of the English Church to make it fully compliant with Protestant precepts. There was, they argued, nothing in Scripture about popes or saints' days; therefore these were works of man, not God.[14] This subversive view of social life was captured in a 14th century rhyme still current: "When Adam delved and Eve span / Who was then the gentleman?" While all Protestants

7 Solt, "Revolutionary Calvinist Parties," 234

8 Trinterud, "William Haller," 37

9 Hill, *Society*, 30-31

10 MacCulloch, "Mumpsimus, Sumpsimus"

11 Nicholas Tyacke, "Puritanism, Arminianism and Counter-Revolution," in *The Origins of the English Civil War*, ed. Conrad Russell (Basingstoke, Hampshire: Macmillan Education, 1973), 129

12 Tobias Gregory, "Runagately Rogue," *London Review of Books* 33, no. 16 (25 August 2011), https://www.lrb.co.uk/the-paper/v33/n16/tobias-gregory/runagately-rogue Accessed 16 December 2018; Hill, *Society*, 257

13 Gregory, "Runagately Rogue"

14 Hill, *Society*, 142; *World*, 325-326

looked to the Bible for definitive religious guidance, many Puritan divines focused on Scripture alone as the word of God. "To a large extent the Puritans were distinguished from other Protestants by differences of degree rather than of kind."[15] At bottom, Puritans were simply orthodox or consistent Protestants.

"Puritan" was nonetheless an ambiguous term. No single manifesto or codified set of principles existed. Rather, Puritans occupied a spectrum of opinions derived initially from Luther, but most heavily from the Reformed teachings of the more radical Frenchman, John Calvin. Calvin, unlike Luther, rejected transubstantiation.[16] Other influences came from German, Swiss or Dutch theologians.[17] Puritanism was, in practice if not in name, pluralist,[18] and there was a great deal of theological debate at the highest levels within it. This was not so obvious at the time, however, in the face of the struggle with anti-Calvinists. When James I came to the throne in 1603, his main ambition was to isolate Puritan extremists by downplaying differences and winning moderates to accept a tranquil conformity.[19] "To each, James offered not toleration but tolerance,"[20] provided they didn't cause trouble.

As is often the case, "Puritan" originated as a term of opprobrium by their opponents, and militant Protestants often rejected the label while still adhering to some version of a Calvinist outlook. "John Pym, during the parliament of 1621, attacked 'that odious and factious name of Puritans...'" The term could be deliberately misused to sully the arguments or reputations of political enemies.[21] But during the 22-year reign of James I it commonly meant anyone within the Church of England who wished to reform it, "... as contrasted with separatists on the one hand, and those who were satisfied with the established discipline on the other."[22]

Given the competing tendencies within the Church, a result of the compromise Elizabethan settlement, such contemporary distinctions depended very much on the point of view of the writer or speaker. "Most of the basic theological and ecclesiological divisions that would show themselves with a vengeance in the later 1640s were already present in embryo within the puritan community prior to 1640."[23] At this early date these multifarious

15 J.T. Cliffe, *The Puritan Gentry: The Great Puritan Families of Early Stuart England* (London: Routledge & Kegan Hall, 1984), 7

16 MacCulloch, "Mumpsimus, Sumpsimus"

17 Leonard J. Trinterud, "The Origins of Puritanism," *Church History* 20, no. 1 (March 1951): 38-39, 41, 46, http://www.jstor.org/stable/3162047 Accessed 1 July 2017

18 David Underdown, *Pride's Purge* (London: Oxford University Press, 1971), 16-18

19 Kenneth Fincham and Peter Lake, "The Ecclesiastical Policy of King James I," *Journal of British Studies* 24, no. 2 (April 1985): 174, 177, 182-183, https://www.jstor.org/stable/175702 Accessed 12 October 2018

20 Fincham and Lake, "Ecclesiastical Policy," 185

21 Tyacke, "Puritanism, Arminianism and Counter-Revolution," 129; Hill, *Society*, 2

22 Hill, *Society*, 5

23 David R. Como, "Secret Printing, the Crisis of 1640, and the Origins of Civil War Radicalism," *Past & Present*, no. 196 (August 2007): 81, https://www.jstor.org/stable/25096680 Accessed 11 November 2018.

differences are not of much concern here, but as the revolutionary period approaches this will change, and the more set internal divisions within Puritanism will become quite important.[24]

People of all classes who identified with Puritanism could hold or advocate a wide span of views, which not infrequently changed with events.

> Puritanism embraced such divergent religious alignments as the moderate Episcopalians, the Presbyterians, the Independents, and the Particular Baptists. Politically Puritanism embraced advocates of a limited monarchy, of responsible parliamentary government, of unlimited rule by parliament, and of recurrent revolution. ... What the advocates of these many ideas had in common made it possible for them to unite in revolution. But, the divergent lines of development which each group had taken since their common beginnings made it impossible for them to unite in creating a Puritan regime in England.[25]

It was no more possible to have a uniformly Puritan regime than it was to have a purely Puritan revolution. The different tendencies reflected different conceptions of how a new society should operate, in line with differing economic interests.

Until the revised King James translation of 1611, it was the Geneva Bible, complete with Calvinist marginal annotations, that predominated in England.[26] Though "Puritan" began as a religious designation, their active opposition to the policies and authority of the Church's Episcopal hierarchy, including its head, the queen, quickly gave it political overtones.[27] In 1572 they appealed to Parliament as the representative of the people for reforms. Since Parliament's Act of Supremacy had created the Church in 1534, Parliament in theory had the power to change it. Puritans thus allied with the "constitutional" opposition to limit the power of the monarch. Elizabeth struck back with prerogative powers to suppress and drive them underground for a time.[28]

> What began as an attempt to reform the Church was deflected by the historical situation into a contest for the right and the authority to make such reforms. This in turn led to a century-long debate over the grounds for claiming such a right, and over who in England had such right and authority.[29]

Protestantism taught that it was not what men did that made them righteous, but how they did it: with a devoted heart, and not mechanically for outward show. "A good man made a good work, not a good work a good

24 See the section in this chapter below "Puritan subdivisions."

25 Trinterud, "The Origins of Puritanism," 38; Hill, *Society*, 7

26 Hill, *Society*, 18

27 Kenneth Shipps, "The 'Political Puritan,'" *Church History* 45, no. 2 (June 1976): 197, http://www.jstor.org/stable/3163717 Accessed 30 January 2017

28 Trinterud, "The Origins of Puritanism," 46-47; Brenner, *Merchants and Revolution*, 664; Solt, "Revolutionary Calvinist Parties," 235, 236

29 Trinterud, "William Haller," 35

man."[30] Given a mostly illiterate population, Puritans emphasized preaching, endorsed by both Luther and Calvin, over prayer and ritual;[31] hence the struggle to control the pulpits. Many also opposed the much-hated collection of tithes.

Before the 1630s, most Puritans sought to reform the Church of England from within; only a very small number broke completely to become separatist sects.[32] Preaching took precedence above all else; "it was the duty of a minister to conform [to Church practices] rather than be silenced," a theologian maintained in 1605, and even King James endorsed it early on, provided what they preached was acceptable to him.[33] The large majority of Puritans thus remained, often uncomfortably, in the official Church, outwardly conforming to its dictates. But it thereby brought Puritan ideas to a large audience.[34] Particularly in London, from at least the 1610s, there was a thriving Puritan subculture that encompassed many congregations and ministers, and even some bishops.[35] In 1611, George Abbot, a Puritan sympathizer, was appointed Archbishop of Canterbury, succeeding the hard anti-Puritan Richard Bancroft.

Unofficial seminaries "maintained in the households of eminent Puritan divines, [were] a common feature of the godly scene..."[36] Doctrinal debates in pamphlets and pulpits, informal meetings and secret conventicles, were rife, only loosely regulated by the government most of the time. The ideological struggles over orthodoxy took place in front of a large godly audience of London laymen who financially supported these activities, and often took an active part. A preacher's reputation could be made or broken by this community. The Puritans' unofficial, semi-underground activities were kept as much as possible within the general Puritan community, and out of official sight, but on rare occasions broke into wider public view. The heterogeneity of conflicting claims bubbling among the London Puritan clergy, closely attended by the lay populace, was the background to the spread of more radical religion during the 1630s persecution. In 1640, these radical ideas exploded into the open.[37]

30 Christopher Hill, "Protestantism and the Rise of Capitalism," in *Essays in the Economic and Social History of Tudor and Stuart England*, ed. F. J. Fisher (Cambridge: Cambridge University Press, 1961), 18. Reprinted in Christopher Hill, *Change and Continuity in 17-Century England* (New Haven: Yale University Press, 1974, 1991)

31 Hill, *Society*, 18, 38-39

32 Christopher Hill, "History and Denominational History," *The Baptist Quarterly* 22, no. 2 (April 1, 1967). Reprinted in *The Collected Essays of Christopher Hill* Vol. 2 (Amherst: University of Massachusetts Press, 1986), 8

33 Tyacke, "Puritanism, Arminianism and Counter-Revolution," 122; Fincham and Lake, "Ecclesiastical Policy," 173, 175, 180; Hill, *Society*, 31-32

34 Cliffe, *The Puritan Gentry*, 6; C. H. George, "Puritanism as History and Historiography," *Past & Present*, no. 41 (December, 1968): 81, http://www.jstor.org/stable/650004 Accessed 17 October 2017

35 Tyacke, "Puritanism, Arminianism and Counter-Revolution," 125-127

36 Peter Lake and David Como, "'Orthodoxy' and Its Discontents: Dispute Settlement and the Production of 'Consensus' in the London (Puritan) 'Underground,'" *Journal of British Studies* 39, no. 1 (January 2000): 40, http://www.jstor.org/stable/175868 Accessed 25 December 2016.

37 Lake and Como, "London (Puritan) 'Underground,'" 34, 64-65, 66-68 fn. 81. This study provides a description of three pre-1630 "public" Puritan disputes. 35-63.

Puritan ideology in a changing society

Puritans wanted to instill in the population a recognition of the necessity for making God an active part of their everyday personal lives, as opposed to a passive, rote acceptance of whatever they were told by church officials. "For the godly, morality should be self-imposed: unquestioning obedience to the priest was a positive hindrance."[38] This activist perspective, which challenged individuals to take responsibility and think for themselves, was most popular among the petty-bourgeois crafts artisans and yeomen to whom it gave an ideological coherence as a class, distinct from the rich and the poor.[39] Middling tradesmen were the most numerous among the separatist sectary groups.[40] But many merchants and gentry, and even a few noblemen were also Puritan adherents or sympathizers. The latter groups' conceptions, however, were usually more conservative than those lower down on the social ladder.[41] The admonition for a "godly" life was analogous to the later emphasis on the more secular term "virtue" as a justification in the 18th century revolutions, and played a similar role.

Luther had firmly relocated religion from obedience to the Church to the belief of the individual, making the laity the equal of the clergy ("'the priesthood of all believers'").[42] He thereby completed the excoriating critique of England's own John Wycliffe.[43] Faith may have been its own justification,[44] but it was no easy matter. Oliver Cromwell committed to Puritanism during the 1630s after what appears to have been a prolonged emotional struggle.[45] It was constantly necessary to examine one's own motives. Only the individual could know whether his intentions and heart were pure. No amount of ritual could make it so. "There is nothing which gives men greater confidence and licence in sinning than the idea that after making confession to priests they can wipe their lips and say, I have not done it," wrote Calvin.[46]

This individualistic theology was an outgrowth of early capitalist economic activity. Free choice in religion flowed from free industry and free trade.[47] It

38 Hill, "Protestantism and the Rise of Capitalism," 21

39 Manning, *English People*, 178, 179-180

40 Keith Lindley, *Popular Politics and Religion in Civil War London* (Aldershot, Hampshire: Scolar Press, 1997), 80; Hill, *World*, 41

41 Underdown, *Pride's Purge*, 11

42 Hill, *Century*, 70; "Protestantism and the Rise of Capitalism," 82-84

43 Trevelyan, *England in the Age of Wycliffe*, 169-182. Wycliffe's works were largely destroyed by the authorities in England after his death, but copies were taken to Germany by his adherents where they influenced Jan Hus, first leader of the Czech Reformation, and his followers. 262, 347. It is an interesting question whether Luther, who certainly knew of Hus, had any knowledge of Wycliffe's writings.

44 Hill, "Protestantism and the Rise of Capitalism," 16-18; *Society*, 422

45 Antonia Fraser, *Cromwell: Our Chief of Men* (St. Albans, Hertshire: Grenada Publishing, 1973), 36-40; Christopher Hill, *God's Englishman: Oliver Cromwell and the English Revolution* (London: Penguin Books, 1970, 1988), 32, 42-43; Charles Firth, *Oliver Cromwell and the Rule of the Puritans in England* (New York: G.P. Putnam's Sons, 1900), 138-145, http://www.gutenberg.org/ebooks/57268 Accessed 6 July 2018

46 Hill, "Protestantism and the Rise of Capitalism," 21-22

47 Hill, *Society*, 423

was by design perfectly suited to the transformation of servile peasants into the wage workers, "free" to be exploited by any employer who would have them, that capitalism requires. Puritans made the dignity of labor a dominant social idea in the early 17th century, simultaneous with the increasing numbers of "masterless" day laborers, and the strategic weight of petty-bourgeois craftworkers and spreading manufacture.[48] The Puritans' severe attitude towards idleness flowed from this individualist outlook. The precept that work profited a man dovetailed all too neatly with the need to instill labor discipline on a population that had formerly lived in the country by the weather, and was unprepared to participate in a competitive money economy. The new workers were unused to the very regular rhythms of an industrializing society, and in this regard the established church was useless to them.[49] The condemnation of idleness was also a handy argument against the large number of royalist aristocrats during the Civil War. While most nobles and high gentry were Protestant, very few were Puritan, and a larger minority were Catholic.

The Puritans aimed to redefine labor as a social duty: that work should profit not only oneself, but one's neighbors. This argument spoke to the need to maximize economic accumulation so that England could compete internationally. Ambitiously, they proclaimed that it was better to increase one's knowledge and worth "'to be ready for every man's service.'"[50] This contrasted with the Catholic view that work was punishment for sin.

Puritans argued that popery encouraged idleness (monasteries and nunneries), population decline (chastity), superstition leading to extravagance and wastes of money (church decoration, images, pilgrimages), an excessive number of holidays (saints' days), and the robbery of alms from the poor by friars.[51] In feudal agricultural society one peasant had little opportunity to become richer than another; thus Catholicism presented poverty as a holy state. But for Protestants in an age of nascent capitalism, "...God helps those who help themselves, in which thrift, accumulation and industry are the cardinal virtues, and poverty very nearly a crime."[52] Thus work prevented one from succumbing to sins that idleness leaves one prey to. Catholicism was a religion for landlords who passively collected rents;[53] active pursuit of profit was justified provided one's motives were pure of heart.[54]

Spreading the word

Bibles in English had been available in cheap editions since 1575. In the early 17th century, a growing educated middle class could read, but the literate still included only a minority of the lay population. To Puri-

48 Hill, *Society,* 112

49 Hill, *Society,* 101

50 Hill, *Society,* 103-104

51 Hill, *Society,* 105-106

52 Hill, *Society,* 106, 229-232

53 Hill, "Protestantism and the Rise of Capitalism," 24-25

54 Hill, "Protestantism and the Rise of Capitalism," 32-33

tans, preaching was the best weapon available in the struggle against the Counter-Reformation. To disparage preaching when Protestantism was fighting for its life in Europe, they charged, was downright unpatriotic as Guy Fawkes' awful example of 1605 had demonstrated. Conservatives hated preaching, and argued that it led to rebellion, pointing to the Peasant War in Germany, the 1535 Anabaptist takeover of Münster, and Kett's peasant army of 1549 in Norfolk. Centrists replied that the people needed learned men to teach them, and that keeping them in ignorance would indeed only lead to more rebellion.[55]

Preaching was seen as the solution to the lower classes' extensive and horrifying ignorance of religion, or anything else, the legacy of the Church of Rome. Particularly in the less developed north and west of the country, which would in the main support the king in the Civil War, the continued existence of popery and superstition was viewed as both a spiritual and temporal threat. In these regions, a knight told Parliament in 1628, "'The prayers of the common people are more like spells and charms than devotions.'"[56] The spread of preaching's popularity mutually reinforced the Puritans' emphasis on it. This led many to view ministers who did not preach as incompetent, illegitimate, unlawful and/or damned. "'A greater part of the people,' said a preacher at Paul's Cross in 1598, hold it 'the only exercise of the service of God to hear a sermon.'"[57] Conservatives charged that listening to sermons, sometimes twice a day, was a lazy way of worship, which accounted for its mania among the common people: "'this insatiate appetite of it is originally founded either in the not having business or not attending to it'" which was why it attracted servants and workmen in particular. Sectarian separatists and many Independent congregations later combatted this charge of passivity by holding discussions after sermons, to which any member of the congregation could contribute.[58]

Such discussions were exactly what the hierarchy feared; the strongest denunciation of Puritanism was that it led to factions (as indeed it did) which disturbed social order. Foreigners, however, were impressed by how many people took notes during sermons, which Puritans approved of so that they could "'help others — children, servants, and neighbors of less understanding.'" Leaving one's own parish church to seek out sermons or better preachers was against the law, the penalty for which was substantial fines, but some braved it. The fears of conservatives were confirmed by the large increase in lay preaching, fed by the shortage of good preachers on the one hand and the view that any true believer was qualified to spread the word of God on the other.[59] The Church hierarchy was naturally shocked by this radically egalitarian notion: that untrained upstarts could propagate their

55 Hill, *Society*, 32-35

56 Hill, *Society*, 40

57 Hill, *Society*, 45

58 Hill, *Society*, 46

59 Hill, *Society*, 47-48

opinions was completely alien to feudal discipline, and directly threatened their own positions.

Puritans were not necessarily opposed to prayer, but most thought preaching more important. "Any minister could make the sign of the cross in baptism, but only a preaching minister could make the parents understand what baptism was really about."[60] Conservatives on the other hand emphasized prayer, which was held to increase devotion as opposed to faction. Catechizing was also upheld over preaching, as rote answers, which could be memorized by illiterate people, were comfortingly reliable. But this lulling passivity exactly subverted the Puritan principle of an "intelligent comprehension of faith."[61]

Puritan subdivisions

From 1629 on, Puritans were actively purged from the Church hierarchy, their teachings suppressed, and their ministers persecuted.[62] "...many court hardliners came to see Calvinist divinity and popular political subversion as two aspects of a seamless whole."[63]

> In the universities, the pulpits, and the press, the defense of predestinarian doctrine was proscribed, while Arminian clerics were steadily advanced to bishoprics, deaneries, and royal chaplaincies. This was a counter-revolution in the Church of England...[64]

Arminians, named for the Dutch theologian Jacobus Arminius, were opposed to key Calvinist beliefs, and regarded by Puritans as crypto-Catholics. In fact, it was under James that a steady increase in the appointment of Arminian bishops had begun: in 1603 there were at most two, in 1621, there were nine, and at his death, twelve.[65] The persecution under Charles not only reinforced the Puritan-parliamentary political alliance,[66] but saw the proliferation of more radical Puritan separatists. Illegal "gathered churches" were organized by like-minded worshipers who totally rejected the church hierarchy, and therefore the king's government which supported it. In the 1630s, Puritanism was both a political and religious tendency working out its ideas in the light of Charles' repression and the progress of events. Soon the lines began to be more clearly drawn between Presbyterians and Independents. (The smaller, more radical Anabaptists were the movement's left wing).

60 Conrad Russell, "Introduction," in *The Origins of the English Civil War*, ed. Conrad Russell (Basingstoke, Hampshire: Macmillan Education, 1973), 19

61 Hill, *Society*, 49-51

62 Tyacke, "Puritanism, Arminianism and Counter-Revolution," 137-140; David R. Como, "Predestination and Political Conflict in Laud's London," *The Historical Journal* 46, no. 2 (June 2003): 268-269, https://www.jstor.org/stable/3133511 Accessed 4 April 2019

63 Como, "Predestination and Political Conflict in Laud's London," 272

64 Caroline Hibbard, "Anti-Calvinists: The Rise of English Arminianism c. 1590-1640 by Nicholas Tyacke," *Albion* 20, no. 4 (Winter 1988): 619, https://www.jstor.org/stable/4050208 Accessed 22 April 2019

65 Harris, "Revisiting the Causes of the English Civil War," 626

66 Shipps, "The 'Political Puritan,'" 204-205

For Puritans of all stripes Laud's Arminian persecution did not just undermine orthodox Protestantism, but was a political attack on the people's liberties.[67]

> The evidence leaves little doubt that it was the Puritan citizens and clergy of the metropolis, and some of the less wealthy City merchants as well as a number of merchants of middle and upper middle rank, who nourished the cause of the parliamentary opposition in the years before 1640.[68]

Prior to 1640, the radical Puritan movement was "nourished" by three London parishes which, unusually, had the right to elect their own ministers and pay them as they saw fit; most official ministers of the state church were appointed by bishops, and supported, poorly, from tithes. A minority among the City clergy, these Puritan ministers were nonetheless respected and popular men whose leading parishioners were sometimes well-known, (such as Alderman Isaac Pennington), well-to–do and, in a very few cases, even titled.

"The rector of St. Anne's, Blackfriars, from 1621 was William Gouge, who for more than thirty years drew huge crowds, more than his church could accommodate, to his Sunday sermons and his Wednesday lectures."[69] A fourth parish church, St. Antholin's, had, since 1559, supported six lectures a week "in full Genevan fashion," making it "the centre of Puritan social and religious activities…a kind of 'missionary' headquarters in the heart of London." The lectures were used as a training ground for young preachers.[70] Those who attended were very likely to be millenarian enthusiasts, holding the expectation that the Kingdom of Jesus on Earth was close at hand: "the doctrine became almost orthodox on the Parliamentary side."[71] Though they understood it in their own way, this widespread belief reflected acute awareness of the unfolding social crisis.

Puritans generally considered some version of a presbyterian system, a strict form of which existed in Scotland, to be the goal for a new church. (An earlier, more directed movement for a Presbyterian church had been suppressed by Elizabeth.)[72] Both wings demanded more local autonomy than episcopacy (rule of the Church by bishops) allowed, but by 1640 they had different conceptions of how this should be implemented.

Presbyterians were more or less orthodox Calvinists who accepted predestination, the belief that god had already chosen the "elect" to be saved on judgement day. Their bias equated this minority with church "elders:" ministers and prominent men of sober and irreproachably respectable status (i.e., wealthy). They envisioned the elders would occupy congregational boards

67 Como, "Predestination and Political Conflict in Laud's London," 271

68 Pearl, *London and the Outbreak*, 160

69 Pearl, *London and the Outbreak*, 162-163

70 Pearl, *London and the Outbreak*, 163-164; Hexter, *King Pym*, 81

71 Hill, *World*, 33-34, 96

72 Cliffe, *The Puritan Gentry*, 6

governing the new church, overseeing the parish through their power to discipline the more ordinary, lower-class souls. Elected as representatives to regional and national synods, these men would be able to mandate decisions for implementation at the local level. All citizens would perforce be members of the new Church, just as had always been the case under feudalism.[73] Independents, informed by their experiences in Holland and America during the 1620s and '30s,[74] went further. They were not opposed to a national church structure *per se*, which they believed necessary for success on a national scale, but they denied it any compulsory authority over individual congregations or what they referred to as "tender consciences."

Independency, or congregationalism, was characterized by a decentralized, democratic structure in which able laymen could preach alongside trained clergymen.[75] Their religion derived from the same Calvinist sources as Presbyterianism, and included many of the same earnest deprecations of anything pleasurable as distractions from a godly life. But the Independent view placed far more emphasis on the individual's rights and responsibilities for his own fate. What was in a person's heart or conscience could not be known by anyone else, and therefore could not be imposed by an outside authority; it must come from a struggle within himself. Only in this way could one be assured of salvation. This conception was in contradiction to the Calvinist teaching that the elect to be saved were predetermined or, as was normally expected, likely part of the wealthy elite. It was also implicitly tolerant, at least to any reformed Christian.[76] These convictions for an absolute freedom of conscience, and against the dictates of any form of compulsion in religious government, made it the more consistently revolutionary wing of Puritanism. In the long run, however, although more democratic relative to Presbyterianism, it was usually less so compared to the Anabaptists and other separatist groups called sectaries.[77]

73 Hill, *Society*, 191-192, 204, 379-380, 423-424; H. N. Brailsford, *The Levellers and the English Revolution* (Nottingham: Spokesman, 1976, 1983), 28

74 Brenner, *Merchants and Revolution*, 395, 416-417

75 Brenner, *Merchants and Revolution*, 415

76 Brenner, *Merchants and Revolution*, 416; Hill, *Society*, 423-424

77 Trinterud, "William Haller," 42-43

5) THE FRANCHISE

Preoccupation with the individual and his rights began in the seventeenth century, with the rise of the bourgeoisie, whose existence and development as a class depended on the freedom of the individual capitalist to buy, and of the individual proletarian to sell, labour power. The rebellion of the rising bourgeoisie against the economic shackles of feudalism found its political, social and ideological expression in opposition to arbitrary political power, to arbitrary restraints on personal liberty, to the violation of human dignity and to clerical obscurantism. The fight was seen as a struggle between reason and unreason.

~Peter Fryer[1]

The Puritan alternative to the established church hierarchy presented a democratic challenge to the feudal political system as a whole. At the end of the 16th century not much electoral activity took place. "...the wishes of the bulk of the population counted for little..."[2] Along with restrictions on the aristocracy, the Tudor promotion of centralization in government affected town governments as well. Royal charters frequently anointed local burgesses as the sole electors, who consequently either elected those of their own circle, or candidates favored by local aristocrats.[3]

Because reform of the English church required government action, Puritans began to seek government offices through popular election, often successfully. In 1586, a Puritan activist forced a town oligarchy to admit him to the local government or face the people's long-disused electoral right.[4] The Tudors had kept the franchise limited on the grounds that "'the people must be governed, not pleased,'" as an oligarchic candidate told an upstart contender for Parliament in 1584.[5] Set by law in 1430, only freeholders worth 40 shillings were qualified to vote.[6] This "excluded smaller freeholders, copyholders, cottagers, leaseholders, and paupers," i.e., the overwhelming bulk of the rural population.[7] Even freeholders in the 16th century were unlikely to travel long distances to vote, and "humble tradesmen" were not going to challenge the nominee of their betters unless

1 "Freedom of the Individual," *Labour Review* 3, no. 4 (August-September 1958): 121, Marxists Internet Archive, https://www.marxists.org/history/etol/newspape/lr/vol03/v03n04-aug-sep-1958-lr.pdf Accessed 1 May 2020.

2 Hirst, *Representative?*, 1

3 Richard L. Bushman, "English Franchise Reform in the Seventeenth Century," *Journal of British Studies* 3, no. 1 (November 1963): 40, https://www.jstor.org/stable/175047 Accessed 29 September 2018

4 J. H. Plumb, "The Growth of the Electorate in England from 1600 to 1715," *Past & Present*, no. 45 (November, 1969): 94, https://www.jstor.org/stable/650049 Accessed 24 April 2020. Reprinted in *Seventeenth-Century England: Society In An Age of Revolution*, ed. Paul S. Seaver (New York: New Viewpoints, 1976).

5 Plumb, "Growth of the Electorate," 94

6 Hirst, *Representative?*, 13

7 Hill, *Century*, 36

some great issue was at stake.[8] By the early 17th century, more towns were represented in Parliament by county gentry than otherwise.[9]

Thus the franchise was "a privilege attached to particular types of property." Without sufficient property a man was not free.[10] But by the 1620s, due to the inflation, someone worth only 40 shillings was now considered poor, and this expanded downward the number of eligible rural voters under the law.[11] The early Stuarts' chronic financial difficulties, and multiple disputes with their parliaments, necessitated the convoking of more parliaments "to replace the ones that had failed before." The greater number of elections by itself raised interest and awareness among the electorate.[12] Further, those areas in which the greatest electoral interest occurred were also those undergoing brisk economic changes, and strongly Puritan.[13]

Beginning with a county election dispute in 1604, the House of Commons entered a course of wresting control over elections away from the king's government.[14] "The efforts of the gentry were aided by indigenous pressures building up in many communities, which culminated in domestic challenges to unpopular urban oligarchies."[15] In the boroughs (towns), now quite larger than a century before, uncertainty about who was eligible to vote, as well as the prestige associated with representing them, increased the number of disputes referred to the Commons.[16] The rebellious House resolved many election disputes during the politically turbulent and economically depressed 1620s, usually to the benefit of the voters. This had the effect of widening the franchise, especially in the boroughs.[17]

The efforts of the Puritans and the Commons effected a slow but steady expansion of voting rights for those of the common people ("'men with no shirts,' a disgruntled noble called them")[18] who were becoming eligible to vote: "yeomen and poorer peasants in the counties and the shopkeepers and craftsmen and some of the poor in many towns."[19] Conservative and royalist gentry, as "men of quality," attempted to resist this trend; their distaste for acknowledging political differences comported with the emphasis

8 Plumb, "Growth of the Electorate," 94

9 Hill, *Century*, 36

10 Hill, *Century*, 37-38; *Reformation*, 32

11 Hirst, *Representative?*, 31

12 Hirst, *Representative?*, 2

13 Richard Cust, "Politics and the Electorate in the 1620s," in *Conflict in Early Stuart England*, eds. Richard Cust and Ann Hughes (London: Longman Group, 1989), 160-161

14 Plumb, "Growth of the Electorate," 95. For a detailed description, see Derek Hirst, "Elections and the Privileges of the House of Commons in the Early Seventeenth Century: Confrontation or Compromise?," *The Historical Journal* 18, no. 4 (December 1975), http://www.jstor.org/stable/2638517 Accessed 11 April 2020

15 Hirst, *Representative?*, 2

16 Hirst, *Representative?*, 25, 91

17 Hirst, *Representative?*, 11-12; Plumb, "Growth of the Electorate," 95-97, 100

18 Hill, *World*, 21; Hirst, Representative?, 33-34

19 Manning, *English People*, 13-14

in feudal ideology on social order and the immutability of rank. They not infrequently found ways of accommodating local sentiment without the necessity of an open contest.[20]

Such subterfuges were facilitated by the fact that no bill was ever passed codifying electoral eligibility, despite some declarations by the Commons' Committee on Privileges. The concerns of most MPs were to insure honest elections, free from interference by the crown and oligarchs, and less a belief in a democratic franchise *per se*. A proposed franchise reform bill in 1621 actually raised the amount of property needed to vote in rural counties[21] (the gentry's home turf). But opposition to the Stuarts, and divisions within the gentry over religion and government matters, made an electoral base of voters an asset to many gentlemen.[22] "Besides the principled desire for honest elections, the anti-Court group in the Commons wished to strengthen their numbers, and aspiring gentry hoped to win seats in Parliament by appealing to the populace."[23]

In particular, the gentry were quite aware of their power over taxation, and of that power's singular status in Europe. The monarchy's use of monopoly patents, forced loans and increased customs duties called into question "the future survival of representative institutions…"[24] If the crown could tax on its own authority, what was the purpose of having a parliament? "Fears lest parliaments should be discontinued, already voiced in 1610 and 1614, were stronger: they were to be repeated in every parliament of the [1620s] decade."[25] Stressing their responsibility to their constituents was a rationale for resisting the absolutist tendencies of the monarchy,[26] while expanding the electorate was believed to be a way of limiting outside influence.[27]

Dominating families in the countryside now had to face actual contests in many places rather than just specifying candidates or assuming the seats themselves. That the increased electorate so often returned anti-court, or at least those who appeared to be anti-court, candidates[28] is easily explained by the political struggles, driven by local and national controversies, taking place in many localities during this time.

> …Parliament, and in particular the Commons, was frequently seen as standing for a purified Protestant commonwealth and the defense of liberties against the corruption and tyranny sometimes associated with

20 Cust, "Politics and the Electorate in the 1620s," 139; Hirst, *Representative?*, 14-16

21 Bushman, "English Franchise Reform," 39; Hirst, *Representative?*, 31; Plumb, "Growth of the Electorate," 96

22 Plumb, "Growth of the Electorate," 103-104

23 Bushman,"English Franchise Reform," 43

24 Hirst, *Representative?*, 8; Tyacke, "Revolutionary Puritanism," 757

25 Hill, "Parliament and People in 17th-Century England," 109

26 Hirst, *Representative?*, 9

27 Hirst, *Representative?*, 11

28 Richard Cust, "Election and Selection in Stuart England," *Parliamentary History* 7, no. 2 (October 1988): 346

"the Court."[29]

For reforming and/or Puritan gentry there was thus a programmatic basis to their campaigns that, in addition to local issues or gentry rivalries, involved national issues to an important degree, particularly religion.[30] "...increasingly in the 1620s it was associated with godliness, opposition to popery and a willingness to speak in defence of the subject's liberties." Candidates who stood on this platform were regarded as "patriots."[31]

The unpopularity of Charles' chief minister, the Duke of Buckingham, who had imprisoned opposition MPs, played a role in the elections of 1626, as did the campaign against popery.[32] The Puritan MP Thomas Scott claimed "'that it is contrarie to the lawe of God, nature and reason, that any king should usurp, or any free state ordaine, absolute and unlimited and lawlesse dominion.'"[33] In the clothing towns of Yorkshire, freeholders "had to be wooed with political arguments. ...very large crowds assembl[ed] on election day, with estimates as high as 10,000 in 1628."[34]

In 1640, "with the Crown making a particularly concerted effort to get its nominees into Parliament almost regardless of the difficulties,"[35] at least 70 constituencies had rival contestants running for a seat in the Commons, with real issues in dispute. "...one of the candidates nominated by the oligarchy was opposed on the grounds that he had promoted the collection of shipmoney, suppressed preaching, and discouraged the education of poor children."[36] Overall 85 returns were referred to the House Committee on Privileges for adjudication.[37] As earlier however, no franchise bill was passed, at least in part because it would have no hope of support in the House of Lords or by the king.[38]

29 Cust, "Politics and the Electorate in the 1620s," 142

30 Hirst, *Representative?*, 145

31 Cust, "Election and Selection in Stuart England," 349-350

32 Cust, "Politics and the Electorate in the 1620s," 142-143

33 Tyacke, "Revolutionary Puritanism," 755

34 Cust, "Politics and the Electorate in the 1620s," 151

35 Cust, "Politics and the Electorate in the 1620s," 154

36 Manning, *English People*, 13-14

37 Hirst, *Representative?*, 111, 216-222

38 Hirst, *Representative?*, 17 fn. 32

6) THE GOVERNMENT OF LONDON

> *Nothing could be more misleading than to suggest that the constitution of the City of London was well defined either in theory or practice. Except among a few antiquarians and lawyers, the form of the constitution was of small interest to those concerned in the working of the City government. They had no Whiggish preconceptions about fixed methods of procedure or "constitutional rights," but adopted what lay to hand in the way that best suited their immediate purposes. For that reason...any general statement about the constitution [is] subject to many qualifications.*
>
> ~Valerie Pearl[1]

Oligarchic rule was most powerful in London. There were "three main Courts or Councils": Lord Mayor and Aldermen, Common Council, and Common Hall. The first was, roughly, the executive; the second, even more roughly, legislative; and the last "acted solely in an electoral capacity."[2] Membership in Common Hall was nominally limited, since 1475, to members of the livery companies (guilds), numbering some 4,000 men in 1640. The establishment of newer guilds in the sixteenth and seventeenth centuries for some "craftsmen working in humbler trades" gave it a more inclusive and popular character.[3] But, unless there was a dispute, during the elections for London's officials "...men who were not entitled to vote frequently stayed and took part in elections. Since voting was usually by show of hands, there was no systematic way of checking on the voters' qualifications."[4]

Most practices of municipal government were ruled by feudal custom, not law, but even where law existed custom often trumped it. At the beginning of the 16th century, the right to nominate and elect the City's four MPs was given solely to Common Hall. But the tradition that the Court of Aldermen and Common Hall each nominate two of the four candidates, whose selections were then ratified by the Common Council, persisted until 1628,[5] a landmark year as will be seen.

The majority of elected office holders came from the twelve main livery companies.[6] The domination of the aldermen in City affairs, including elections, dated back to the 14th century. Freemen and householders could nominally vote for and serve as common councilors, but in practice only liverymen normally held the office.[7] In the early 17th century, parish church vestries often controlled the local electoral process.[8] The powers of

1 *London and the Outbreak*, 49

2 Pearl, *London and the Outbreak*, 49

3 Pearl, *London and the Outbreak*, 50

4 Pearl, *London and the Outbreak*, 50-51

5 Pearl, *London and the Outbreak*, 52-53, 109

6 Pearl, *London and the Outbreak*, 116

7 Pearl, *London and the Outbreak*, 53-55

8 Pearl, *London and the Outbreak*, 55

the Council were ill-defined and weak, and only its wealthiest members, in conjunction with the aldermen and Lord Mayor, had any real influence. Not only did the aldermen participate in the Council's discussions, "Only those measures proposed to the assembly on the initiative of the Court of Aldermen were in fact discussed," and they held veto power over it. Disputed elections were also resolved by them, and only the Lord Mayor had the power to call or dismiss a Council meeting. Whereas the aldermen met twice a week in the early 17th century the Council sat no more than 6 times a year, and often much less.[9]

> So skillfully balanced was the City constitution that the Privy Council in 1621 commended it to the magistrates of Norwich (one of the few corporations where the citizens as a whole still exercised substantial influence) pointing out the admirable advantages of the constitution in excluding the lower orders, while maintaining a show of more liberal government.[10]

Elections to Norwich's more open aldermanic council were gradually suppressed by the Privy Council during the 1620s,[11] but in 1642 the powers of the London aldermen and Lord Mayor over the Common Council were done away with in practice by the revolution.

The much smaller Court of Aldermen controlled the selection process of its own members, who served for life, and were usually members of one of the twelve major livery companies. A property qualification of £10,000 was required to hold office. The aldermen oversaw all of the subsidiary courts and City government functions, and some senior members also sat as judges or Justices of the Peace (JPs). All guild ordinances had to obtain their approval, and they "enjoyed the special privilege of presenting petitions to the throne, and at the hands of the Sheriffs, to the House of Commons." They also had the power to appoint, or sell, some 140 municipal positions. The aldermen's discussions occurred in secret, and they did not have to explain their decisions.[12] In this way, they were able to maintain their complete control of London's government.

9 Pearl, *London and the Outbreak*, 56-58

10 Pearl, *London and the Outbreak*, 67

11 Hirst, *Representative?*, 48

12 Pearl, *London and the Outbreak*, 59-61

7) ENGLAND AND THE EARLY STUARTS (1603-1640)

The citizenry of the towns used money as a carpenter uses his plane: as a tool to level political inequality. Wherever a personal relationship was replaced by a monetary relationship, a rendering of goods by a rendering of money, that was the place where a bourgeois pattern took the place of a feudal pattern.

~Frederick Engels[1]

James I and VI

In 1603 James VI of Scotland (son of Mary Stewart, Queen of Scots) came to the throne of England as James I. For the first time in history the two nations were subject to the same ruler, but otherwise remained entirely separate. This odd situation would have momentous political consequences later in the century.

"By 1600 gentlemen, new and old, occupied a far greater proportion of the land of England than in 1530 — to the disadvantage of crown, church, aristocracy [nobility] and peasantry alike."[2] The landed gentry in England, staunchly Protestant, was by now generally, if conservatively, influenced by Puritanism; Parliament, for the first time, refused to sit on Sundays.[3] "... the Puritan group in the House of Commons made persistent efforts to secure the passage of legislation aimed at punishing such evils as swearing, drunkenness and adultery."[4] Even in 1586, London aldermen were directed to select men for the Trained Bands from "householders and able-bodied children and servants 'who openly profess and show themselves to love the Gospel and hate Popery'..."[5] There were early hopes that the new king would reform the church, and limit or eliminate the influence of the bishops. James recognized, however, that the established church was an essential prop of the monarchy: not for nothing were kings the anointed of God. He had previously contended with the democratic aspirations of the Scottish Reformation, and promoted the introduction of bishops into the Presbyterian church structure there. "No bishops, no king" was his succinct, and prophetic, reply to reformers.[6]

The Scottish king was nevertheless, much like the English gentry, a conservative Calvinist. He was opposed to both Puritanism (especially Presbyterianism) and Catholicism.[7]

1 "The Decline of Feudalism and the Rise of the Bourgeoisie," Marx and Engels, *Collected Works* Vol. 26 (London: Lawrence & Wishart, 1884, 1990), Marxists Internet Archive, https://marxists.architexturez.net/archive/marx/works/1884/decline/index.htm Accessed 27 October 2021

2 Hill, *Reformation*, 64

3 John Richard Green, *History of the English People* Vol. 5 (New York: Wallachia Publishers, 1874, 2015), 39, Kindle. Reprinted as *Green's England* (New York: Peter Fenelon Collier & Son, 1900); Trinterud, "William Haller," 38; Hill, *Society*, 7

4 Cliffe, *The Puritan Gentry*, 7

5 Nagel, "The Militia of London," 11

6 Hill, *Century*, 67-68; Fincham and Lake, "Ecclesiastical Policy," 174

7 Fincham and Lake, "Ecclesiastical Policy," 170-171, 173-174

> James...was prepared to give favour and preferment to anti-Calvinists and to allow a range of theological opinion within the establishment of the church. But he did not want open theological debate or dispute, and in order to avoid it he imposed silence on the anti-Calvinists, while at the same time distancing himself from the excesses of hyper-Calvinism. ... James had no desire to sponsor an extreme Calvinist heresy hunt.[8]

As a practical matter, the Church was thus largely kept as Elizabeth had left it, with multiple tendencies smothered under a pretended uniformity.

Christopher Hill comments that it took the Tudors 100 years to subdue the aristocracy. Nonetheless, the nobility was still the linchpin that counterbalanced the monarchy. "...the landed class had won a position rare in Europe...virtually independent of a [central] government..."[9] Only now, the nobles' power "was no longer measured principally by the number of their followers, the men who would fight for them: it was determined by their wealth."[10] Landowners, even if ennobled, had long since been forced to adapt to the bourgeois manner of conducting business, and by 1600 the titled peers were mostly no longer a military caste with private armies of thugs at their command.[11] The Parliament of 1628 repealed most (Tudor) laws that regulated or limited the nobles' military retainers as obsolete.[12] But in exchange for a reduction in their power, and the frightened deference it had elicited, they all the more fiercely defended their privileges.[13] Whereas Elizabeth had granted only a handful of new titles, James was so prodigious in bestowing or, worse, selling titles, that nobles and knights felt their prestige injured.[14] James, from a much less developed country closer to its feudal past than England, was infuriated that he had to put up with a semi-independent Parliament and judiciary.

> "So long as his bishops were 'my bishops,' his judges were 'my judges' and his parliament was 'my parliament,'" he was happy to engage in lengthy, good-natured debate with them; but he was allergic to any suggestion that they enjoyed a standing separate from the ultimate will of the crown.[15]

A 1610 work in Latin argued that "men are not by nature born free. On the contrary, the relationship of subjects to their rulers is equivalent to that of children to their parents. Sovereignty is indivisible, and under a monarchy parliaments are merely consultative bodies." James' work, *The Trew Law of Free Monarchies*, published in England in 1603, contained an "unequivocal

8 Peter Lake, "Calvinism and the English Church 1570-1635," *Past & Present*, no. 114 (February, 1987): 51, http://www.jstor.org/stable/650960 Accessed 10 August 2015

9 Hill, *Century*, 87

10 Hill, *Reformation*, 19, 29-30

11 Anderson, *Absolutist State*, 125-126; Hill, *Reformation*, 34

12 Hexter, "Storm Over the Gentry," 145-146

13 Hill, *Reformation*, 48

14 Stone, *Crisis of the Aristocracy*, 41-43, 48-52, 56, 58; Hill, *Reformation*, 107

15 Colin Kidd, "Royal Panic Attack," *London Review* of Books 33, no. 12 (16 June 2011), http://www.lrb.co.uk/v33/n12/colin-kidd/royal-panic-attack Accessed 22 May 2013, quoting Conrad Russell.

assertion of royal absolutism..."[16]

The limitations on the crown did not mean it was feeble. "It was the reverse, for these circumstances preserved the supremacy of the aristocratic society in which the monarchy was embedded and from which it drew its strength."[17] The "King in Parliament" was the theoretical formulation that codified the unsteady relationship between the two wings of the outmoded feudal ruling class, neither of whom could yet do without the other. In the absence of a parliament, the monarch's will was law. Only he could bring Parliament into being, and he could dismiss it any time. He could also veto any measure it passed. The monarch's prerogatives were absolute and sacrosanct, his authority dominant, his person the repository of the nation's sovereignty, its unifying symbol, the apex of church and state.

> The king really ruled; he was the ultimate responsible party. Yet the king could do no wrong: more than a legal fiction, it was the article of faith on which the polity rested. To remove or even question it was virtually an act of rebellion.[18]

In the face of this defining supremacy, the traditional subordination of Parliament within the rigid feudal hierarchy made it particularly difficult for gentry MPs to legitimate their criticisms. As the Earl of Manchester, head of a Parliamentary army, expressed it in 1644, "If we beat the King ninety and nine times yet he is King still and so will his posterity be after him; but if the King beat us once we shall all be hanged, and our posterity made slaves." To which Oliver Cromwell famously replied, "My Lord, if this be so, why did we take up arms at first? This is against fighting ever hereafter."[19]

The English gentry, an anomalous class

The landholding knights and squires who populated the House of Commons constituted the lower nobility;[20] legally commoners, they were nonetheless highly privileged ones.

> All that the gentry had in common was their gentility, their status as gentlemen. But, although this status was not based on the size of income, it was founded on the source of income, that it came from land and not from trade or industry.[21]

They were thus an intermediate class, but not a homogeneous one, as their incomes could range anywhere from £50 to £10,000 per year.[22] Lower gentry ran the local affairs of the parish, higher gentry those of the county.

16 Tyacke, "Revolutionary Puritanism," 753; Johann Sommerville, "Ideology, Property and the Constitution," in *Conflict in Early Stuart England*, eds. Richard Cust and Ann Hughes (London: Longman Group, 1989), 51-52

17 Manning, "The Nobles, the People and the Constitution," 50

18 Zaller, "The Concept of Opposition," 233

19 Hill, *Century*, 108; *God's Englishman*, 69; *1640*, 59; Fraser, *Cromwell*, 138

20 Hill, *Century*, 37

21 Manning, *1649*, 51

22 Manning, *1649*, 51; Stone, *Crisis of the Aristocracy*, 68

The former served as undersheriffs or other assisting officials, and grand jurors; the latter were sheriffs, Justices of the Peace (JPs) or judges. The highest of these were appointed Lords Lieutenant and deputies by the king, or might even be given an office at Court.[23] Enforcement of the crown's policies was entirely dependent on these men (backed up by church courts and officials).

The economic changes in Elizabethan England caused major social shifts that were beginning to solidify and become more visible under the Stuarts. The first decades of the 17th century saw a continuation of the 16th-century inflation, which adversely affected aristocrats whose lands were occupied by copyholders on long leases at low rents. To preserve their idle livings the landlords needed to increase their incomes. Peers and greater gentry, who were used to sumptuous living, had an almost unlimited ability to obtain loans from "the great London aldermen and merchant financiers on the security of aristocratic mortgages, statutes, and bonds,"[24] and nobles were immune to arrest for non-payment of debts.[25] Some of the nobility invested in overseas trade,[26] urban building,[27] mining and industrial ventures, but they were also greatly concerned to preserve their social position and privileges. They "sought to indirectly profit"[28] from industrial production, and usually kept their distance from any direct involvement.[29]

> Active personal occupation in a trade or profession was generally thought to be humiliating. The man of business was inferior to the gentleman of leisure who lived off his rents. Retail trade was always degrading, and overseas trade only a respectable occupation for a son and heir if pursued as a hobby rather than as a profession.[30]

"It was perfectly in order for Sir Percival Willoughby to own ships and transport his coal down the Trent to Lincolnshire, but disreputable to buy corn there to provide a return freight for resale in Nottingham."[31] The nobility and higher gentry were thus resistant to the steady distortions capitalist markets introduced which undermined their medieval social standing, and which characterized the bourgeois mode of living. The price pinch was especially felt by those below the top rung of gentry, who had less stake in rank, and therefore were more willing to accept an active managerial role. Like the

23 Underdown, *Pride's Purge*, 25; Stone, *Crisis of the Aristocracy*, 28; Manning, *1649*, 54-55

24 Stone, *Crisis of the Aristocracy*, 162

25 Hill, *Reformation*, 48

26 Based on surviving records from 1600-1630, one study found approximately 23% of those who invested in overseas monopoly trading companies were aristocrats. Theodore K. Rabb, "Investment in English Overseas Enterprise, 1575-1630," *The Economic History Review* 19, no. 1 (1966): 74, https://www.jstor.org/stable/2592793 Accessed 7 February 2019

27 Pearl, *London and the Outbreak*, 12

28 Engels, Introduction to *Socialism: Utopian and Scientific*, 389

29 Stone, *Crisis of the Aristocracy*, 89, 91, 157-159, 161-162, 165-172; Hill, *Reformation*, 66; Grassby, "Social Mobility and Business Enterprise," 355-356

30 Stone, *Crisis of the Aristocracy*, 24; Manning, *1649*, 56

31 Stone, *Crisis of the Aristocracy*, 161. In George Bernard Shaw's play *Major Barbara*, the 24-year old son of a weapons industrialist, circa 1900, sneers at his father for being "in trade." His mother reproaches him: "Cannons are not trade, Stephen. They are enterprise."

nobility, the gentry had been selling the agricultural produce of their estates at market for well over a century, and those with capital or the ability to borrow it searched for metals to mine, or developed other industries (such as iron or lead works) on their land.[32] A variety of methods provided opportunities to improve their holdings: consolidation or expansion of lands, enclosures of commons and waste (unused) lands, modernizations, drainage, new crops and techniques, and clearing forests, as well as rack rents, short leases, calculated marriages[33] and other means. But the lesser men, more in need, were often better placed to take advantage.

> Generally it was the larger and more scattered estates which proved the most difficult to reorganize; the medium-sized land-owner alone had both the personal interest and the technical possibility of supervising all his estates. The larger owners, and the less efficient, those who had failed to adapt themselves in time, trailed further and further behind, dragging on from hand to mouth on "unimproved" estates, heavily mortgaged and involved in lawsuits, miserably unfit but surviving.[34]

Improving gentlemen were the most sensitive to the crown's prerogative powers, which kept property ownership insecure and individual freedom of action (i.e., their own) restricted. This gave them much in common with yeomen, domestic manufacturers, artisans, and merchants:

> The cry of property in danger united a wide movement behind the nobility and gentry, not only the urban middle class, but the small producers in town and country, the mass of the people. ... No longer was the idea of property merely a defence of the old order but a challenge to that order — a demand to free the small producers from the exploitation of the existing system. This merged with the middle class hostility to government interference with economic activities and their demand for the removal of restrictions on production. It further embraced...a régime of economic freedom which would give a free hand to landlords.[35]

Importantly, the landlords' freedom to carry out enclosures without interference, as both the Tudors and Stuarts (for different reasons) had made obstructive, but largely ineffective, efforts to curb the practice.[36] Parliament passed 11 Acts against enclosure between 1489 and 1624,[37] but "...the process was carried on by means of individual acts of violence against which legislation, for a hundred and fifty years, fought in vain."[38] Especially under

32 Stone, *Crisis of the Aristocracy*, 161-162

33 Hill, *Century*, 12; Stone, *Crisis of the Aristocracy*, 91; Buchanan Sharp, "Village Revolts: Social Protest and Popular Disturbances in England, 1509-1640 by Roger B. Manning," *Albion* 21, no. 1 (Spring 1989): 101, https://www.jstor.org/stable/4049875 Accessed 12 July 2018

34 Hill, "Land in the English Revolution," 27

35 Manning, "The Nobles, the People and the Constitution," 58

36 Hill, *Century*, 13; *Reformation*, 69; "Land in the English Revolution," 29; Marx, *Capital* Vol. 1, 719-721; Fisher, "Commercial Trends and Policy," 103

37 Nicholas Blomley, "Making Private Property: Enclosure, Common Right and the Work of Hedges," *Rural History* 18, no. 1 (April 2007): 4, https://www.proquest-com/docview/211060271/fulltextPDF/643D9D8DBFB44BCPQ/1? Accessed 10 May 2021

38 Marx, *Capital* Vol. 1, 724

Charles I, fining for enclosure allowed the crown to pose (unsuccessfully) as friend to the peasantry, while (successfully) irritating the gentry. Meanwhile, the latter "continued to exploit its tenantry through manor courts..."[39]

> The freezing reception given by the Long Parliament to petitions from the peasants for the redress of agrarian grievances is hardly surprising, when it is remembered that one in every two of the members returned, up to the end of 1640, for the five Midland Counties which were the disturbed area of the day, either themselves had been recently fined for depopulation [enclosure] or belonged to families which had been.[40]

The pace of enclosure would pick up after the Civil War when government interference ceased.[41] But the progress of enclosure, which eventually converted the aristocracy to proprietary capitalist farmers and the peasantry to proletarians, nevertheless was slow.[42] "Even in the last decade of the 17th century, the yeomanry, the class of independent peasants, were more numerous than the class of farmers."[43] The use of enclosure for economic reasons that began in the late 15th century would last to the end of the 18th century.[44]

Yeomen, the largest of whom might be as wealthy as some of the lower or even middle gentry by 1640,[45] were working, capitalist farmers not idle socialites or remote investors. They enjoyed no legal privileges, so had no personal attachment to the feudal order. Like larger yeomen, gentry might also directly employ agricultural labor on their estates, or lease land directly where they were able to (e.g., to expanding yeomen or investors), further manifesting themselves as rural capitalists. But feudal land tenures operated upwards as well as downwards: directly or indirectly "'...most of the great families of the nation were tenants of the crown...'"[46] The complex and overlapping tenures acted as a drag on land transfers.

Not until after the First Civil War in 1646 would Parliament do away with feudal tenures (reiterated in 1656 and 1660), giving the aristocracy "absolute ownership of their estates,"[47] but leaving them in place for the

39 Hill, "A Bourgeois Revolution?," 130

40 R. H. Tawney, "Rise of the Gentry," 34-35; Hill, *Century*, 13

41 Hill, *Reformation*, 151; "Land in the English Revolution," 42-43

42 Hill, *Reformation*, 70; Hilton, "Feudalism and the Origins of Capitalism," 21; J. R. Wordie, "The Chronology of English Enclosure, 1500-1914," *The Economic History Review* 36, no. 4 (November 1983): 503, http://www.jstor.org/stable/2597236 Accessed 1 July 2017

43 Marx, *Capital* Vol. 1, 722

44 Hill, "The English Civil War Interpreted by Marx and Engels," 139; *1640*, 70; Marx, *Capital* Vol. 1, 727-728

45 Manning, *1649*, 57-58

46 Hill, *Reformation*, 101, 146-147; "Land in the English Revolution," 28

47 Hill, *Reformation*, 146; *Century*, 126-127; Marx, *Capital* Vol. 1, 723. "This was the decisive change in English history which made it different from that of the continent. From it every other difference in English society stemmed." H. J. Perkin, "The Social Causes of the British Industrial Revolution," *Transactions of the Royal Historical Society* 18 (1968): 135, http://www.jstor.org/stable/3678958 Accessed 11 December 2016

copyholders who "remain[ed] in abject dependence on their landlords..."[48] Feudal fees such as "...reliefs, arbitrary fines, merchets, heriots and other payments due from tenants to their lords were left intact and explicitly confirmed" by legislation in the 1640s and 1650s.[49] The replacement of customary tenures with capitalist leases would not become decisive until the second half of the 17th century, since "The improving landlord was not typical before 1660."[50] Those gentry who did embrace the new Puritan emphasis on thrift and capitalist accumulation did not therefore accept any idea of doing physical labor themselves. Outward displays of conspicuous wealth, such as lavish feasting or elegant clothing, fell out of favor with many gentry by the early 17th century, but they did not abandon their commitment to their feudal status as privileged idlers. They still regarded themselves as the natural rulers in the countryside. Anachronistic and antagonistic personal relations continued to exist as part of the tenant-landlord relationship for as long as copyhold remained in force, and were keenly felt by the peasants as demonstrated by their actions in the lead-up to the Civil War.[51]

Copyhold tenants were "'the body of the kingdom'" according to a Buckinghamshire petition to General Fairfax at the end of the Civil War.[52] The greater part of the aristocracy whose tenants still maintained their rights in the decades before the Civil War were therefore in a highly peculiar position: their participation in the swelling money economy habituated them to business and finance, yet they still retained a conflictive status vis-à-vis the peasantry. As landlords, the gentry subordinated tenants (whom they called "their people") through their feudal rank and legal power over them.[53] This dual role of the gentry came from having a foot in each of two incompatible social systems, feudalism and capitalism, which could not indefinitely coexist.

Social consequences of growth in the capitalist economy

By the time of James' ascension it was an article of faith in England "that commerce, shipping and manufactures were the El Dorado of the future..." To command the sea was to command the world. This conviction, widely accepted in the ruling class, only strengthened as the 17th century proceeded.[54] It is difficult to overstate the degree to which London, with its busy port and a population of around 200,000 in 1600, (nearly ten times its nearest competitors), economically dominated the country.[55] "Consumption of corn in London is estimated to have grown by 230 per cent between 1605

48 Hill, *Reformation*, 147; *1640*, 69-70; Marx, *Capital* Vol. 1, 723

49 Hill, "Land in the English Revolution," 41

50 Hill, *1640*, 29

51 See Chapter 14 below.

52 Manning, *English People*, 205

53 Hill, "Recent Interpretations of the Civil War," 71; "Land in the English Revolution," 24-25; Underdown, *Pride's Purge*, 28-29

54 R. H. Tawney, *Business and Politics Under James I* (London: Cambridge University Press, 1958), 3

55 Pearl, *London and the Outbreak*, 13-14; Tawney, *Business and Politics Under James I*, 75-76; Hill, *Reformation*, 26

and 1661... Grain imports to London from three north-eastern counties rose fourteen times in the sixty years before the civil war."[56] The city's population would almost double again by 1642.[57]

The need to feed London's growing population stimulated the commercial expansion and improvement of agriculture, as well as industry.[58] This growing market, as well as the steady inflation, meant agricultural prices rose continuously in the late 16th and early 17th centuries to the benefit of the peasantry.[59] But it was a detriment to gentlemen who let their lands to copyhold tenants at low rents for long periods. Landlords, in order to take the agricultural profits for themselves, retaliated through the use of enclosures, rack-rents (large increases), short leases, and the revival of every obsolete feudal tax they could find, supported by new legal claims, interpretations, and laws.[60] Through these methods they forced tenants off the land, and caused an immense redistribution of wealth to the landowning class, including the crown.[61]

Many dispossessed tenants took to the forests to live semi-legally as cottagers, but most migrated to the edges of villages and towns, especially London, where they constituted a pool of desperately poor casual labor.[62] In 1602 a judge thought that some 15% of London's population was unemployed; it may well have been higher.[63] A self-perpetuating cycle was set in motion as capitalist market relations expanded in the countryside, and continued virtually unchecked through the 17th century.[64] By the mid-18th century the small peasantry and yeomanry had mostly disappeared,[65] and mass vagabondage became the most pressing social problem in England.

In pastoral areas where the chief occupation was raising livestock, farmers or their wives could earn extra money by weaving cloth at home and selling it to local traders on a weekly basis. Domestic manufacture of this sort was the predominant norm for decades.[66] After 1600 some rural parts, like the West Riding in Yorkshire, parts of East Anglia, and Worcestershire

56 Hill, *Reformation*, 62; Stephen Porter, "The Economic and Social Impact of the Civil War Upon London," in *London and the Civil War*, ed. Stephen Porter (New York: St. Martin's Press, 1996), 183

57 Coward, "London and the English Civil War," 9; Weinstein, "London at the Outbreak of the Civil War," 31

58 Hill, *Reformation*, 61-62, 85; Stone, *Crisis of the Aristocracy*, 89

59 Hill, *Century*, 11; Marx, *Capital* Vol. 1, 742-744; *Capital* Vol.3, 799

60 Hill, *World*, 54-55; *1940* 28; Christopher Hill, "The Inns of Court," *History of Education Quarterly* 12, no. 4 (Winter, 1972): 544, https://www.jstor.org/stable/367344 Accessed 2 August 2020. Reprinted in Hill, *Change and Continuity in 17th-Century England*. Stone, *Crisis of the Aristocracy*, 152-153; Manning, *English People*, 131-133

61 Manning, *English People*, 134-135; Hill, *Reformation*, 65

62 Hill, *World*, 40-41, 43

63 Hill, *Reformation*, 45-46

64 Hill, *Reformation*, 26-27; *Century*, 127

65 Engels, Introduction to "Socialism Utopian and Scientific," 389; Marx, *Capital* Vol. 1, 723; Thirsk, "Seventeenth-Century Agriculture and Social Change," 80-81

66 Thirsk, "Seventeenth-Century Agriculture and Social Change," 99

in the west Midlands, became centers of cloth and clothing manufacture.[67] Smallholders, who could only engage in subsistence farming and who might have one or two animals they grazed on the common land, would hire themselves out to larger yeomen or find other by-employment to supplement their incomes. This was enough to keep them from qualifying as poor, at least until enclosure doomed them.[68]

Journeymen worked for wages; as skilled craftsmen who had completed apprenticeships they were an intermediate stratum. Few, however, had or could obtain the capital to set themselves up as masters in their own workshops. They therefore had to go wherever they could find work — part of the mobile "masterless men."[69] Those with no land and no skill were forced to work for wages either as agricultural labor, which was often seasonal, or in industry, mining for coal, iron, or copper, or making steel. Dependence on wages alone, which were set by JPs,[70] was considered no more than slavery.

The merchant princes controlled the town governments as their private fiefs through self-perpetuating oligarchies, most especially London. They served as bankers to the aristocrats who were often indebted to them for large sums.

> As the chief market for the larger transactions by mortgage and sale in real estate, London had its thumb on a considerable section of the landed gentry. The whole increasing mass of Government financial business, with its formidable reactions on public revenues and private fortunes, was virtually its monopoly.[71]

> What first strikes the eye is the very high degree of specialization among a restricted circle of great London merchants, men who first made their money in overseas or retail trading and who then turned to the money-lending business. The most favourably placed for this business were the leading mercers, silkmen, jewelers, and goldsmiths...drawn into money-lending between 1580 and 1620.[72]

Above all, the close financial connection between the monarchy and the London company merchants made each dependent on the other. The overseas merchants derived their monopoly privileges from the king and enforced his edicts, while they supported him financially through customs duties, loans and gifts.[73] James consulted them, even if reluctantly, on economic matters which, as business men, they were professionally able to assess. Moreover, they possessed liquid commercial capital which could easily be

67 Hill, *Reformation*, 86, 90, 96; Porter, "Impact of the Civil War Upon London," 184-185

68 Manning, *English People*, 133-134; *1649*, 60-61; Thirsk, "Seventeenth-Century Agriculture and Social Change," 96-98

69 Hill, *World*, 41

70 Hill, *Century*, 15, 19

71 Tawney, *Business and Politics Under James I*, 76

72 Stone, *Crisis of the Aristocracy*, 241

73 Robert Ashton, "Insurgency, Counter-Insurgency and Inaction: Three Phases in the Role of the City in the Great Rebellion," in *London and the Civil War*, ed. Stephen Porter (New York: St. Martin's Press, 1996), 47

moved from one area of investment to another, unlike the aristocracy whose wealth derived mainly from land.[74] Such economic mobility by the *haute* bourgeoisie cut across normal feudal social divisions, just as the movement of the dispossessed in the countryside did.

> The merchants had little formal power but their economic interests closely interlocked with those of the landed classes, thanks to the dependence of the price of land on the price of wool, in turn dependent on the cloth export trade. The maintenance of this trade was also of vital concern to the government, since a slump not only created a threat to social stability in the clothing areas due to unemployment, but also reduced government revenue from the customs. … As a result, foreign, military, and economic policies were increasingly conducted with an eye to the interests, and with the advice, of this merchant elite.[75]

As previously described, England's economy was primarily capitalist by the time of James' ascension. This is not to say that its continued development could not have been arrested or collapsed as, for example, happened to the Italian statelets.[76] The English economy had yet to solve numerous issues, but a critical precondition for its success — the expansion to a world economy — already existed.[77] There is no other meaning to categorizing this period the "early modern era," as historians commonly do, than the penetration of agrarian societies by capitalist market relations through urbanized commerce, finance, and manufacture. The only variations are the rate at which this process proceeded, and the uneven extent of its progress at any given time in different geographic areas.

Emanating out from London, the south and east of England were much more advanced than the north and west. Nonetheless by 1640, these more backward regions contained pockets of manufacturing towns. Many of these were cloth and clothing centers, such as the West Riding in Yorkshire. The towns and the areas around them largely supported Parliament in the Civil War; the "darker" parts would follow the king.

In 1603, however, the major European powers were financially exhausted. Spain declared bankruptcy in 1557, 1575 and 1596, and in 1607 declared a moratorium.[78] France was in no better shape after 36 years of internal religious war, and Elizabeth left debts of £400,000, nearly twice what she had inherited.[79] Peace and prosperity (that is to say, trade) became the

74 Tawney, *Business and Politics Under James I*, 79-81

75 Lawrence Stone, "Social Mobility in England 1500-1700," *Past & Present*, no. 33 (April, 1966): 52, http://www.jstor.org/stable/649801 Accessed 10 August 2015. Reprinted in *Seventeenth Century England: Society in an Age of Revolution*, ed. Paul S. Seaver (New York: New Viewpoints, 1976). J. P. Cooper, "Economic Regulation and the Cloth Industry in Seventeenth-Century England," *Transactions of the Royal Historical Society* 20 (1970): 84, https://www.jstor.org/stable/3678763 Accessed 2 February 2019

76 Marx, *Capital* Vol. 1, 716 fn. 1

77 Marx, *Capital* Vol. 3, 333

78 Anderson, *Absolutist State*, 76

79 Tawney, *Business and Politics Under James I*, 13-14; Russell, "Parliament and the King's Finances," 98; Hill, *Century*, 39. Elizabeth, like her father, had been forced to sell crown lands acquired by the dissolution of the monasteries to help pay for the Spanish and Irish wars.

order of the day, and within a year James signed a peace treaty with Spain. Over the next few years, a series of bilateral trade treaties were signed between various countries of Europe, including one between France and the Ottoman Empire. In 1609 a twelve-year truce was declared between Spain and the United Netherlands.[80] During the first decade and a half of James' rule, there was peace in Europe and commercial trade and production did indeed boom, much to England's benefit.[81]

> But the conflicts of early Stuart England were aggravated by the fact that the world of commerce and finance was interpenetrated by privilege and by legal prohibition — by patents and monopolies, companies and licences, guaranteed markets and favoured relationships.[82]

And by the fact that James I was "one of the most extravagant kings ever to occupy" the throne.[83]

A major source of friction had existed since the 16th century in the cloth industry where the Merchant Adventurers had been granted substantial supervisory authority over the cloth manufacturers. (Similar conflicts existed in other segments of the economy where noble courtiers had been granted monopoly licenses or patents.)[84] Laws regulating the quality of broadcloth with great specificity were resented by the manufacturers, especially as mechanical improvements were banned by the government. Any dip in the Adventurers' exports or profits was blamed on the craftsmen for producing poor quality goods.[85] Clothiers responded by blaming high taxes and customs duties for low profits, and market depressions on the monopoly. They also attacked the necessity of transporting goods to London when provincial ports lay closer to the sources, a complaint which would be included in the Grand Remonstrance in 1641.[86]

The monopolists limited the number of merchants who could buy cloth in England and sell it abroad to between 20 and 30 investors,[87] and set the prices and quantities of purchases to keep their costs low and profits high. This absence of competition kept down the volume of product that could be sold. The manufacturers, on the other hand, wanted to increase their volume of output, and believed competition among buyers would increase their prices. For obvious reasons they had the sympathy of smaller domestic traders who were also excluded from the company. The gentry too were unhappy with the siphoning of wealth from their local areas to the great merchants in

80 Tawney, *Business and Politics Under James I*, 14-15; Anderson, *Absolutist State*, 70

81 Stone, *Crisis of the Aristocracy*, 89; Hill, *Reformation*, 72

82 Barry Supple, "Class and Social Tension: the case of the merchant," in *The English Revolution 1600-1660*, ed. E. W. Ives (New York: Barnes & Noble, 1969), 139; Hill, *Reformation*, 95

83 Russell, "Parliament and the King's Finances," 98; Brenner, *Merchants and Revolution*, 641

84 Stone, *Crisis of the Aristocracy*, 203-205

85 Manning, *English People*, 155-156

86 Manning, *English People*, 158-159, 161; Cooper, "Economic Regulation," 76-77

87 Cooper, "Economic Regulation," 78

London. First attempted in 1604,[88] the Parliaments of the early 1620s finally got the regulations significantly liberalized in favor of free trade, but this would be reversed in the 1630s by Charles I's government.[89]

The parliamentary gentlemen must have thought it was in their own interest: between 1575 and 1630, "Almost half of all the gentry who invested in trade also sat in Parliament, and most of them attended the Commons before they joined a company."[90] That aristocrats invested in trade or manufacture did not make them bourgeois; they remained privileged landowners, which their rank depended on in the existing social system. What it did do was to substantially align their economic and political interests with those of the bourgeoisie, especially its well-to–do middle layers who favored free trade and opposed arbitrary government.

Early political conflicts

In 1606 a court held that James had the legal right to raise impositions, special customs duties on trade, on his own authority. At the next Parliament in 1610, the House of Commons responded that, under the common law, "...English subjects had 'such a propriety' in their goods 'as may not without their consent be altered and charged.'" Said an MP, "'If...their lands and goods be any way in the king's absolute power to be taken from them, then they are...little better than the king's bondmen.'"[91] Unparliamentary taxation and property rights would be a central bone of contention between the Commons and the crown right up to the revolution in London in 1641-1642.

The dominant role of the king in the state was obvious to all.

> In 1610, when the members denounced the extravagance of his Scottish favorites, James was with difficulty restrained from arresting some of them. After he dissolved Parliament in 1614, he was not restrained. He jailed four members, including one who made unfriendly mention of courtiers who were "spaniels to the King and wolves to the people." In 1621, after adjournment, James jailed the two most effective members of the House, Sir Edward Coke, a privy councillor, and Sir Robert Phelips.[92]

John Pym, the step-son of a knight and an oppositionist, was himself subjected to house arrest following the Parliament of 1621.[93]

James' peace policy had the benefit of promoting "social order and

88 "III. Free Trade and Parliament," The History of Parliament, https://www.historyofparliamentonline.org/volume/1604-1629/constituencies/london Accessed 13 August 2020

89 Manning, *English People*, 159-160; Hill, *Reformation*, 95-96; Cooper, "Economic Regulation," 85-86

90 Rabb, "Investment in English Overseas Enterprise," 72

91 Sommerville, "Ideology, Property and the Constitution," 57-58

92 J. H. Hexter, "Power Struggle, Parliament, and Liberty in Early Stuart England," *The Journal of Modern History* 50, no. 1 (March 1978): 26, http://www.jstor.org/stable/1878705 Accessed 16 December 2016. Reprinted "in slightly different form" as "Power, Parliament and Liberty in Early Stuart England," in *Reappraisals in History* (Chicago: University of Chicago Press, 1979).

93 Hexter, "Power Struggle, Parliament, and Liberty in Early Stuart England," 26; *King Pym*, 85

monarchical legitimacy in a world threatened by Dutch and Presbyterian republicanism." The extreme indebtedness of the state meant there was no money to conduct a war unless Parliament agreed to provide funds, which it would not do unless James made concessions. Instead, James spent years maneuvering for a "Spanish match," marriage between Prince Charles and the royal Infanta, in the hopes of reaping a munificent dowry. The policy provoked much opposition among the nobles and gentry, as it necessarily implied increased tolerance for Catholic recusants. This added religious polarization of the English ruling class to the already existing political differences.[94]

Two important events occurred in 1618. A Protestant party of Hussites (political descendants of Jan Hus) led a successful revolt in Bohemia against the new Catholic Hapsburg king, Ferdinand II. They chose instead Frederick V, Protestant Elector of the Palatine in Germany, who accepted. The rebellion kicked off the highly destructive Thirty Years' War. Frederick happened to be James I's son-in-law, placing James in an embarrassing position with the Hapsburg rulers of Spain.

Puritans on the Privy Council, in Parliament, and the Church of England hierarchy enlisted Calvinist clergy and London citizens to raise money for the defense of the Palatinate.[95] Clergymen were encouraged to attack the ungodly policies of the government, and many did so. The government retaliated through repressive measures against dissent, including arrests of a number of Puritan ministers, while simultaneously suspending the penal laws against Catholics. James' apparent hard turn against Calvinists in the Church threatened the acceptance of multiple viewpoints within English Protestantism that had existed up to this time.[96]

> The Spanish match and the drive towards war with Spain served to overturn the careful balance of the mid-Jacobean period. It served to politicize once again differences of religious opinion by giving them a direct relevance to policy options now of crucial interest to the king. The public agitation against the Spanish match…served to reawaken in James his latent fear of a populist Puritanism.[97]

James refused to lead a war for the "Protestant Cause," deluding himself that diplomacy could be used to defend his son-in-law's position, but Frederick was badly defeated by the Spanish army. During the same time Louis XIII was pressing a campaign against the Huguenots (French Protestants), and the truce between Spain and the United Provinces (Holland) was expiring.[98]

Also in 1618, England's cloth trade was hit by depression: this was partly due to overproduction, but also to saturation of European demand, which

94 Brenner, *Merchants and Revolution*, 247

95 Brenner, *Merchants and Revolution*, 247

96 Brenner, *Merchants and Revolution*, 247-248; Fincham and Lake, "Ecclesiastical Policy," 199-201

97 Lake, "Calvinism and the English Church," 70

98 Brenner, *Merchants and Revolution*, 248

beset Dutch, Flemish and Italian textile trades as well. The outbreak of the Thirty Years' War made Continental markets inaccessible.[99] With the Privy Council, Parliament and the Church all split over religious and political issues, a debate on foreign policy ensued. Archbishop Abbot in 1619 had openly opposed the Spanish match, and pronounced the Bohemian Revolution the beginning of the final struggle against the Antichrist in Rome. James, by contrast, "wrote to the pope as 'his holy father' to request his cooperation in the restoration of European peace."[100] In 1621, a new Parliament was called. James' policy of seeking an alliance with Spain had come to nothing due to the monkey wrench of Frederick, and the impossibility of reconciling the various factions in both governments. He nonetheless continued to pursue it.[101]

A "Blue Water" program of war on Spanish shipping was presented in Parliament as a diversionary strategy toward saving the Palatinate for Protestantism (and thereby Frederick, whom James wished to help). This would open the West Indies to English shipping, and relieve Spanish pressure on Bohemia and other parts on the Continent, while providing financing (via plunder) for more military actions. James adamantly opposed war with Spain or any action which might provoke it. As a compromise, John Pym got a bill passed providing some money ("a gift") for defense of the realm, but less than full financial support until such time as England declared war on Spain.[102]

Negotiations for the Spanish match, broken off in 1618, resumed in the years 1620-1623. During the interval the Earl of Warwick set up a small colony in Guiana (Guyana) as a base to privateer against the Spanish in the Caribbean. The resumption of negotiations forced him to give this up. Nathaniel Rich, the earl's kinsman, became a leader in the 1621 Parliament for an international Protestant alliance emulating the one among Catholic countries, and he proposed that it should be confirmed by an act of Parliament. Such a direct intervention into foreign affairs would have been a novelty, certain to outrage the king. It gained no support.[103]

Instead, the Commons voted on 3 December 1621 to petition James "to declare war for the defense of the Protestant religion, to employ a diversionary strategy for the restoration of the Palatinate, to forge an international Protestant alliance, and to marry Charles to a Protestant princess." James promptly dismissed Parliament.[104] This was essentially the first bid for greater power in the government by the gentry-Puritan opposition. It combined an appeal for Protestantism with a viable program to restore England's military power in international affairs. Three years later, with a new Parliament and

99 Brenner, *Merchants and Revolution*, 33-39; Hill, *Century*, 27-28

100 Fincham and Lake, "Ecclesiastical Policy," 198

101 Brenner, *Merchants and Revolution*, 248-249

102 Brenner, *Merchants and Revolution*, 250-251

103 Brenner, *Merchants and Revolution*, 251-252

104 Brenner, *Merchants and Revolution*, 252

the Spanish match now a complete fiasco,[105] James reluctantly acceded to readying the country for war, and "assisting" the Low Countries as the price of financial support to the crown. A total of some £300,000 was allocated for a war in defense of the Palatinate, but Parliament put restrictions on what the money could be used for. To make sure, they entrusted it to their own appointed commissioners to administer.[106] James also approved a Parliamentary petition to enforce the recusancy laws against Catholics for the same reason. However, a new dispute over religion broke out when an Arminian royal chaplain, Richard Montagu, published an openly anti-Calvinist pamphlet, meant to propagate James' religious views and support him politically in the on-going public debate.[107] Pym investigated and the Commons sent a protest petition to Archbishop Abbot directly, bypassing the House of Lords. James, in retaliation, arrested two East Anglian Puritan ministers, and defended the repressive Bishop of Norwich (a post later held by Montagu) against the Commons' attacks. He then began to back away from war with Spain.[108]

England made only one half-hearted effort, by land, to defend the Palatinate during 1624-1625. James ordered the force to refrain from attacking Spanish troops, rendering it all but useless.[109]

Charles I, Parliament and the Church

Early in 1625, James suddenly died. Charles immediately began seeking loans in part to pay debts left by his father's profligacy. To raise new loans from the City he was forced to turn "over to them a vast quantity of crown lands" as security.[110] He married a French Catholic princess shortly thereafter, requiring him to break his previous promise to intensify enforcement of anti-Catholic laws against recusants in England. The dynastic alliance with France eliminated any possibility of English help for the Huguenots, who suffered renewed repression from Louis XIII as a result.[111]

Almost as quickly, confrontations occurred between Parliament and the new king over religion, foreign policy and his demands for money. During the 1620s "...the Crown had in fact alarmingly little business that it wanted done in Parliament, other than obtaining money..."[112] Charles in particular

105 For a detailed discussion, see Brennan C. Pursell, "The End of the Spanish Match," *The Historical Journal* 45, no. 4 (December 2002), https://www.jstor.org/stable/3133525 Accessed 3 July 2021

106 Christopher Thompson, "The Origins of the Politics of the Parliamentary Middle Group, 1625-1629," *Transactions of the Royal Historical Society* 22 (1972): 73-74, http://www.jstor.org/stable/3678829 Accessed 30 January 2017

107 Fincham and Lake, "Ecclesiastical Policy," 202

108 Brenner, *Merchants and Revolution*, 253-255; Kennedy, "the Parliament of 1624," 45-46, 50, 52-53, 53-54

109 Brenner, *Merchants and Revolution*, 255

110 Pearl, *London and the Outbreak*, 72-73

111 Brenner, *Merchants and Revolution*, 255

112 Derek Hirst, "Unanimity in the Commons, Aristocratic Intrigues, and the Origins of the English Civil War," *The Journal of Modern History* 50, no. 1 (March 1978): 58, http://www.jstor.org/stable/1878706 Accessed 11 August 2016, citing Conrad Russell.

"measure[d] the goodness of Parliaments by the degree of their subservience to him..."[113] The new king appointed Sir Edward Coke, Sir Robert Phelips and other opposition figures to minor posts which prevented them from standing for election in 1626. Before the Parliament had adjourned he arrested two sitting members.[114]

Similar to 1621, the Commons and the Privy Council discussed setting up a West India Company to be financed privately, but under Parliament's direction, to attack Spanish shipping. "In practice, the proposed company would have been beyond the reach of royal authority and English foreign policy would have been partly in its [Parliament's] hands."[115] Like James, Charles rejected the Blue Water strategy to attack Spanish shipping. He was not helped by an ignoble defeat at Cadiz organized by Buckingham in 1625, or the looming prospect of war with France. Members of Parliament were alienated by Charles' defense of his chaplain, the same Richard Montagu who had served James, and who had been held in contempt by the Commons for his anti-Calvinist pamphlet. Charles refused to repudiate his aide or Arminianism. The 1626 Parliament was called to fund armies for war. The Commons again offered money to Charles in exchange for the Duke of Buckingham's ouster as chief minister, and Parliament's review to stabilize the king's finances.[116]

The Earl of Warwick (who would provide many positions to Puritan clergymen in the 1630s)[117] and Viscount Saye requested a conference be held to debate religious doctrine. "Puritans assumed correctly that a rapprochement with Roman Catholicism was involved here and that they were likely to be the losers."[118] Not only did the York House Conference bring no agreement, it only demonstrated the royal government's commitment to Arminianism, solidifying the parliamentary opposition to a greater extent.[119] Charles consented to the Commons investigation of Buckingham, but upon their impeachment of him the king dismissed Parliament before it had voted him any money to live on and run his court.[120]

The king then made matters far worse by trying to bully the counties for a so-called "free gift" of money already denied him by Parliament, provoking

113 Hexter, *King Pym*, 56; David Johnson, "Parliament in Crisis: The Disintegration of the Parliamentarian War Effort During the Summer of 1643" (PhD diss., University of York, June 2012), 70, http://etheses.whiterose.ac.uk/14226/ Accessed 25 January 2019 71

114 Hexter, "Power Struggle, Parliament, and Liberty in Early Stuart England," 26

115 Thompson, "Parliamentary Middle Group," 80; Brenner, *Merchants and Revolution*, 257-259

116 Brenner, *Merchants and Revolution*, 258

117 Shipps, "The 'Political Puritan,'" 204

118 Tyacke, "Revolutionary Puritanism," 755

119 Thompson, "Parliamentary Middle Group," 79-80; Richard Cust, "Charles I, the Privy Council and the Parliament of 1628," *Transactions of the Royal Historical Society* 2 (1992): 35-36, https://www.jstor.org/stable/3679098 Accessed 5 November 2018; Jesse McCarthy, "The Emergence of English Arminianism: Richard Montagu 1624-1629," Senior Honors Thesis, UC Santa Barbara, (June 14, 2013), 38-39, https://jessekmccarthy.files.wordpress.com/2013/12/the-emergence-of-englis-arminianism.pdf Accessed January 27, 2019

120 Brenner, *Merchants and Revolution*, 260

opposition across the land. The crown next pressured London and the counties for the infamous forced loan early in 1627.

> The [London] Court of Aldermen agreed to subscribe to the loan personally and submit lists of those men in their wards who were prepared to contribute and those who refused. This led to a demonstration of protest by parliamentary puritans who covered the City with placards denouncing the Guildhall as the "Yield-all."[121]

Twenty gentlemen, sixteen of them knights, and nearly all future members of the Long Parliament, refused to pay and were imprisoned. In the Five Knights Case, argued near the end of 1627, gentlemen sought a writ of *habeas corpus* for release from prison. A few months later the court "reaffirmed the principle laid down in 1591, that the king had the right to commit men to prison without cause shown."[122]

In London, the installment levied for 1628 of £120,000, was met by extensive opposition from some of the livery companies who were its first targets.

> Prominent members of the Vintners' Company, twenty or thirty members of the Saddlers', including the Master and Wardens, and the officers of the Founders', Glaziers', Plumbers', and Joiners' Companies, were committed to Newgate "for not having used their best endeavours" in promoting the loan.[123]

The issue played a significant role in the parliamentary elections later that year:

> ...in the shires and large boroughs, at least, a crucial determinant was often a candidate's response to the forced loan. ...it was widely regarded as a crucial test of an individual's ultimate loyalties. ... Several of the regular knights of the shire were themselves loan refusers, and alongside these there were several refusers being elected for the first and only time.[124]

Charles' resort (not for the last time) to a forced loan and unauthorized taxes was meant to pay for the war with Spain. But as relations worsened with France, new negotiations with Spain resulted in even greater favoritism being shown to anti-Calvinist Arminians. They "alienated the country further when they preached that Englishmen must comply with Charles' attempt to collect a loan in 1626 or be damned for disobedience."[125] Arminian clergy rejected the view that the pope was Antichrist and accepted Catholicism as a legitimate religion. "The notion that kings might tax without consent was underpinned by the contention that the monarch is entrusted by God alone to govern the country."[126]

121 Pearl, *London and the Outbreak*, 74

122 Hill, *Century*, 8

123 Pearl, *London and the Outbreak*, 75; Hexter, *King Pym*, 83 fn. 51

124 Cust, "Politics and the Electorate in the 1620s," 156-157

125 Shipps, "The 'Political Puritan,'" 201

126 Sommerville, "Ideology, Property and the Constitution," 60

In July 1626 Charles "effectively outlawed Calvinist teaching on a national basis." Buckingham had become Chancellor of Cambridge, putting him in charge at one of only two universities turning out authorized ministers and theologians. Archbishop Abbot was stripped of his powers, and William Laud and other Arminians were promoted to the Privy Council in 1627. Pro-absolutist propaganda in sermons and pamphlets followed forthwith.[127] The following year Laud was made Bishop of London.

The financial problems of both James and Charles were to no small extent due to the opulent courts they kept. "By the end of the 1630s the queen and the royal children had almost 400 servants."[128] Sent to London as a diplomat in 1629 (where Charles prevailed on him to paint a glorification of monarchy on the ceiling of the palace Banqueting House), Peter Paul Reubens wrote:

> "The first thing to be noted is the fact that all the leading nobles live on a sumptuous scale and spend money lavishly, so that the majority of them are hopelessly in debt. … Splendour and liberality are of primary consideration at this Court."[129] [Ellipsis in original]

To reforming MPs and militant Puritans alike, such profligacy was irrational, and came at the expense of the state, not just in cost, but in prestige and influence abroad. Such wasteful ostentation, so characteristic of Catholicism, was a dangerous affront to those who championed thrift, investment and accumulation of wealth, backed up by sincere religious feeling.

> Both James and Charles showed that…their sympathies were wholly with the privileged, provided that they exercised their power judiciously. … What was worse was that in a period of hardship and depression, the closed bodies appeared to become tighter and even more oppressive…[130]

The early Stuart kings disputed with, and then dismissed, Parliaments which sought to elicit reforms or policy changes from them in exchange for money. This was no more than the customs farmers, private merchants contracted by the crown to collect duties on overseas trade, did with far less justification.[131] From the late 16th century on, the incomes from the estates of large landholders were mostly declining due to inflation, forcing many, including the monarchy which was the largest, to sell land.[132] This put them in a losing struggle with bourgeois and improving aristocratic elements, whose continuously growing wealth led them to demand greater political power in the state.[133]

127 Brenner, *Merchants and Revolution*, 261; Tyacke, "Puritanism, Arminianism and Counter-Revolution," 133; Hill, *Society*, 27

128 Porter, "Impact of the Civil War Upon London," 188

129 Charles Hope, "England: How the Masterpieces Came and Went," *New York Review of Books* 61, no. 2 (February 6, 2014), https://www.nybooks.com/articles/2014/02/06/england-how-masterpieces-came-and-went/ Accessed May 10, 2016; Porter, "Impact of the Civil War Upon London," 189

130 Hirst, *Representative?*, 50

131 Donald Pennington, "The Making of the War, 1640-1642," in *Puritans and Revolutionaries*, eds. Donald Pennington and Keith Thomas (Oxford: Oxford University Press, 1978), 165

132 Hill, *Century*, 11, 39-40

133 Hill, *1640*, 41-42

The spread of opposition

Almost from the time of Charles' accession, London was in a state of "growing turbulence and defiance of authority."[134] Economic depression, threats of war, the crown's high-handed actions to raise money, and open friendliness to Catholic or semi-Catholic adherents, made MPs in particular aware of the possibility of popular rebellion.[135] In 1626, 300 sailors from the bungled attack on Spain broke into the house of the Treasurer of the Navy demanding to be paid. Even more bitter demonstrations broke out against the Duke of Buckingham; one of his followers was killed by a mob, and the Duke was assassinated not long after. "...the king's subjects openly drank toasts to the assassin in taverns throughout England. [John] Felton was cheered by crowds of well-wishers as he was conveyed from Portsmouth to the Tower of London."[136] Buckingham's state funeral had to be held at night for fear of what the citizenry might do.[137]

Charles also managed to provoke opposition from the ranks of company merchants for a time by unilaterally raising customs duties on imports, known as impositions. "By the end of 1628, thirty 'prime merchants' were under arrest."[138] The General Court of the Levant Company voted to overrule their Board of Governors and petition the House of Commons rather than the Privy Council. Merchant opposition reached a climax during 1628 and 1629 by going on "strike," i.e., refusing to ship goods to deprive the crown of customs duties; but compliance was not uniform and eventually petered out. Although impositions remained high, the economic picture for trade improved after 1630, and future increases in royal revenue were extracted from London rather than the monopoly companies.[139]

Government interference in the economy was specifically designed to arrest the destabilizing growth of capitalism.[140]

> In 1624 the government ordered the destruction of a needle-making machine, together with the needles which it had made. Nine years later Charles I prohibited the casting of brass buckles and in 1635 the use of a windmill for sawing wood.[141]

The longstanding division between the Merchant Adventurers and regional clothing manufacturers also came to a head during the 1630s. The Adventurers were losing ground to cheaper competitors on the Continent, creating a depression in England which forced the manufacturers to cut

134 Pearl, *London and the Outbreak*, 76

135 Hill, "Parliament and People in 17th Century England," 115-117

136 Como, "Predestination and Political Conflict in Laud's London," 274-275

137 Pearl, *London and the Outbreak*, 77

138 Pearl, *London and the Outbreak*, 77

139 Pearl, *London and the Outbreak*, 77-79; Brenner, *Merchants and Revolution*, 227-239

140 Manning, "The Nobles, the People and the Constitution," 49

141 Hill, *Reformation*, 95

costs, "which meant evading the statutory regulations."[142] In 1630, the Company successfully petitioned Charles' government to appoint a commission to investigate and enforce cloth laws in four counties west of London. However, the commission "aroused wide-spread and persistent opposition in the west country clothmaking region, and on one occasion...[a commissioner] was seized and flung into the river."[143] Two local gentlemen, both JPs, were brought before the Star Chamber for obstructing the commission's work and encouraging others to disobedience.[144]

> Many of the justices of the peace supported the clothiers: some of them were clothiers themselves or had "social or economic ties with the cloth manufacturers;" some were producers of wool for the industry or had tenants who were clothmakers, and so were interested in the prosperity of the trade, and as local men...they were influenced by the belief of the clothiers that strict enforcement of the regulations would worsen rather then cure the depression; and they all resented governmental interference and the subjection of the industry to central rather than local control.[145]

With no other resource than the JPs to enforce the law, the government was forced to make concessions,[146] but only for a time: "In 1634 the Merchant Adventurers had their monopoly of the export of all types of cloth restored," and additional restrictions on the clothiers were implemented during the 1630s to the London merchants' advantage.[147]

Charles' need for funds was still great, forcing him to summon Parliament in early 1628. The House of Commons was quite unhappy that the City magistrates had granted the king a loan before he called Parliament into session. The House received two petitions from guild members who had been imprisoned for nonpayment, and voted to petition the king for their release.[148] More significantly, in response to the court decision in the Five Knights case, Parliament passed the Petition of Right. It was preceded by two months of debate and negotiations with the Lords and the king, (who would not have accepted a legislative act).[149] The document this produced invoked Magna Carta; re-asserted Parliament's control over taxes including, for the first time, customs duties (which since the early Tudor era had accounted for half of state revenues);[150] and declared arbitrary imprisonment illegal.[151] Its passage was met with "widespread lighting of bonfires and ringing of church

142 Manning, *English People*, 157

143 Manning, *English People*, 156

144 Manning, *English People*, 157

145 Manning, *English People*, 156

146 Manning, *English People*, 157

147 Cooper, "Economic Regulation," 85-86. "Cloth valued at roughly £1,150,000 was exported from London in 1640, three-quarters of the national total, and that was a poor trading year." Porter, "Impact of the Civil War Upon London," 184

148 Pearl, *London and the Outbreak*, 75-76

149 Thompson, "Parliamentary Middle Group," 82-85

150 Hill, *Reformation*, 105

151 Thompson, "Parliamentary Middle Group," 82

bells when the King's final assent to the Petition was announced."[152]

Despite being careful not to explicitly infringe the king's prerogative, or assign absolute rights to the subject,[153] this lengthy document was the first formal statement in the new century that codified protections for Parliament and the citizen (including *habeas corpus*) against the powers of the feudal monarchy.

> ...by placing them [Parliament's grievances] within the framework of the common law, and asserting that these rights were pre-existent independently of the grace of the monarch, it became a broader assertion of the rule of law and the ancient constitution.[154]

Regardless of the extended wrangling needed to get the Petition approved, it established the political basis of the Commons' anti-absolutist struggle, the opening shot that would culminate in war in 1642.

The political crisis engendered by the Stuart monarchy's attempts to uphold and reinforce the feudal system against the social subversion of expanding capitalist relations, was becoming more acute. The more the government attempted to centralize power, the more of a hindrance it was to the expansion of capitalist ventures; the more the improving gentry insisted on doing as they liked with their own property, the more they resisted that centralization. They were already long used to ruling over their local areas, and now used their power of the purse to bend the king to their will. Charles was forced to approve the Petition of Right's provisions in order to obtain money.[155] But in 1629, the antagonism between Charles and Parliament became even sharper.

> In the House of Commons...men said that the king possessed only those powers which the law granted to him, and that he need never be obeyed if he commanded against the law. ...the House proceeded against customs officers...though the King made it perfectly clear that they had been acting on his command. In effect, the doctrine that the king's servants are punishable for executing his commands permitted active resistance to the king's will.[156]

Upon learning of Parliament's sudden dissolution, MPs forcibly held the Speaker in his chair while they hastily passed several reform resolutions. Nine leaders were afterwards jailed.[157] Their trials

> took the better part of the year and succeeded only in inflaming the political situation. More importantly, the monarch never received the obedient

152 Cust, "Politics and the Electorate in the 1620s," 143

153 Thompson, "Parliamentary Middle Group," 85; Brenner, *Merchants and Revolution*, 266

154 Foxley, "Magna Carta," 67

155 Woolrych, "The English Revolution: an introduction," 13; "The Parliament of 1628-1629," The History of Parliament, http://www.historyofparliamentonline.org/volume/1604-1629/survey/parliament-1628-1629 Accessed 10 August 2018

156 Sommerville, "Ideology, Property and the Constitution," 61

157 Hexter, "Power Struggle, Parliament, and Liberty in Early Stuart England," 26; "The Parliament of 1628-1629," The History of Parliament

> submission of Sir John Eliot and two other M.P.s, whose indefinite imprisonment transformed them into popular martyrs.[158]

In response to the parliamentary alliance of the anti-absolutist aristocrats with the Puritan and merchant opposition, the early Stuarts turned to Catholic aristocrats to shore up the monarchy, and to promote the economic power of the Church of England. The Church had been "continuously undermined in favour of the crown and the lay landlords during the sixteenth century." What became the Arminian high church movement was intent on promoting the power and independence of the church vis-à-vis the state, against its social decline and the rise of Puritanism.[159] Notwithstanding the proscription on debate over Calvinism in 1626, ministers had still been afforded a good deal of slack due to Charles' need to appease Parliament. In 1629, this leniency ended.[160] Opprobrium and arguments formerly used against Catholics alone were now being employed by Church officials against Puritans.[161]

Charles made Arminians his allies, and their dependence on crown patronage made them the most ardent supporters of the king's prerogatives. The Church provided the king with "the nearest thing to an independent bureaucracy."[162] But his policies only increased fears of popery within the ruling class, among nobles and gentry: much of their lands had once belonged to church monasteries, giving them economic incentive to fear a restoration of ecclesiastical power. They therefore wanted both church and monarchy subordinated to themselves.[163]

The moderate language of the Petition of Right, acquiesced to by the House of Lords, was deliberately written so as not to encourage rebellion by the lower classes.[164] Charles however chose this moment to modify the Forest Law to his own advantage. Along with bad harvests and plague, this caused peasants in the west country to revolt and break down enclosures between 1628-1631. It was the largest popular disturbance in the countryside prior to the Civil War.[165] But at the same time,

> John Pym himself, leader of the "popular party," was as a Receiver General for Crown revenues deeply involved in royal forest enclosures of the 1620s, and remained committed to that policy as one means of solving the Crown's financial problems.[166]

158 Thomas Cogswell, "Charles I and the Road to Personal Rule by L. J. Reeve," *Albion* 22, no. 4 (Winter 1990): 670, https://www.jstor.org/stable/4051403 Accessed 25 April 2019

159 Manning, "The Nobles, the People and the Constitution," 56

160 Como, "Predestination and Political Conflict in Laud's London," 267-268

161 Michael Questier, "Catholic Loyalism in Early Stuart England," *The English Historical Review* 123, no. 504 (October 2008): 1162, http://www.jstor.com/stable/20485375 Accessed 14 July 2020

162 Hill, *Reformation*, 122

163 Manning, "The Nobles, the People and the Constitution," 56; Brenner, *Merchants and Revolution*, 690; Hill, "Henrician Reformation," 35, 42-43

164 Hill, "Parliament and People in 17th-Century England," 116-117

165 Manning, *English People*, 135-136; Hill, *Reformation*, 69

166 Sharp, "The Place of the People in the English Revolution," 106

Personal Rule of the 1630s

The passage of the Petition of Right in 1628, and the unruly end to the Parliament in 1629 completed the open rupture between the king and a large part of the aristocracy. "The point had been reached beyond which the King could retreat no further without a virtual abdication to the bourgeoisie,"[167] i.e., those engaged in capitalist endeavors. In the face of Parliament's antagonism, Charles tried to freeze the situation. After 1629, he refused to call another parliament for eleven years, a period known as the Personal Rule. The Tudors had generally deigned to observe the niceties of parliamentary legality, however grudgingly and hypocritically, because it was to their advantage.[168]

> ...the very people who would have to be relied on to collect unparliamentary taxes were the same ones who would be asked to consent to parliamentary ones, and their co-operation was much the more easily achieved if the King had consulted them.[169]

Even Bloody Mary Tudor waited eighteen months for Parliament to reauthorize the laws, circa 1400, permitting heretics to be burned at the stake, before she committed Protestant martyrs to the flames (at an average rate of two a week for the rest of her reign). MPs had made papal absolution a precondition to protect themselves for their infidelity to Rome under Edward VI.[170]

Charles defended his dismissal of the 1629 Parliament in writing, attributing its necessity to "'ill-affected men'" whose aim was to "'break... through all respects and ligaments of government, and to erect an universal over-swaying power to themselves, which belongs only to us, and not to them.'"[171] King James had similarly "blamed the failure of the 1621 parliament on the activities of certain 'fiery and popular spirits'" who impinged the royal prerogative.[172] In fact, however, as early as the summer of 1626, "...Charles had spoken 'of the means used by the Kings of France to rid themselves of Parliament.'"[173] His personal rule was characterized by repeated attempts to illegally impose taxes without the benefit of Parliament; his shift of the Church of England in a sharply more Catholic direction, with consequent purging and persecution of Puritans; suspension of the recusancy laws; promotion of monopolies and other economic distortions; continuation of a pro-Spanish foreign policy; and attempts to reinforce social rankings and stymie social mobility, a Sisyphean labor but one with dire consequences.

167 Hill, *1640*, 47. Hill is here principally referring to gentry MPs in the House of Commons, whom he terms bourgeois, along with merchants then in opposition, who actually were. See the Preface, and the section "The English gentry, an anomalous class" above regarding the distinction.

168 Hill, *Reformation*, 30

169 Russell, "Parliament and the King's Finances," 94

170 Ridley, *Bloody Mary's Martyrs*, 60

171 "Declaration Showing the Causes of the Late Dissolution of the Parliament," quoted in Lake, "From Revisionist to Royalist History," 671-672 [Ellipsis in original]

172 Lake, "From Revisionist to Royalist History," 672

173 Richard Cust, "Charles I, the Privy Council, and the Forced Loan," *Journal of British Studies* 24, no. 2 (April 1985): 212, https://www.jstor.org/stable/175703 Accessed 25 February 2019

In 1637 two draymen were acquitted of running down the Earl of Essex's carriage. The Privy Council immediately intervened with prerogative powers to have them publicly flogged and committed to hard labor. In another case, "A gentleman called a tailor a 'base fellow' for demanding payment of his bill, but when the tailor replied 'that he was as good a man as the other,' he was forced by the Earl Marshal's court to pay damages to the gentleman."[174]

Many churchmen were made JPs, and the Bishop of London was appointed to the powerful office of Lord Treasurer.[175] In 1633 Charles appointed the Arminian, William Laud, Archbishop of Canterbury. Many Catholics had been appointed to high court and government posts, and the French Catholic queen wielded great influence at court. In 1637, the first Vatican representative in nearly 80 years was received.[176] Laud embraced many aspects of Catholicism which Puritans hated: outward shows of ostentatious display; prescribed rituals; limiting sermons to rote catechizing; and proscription of preaching by laymen, while opposing the strict Sunday sabbath and also enclosure. He restored such church accoutrements as altar rails separating the minister from the congregation, symbolic of the latter's subordination, and requiring parishioners to kneel at them, giving renewed prominence to the ritual of communion.[177] An apocryphal story long had it that Oliver Cromwell was all set to debark for America when he learned that Laud had reintroduced the use of candles during services, and decided to stay and fight.

A Catholic resurgence in England would have been a devastating blow to the Protestant cause, still under worrying attack on the Continent as the Thirty Years' War raged on. Secret meetings or conventicles of the godly were illegal, and many well-known Puritan preachers were forced to emigrate to Holland or America. Some took their congregations with them (such as those later called the Pilgrims). Others were not so fortunate. William Prynne, a fervid Puritan pamphleteer, and two others were convicted of sedition by the Star Chamber in 1637, and sentenced to having their ears cut off, cheeks branded, and imprisonment for life.[178] The following year, John Lilburne, the future Leveller leader, was sentenced to be publicly whipped through the streets of London, pilloried and imprisoned. Lilburne steadfastly refused, as Puritans had begun to do in church courts, to be "put on oath" which would have required him to give testimony incriminating himself.[179]

174 Manning, *English People*, 175

175 Manning, *Aristocrats, Plebeians*, 26

176 Hill, *Century*, 50

177 Hill, *Century*, 70; Manning, *Aristocrats, Plebeians*, 14; Hill, *Society*, 32, 54; Christopher Hill, "The Many-Headed Monster," in *Change and Continuity in 17-Century England* (New Haven: Yale University Press, 1974, 1991), 202

178 "William Prynne, 1600-69," BCW Project, http://bcw-project.org/biography/william-prynne Accessed 10 June 2016

179 Eduard Bernstein, *Cromwell and Communism: Socialism and Democracy in the Great English Revolution* (New York: Schocken Books, 1895, 1963), 38-39; Brailsford, *The Levellers and the English Revolution*, 80. See Hill, *Society*, Chapter 11 on the importance of and resistance to oaths.

In 1635, Charles ordered the collection of ship money, traditionally an extraordinary tax raised from coastal areas for their defense at times of imminent danger. Not only was there no threat of invasion, but Charles imposed it far inland on an annual basis, permanently making it an unparliamentary tax.[180] The tax fell more heavily on the middle sort, the poor and the peasants than on the aristocrats, according to William Prynne,[181] and would become an issue in the elections of 1640.[182] The government justified its collection by pointing to the audacious raids by Barbary pirates, not only in the Mediterranean far from home, but along the southwest coasts of England itself. This much was true. Between 1629 and 1638, at least seventy-three English ships were attacked and 1,473 English subjects were held captive or sold as slaves in North Africa.[183] This state of affairs and the new tax were particularly galling to merchants, as it was the Stuart policy of neglect of the navy that allowed piracy to thrive.[184] While a portion of the money collected was used for a punitive expedition to Morocco in 1637, pirate raids in English waters continued to increase.[185]

Despite royal attacks on themselves, the slavishly loyal London Aldermen enforced the collection of ship money, and imprisoned those who would not pay. Under increased pressure to meet collection targets, municipal officers were authorized to seize and sell the household articles of refusers. Opposition came from all social classes. In 1636, two Puritan nobles, the Earl of Warwick and Lord Saye and Sele, refused to pay ship money, "and both attempted to rouse their tenants to further resistance." John Hampden's legal challenge of 1637 was defended by Oliver St. John (later Pym's successor as leader of the opposition in the Long Parliament). The court upheld the king. All five of these men were members of the Providence Island Company, owner of a Puritan colonial refuge, and would be active leaders of Parliament in 1640. (Hampden was Oliver Cromwell's cousin.)[186] Several Atlantic merchants also refused to pay, two of whom were partners of Maurice Thomson. All would come to play leading roles in London's revolution in 1641-1642.[187] "The Founders' Company of London seems to have paid no Ship Money after 1637, the Society of Apothecaries none after 1638. Refusal to pay became general."[188] In 1638, London's sheriff, Alderman Thomas Soames, refused to collect it. So widespread was the resistance throughout the land that each succeeding year brought in less money than before.[189] But the many attempts

180 Woolrych, "The English Revolution: an introduction," 14

181 Brian Manning, "Religion and Politics: The Godly People," in *Politics, Religion and the English Civil War*, ed. Brian Manning (London: Edward Arnold, 1973), 107

182 Hirst, *Representative?*, 150-151

183 Adrian Tinniswood, *The Rainborowes* (New York: Basic Books, 2013), 95

184 Hill, *Century*, 30-31; "A Bourgeois Revolution?," 126

185 Tinniswood, *The Rainborowes*, 42, 95-96

186 Hexter, *King Pym*, 78; Fraser, *Cromwell*, 97; Brenner, *Merchants and Revolution*, 156

187 Brenner, *Merchants and Revolution*, 291-292

188 Hill, *Reformation*, 108

189 Brenner, *Merchants and Revolution*, 297-298; Pearl, *London and the Outbreak*, 88-91, 192; Hill, *Century*, 46

to levy unparliamentary taxes did bring in considerable sums to early Stuart governments, more "than they ever did from Parliament — a fact which put the continued existence of that institution in jeopardy."[190] Thus the struggle over the power to tax, like the struggle over religion and church governance, and the legal and property rights of individuals, were all magnified and intensified by the crown's steps toward absolute rule.

In London, the aldermen were often high officers in the Levant, East India and other overseas merchant companies. There were innumerable ties between them "as City magistrates and holders of public offices, customs farmers, lenders" and the monarchy. These men "were nominated to royal commissions on commercial and governmental matters..."[191] The aldermen could thus be counted upon to be far less combative than the merchant company members. "Until 1629, the City Aldermen had a strong reputation for Puritanism." But once the latter came under attack from Bishop Laud they ceased their support, "and began to contribute towards Laud's favorite scheme for rebuilding City churches, particularly St. Paul's."[192] Some of the merchant oligarchs also invested in sizable amounts of land.[193]

The king's government frequently sought to influence merchant company elections on behalf of preferred candidates. In return, the Directors appealed to royal support against internal critics, particularly the Puritan nobles Brooke, Saye and Warwick. The Chamberlain of the City from 1625 to 1643 was the Treasurer of the East India Company.[194] The oldest and wealthiest City families, "all closely interconnected by marriage," dominated the monopoly trading companies, and some had close connections to the landed gentry or the royal court. For the most part, the ruling bodies of the livery companies also acquiesced to the king.[195]

The conflicts between the early Stuart kings, their supporters in the monopoly merchant companies and conservative wing of the Church, versus the gentry/Puritan alliance in and out of Parliament, set the historical stage. On the issues of taxation, political rights, and religion, the latter made themselves the champions of the new economy's progress, which, in their various ways, they saw as more open, more constructive and advantageous, more moral and rational. The fidelity of James and Charles to the theological doctrine "divine right of kings" was a defensive, feudal, Catholic resort. As the crisis of the old regime deepened, a new and audacious component of bourgeois leadership was emerging, that would soon provide the oppositional movement with funds, breadth and drive.

190 Sommerville, "Ideology, Property and the Constitution," 56

191 Pearl, *London and the Outbreak*, 91

192 Pearl, *London and the Outbreak*, 79

193 Pearl, *London and the Outbreak*, 93

194 Pearl, *London and the Outbreak*, 92

195 Pearl, *London and the Outbreak*, 93-94

8) THE ATLANTIC MERCHANTS

The discovery of America, the rounding of the Cape, opened up fresh ground for the rising bourgeoisie. The East-Indian and Chinese markets, the colonisation of America, trade with the colonies, the increase in the means of exchange and in commodities generally, gave to commerce, to navigation, to industry, an impulse never before known, and thereby, to the revolutionary element in the tottering feudal society, a rapid development.

~*The Communist Manifesto*[1]

An historic change took place during the reactionary period of Charles' personal rule, which resulted in solidifying a bourgeois opposition to the monarchy and its adherents. Under James I, regular trade across the Atlantic was undertaken. The Virginia Company, first chartered in 1609 to Levant Company-associated personages, engaged on the usual monopoly terms to trade in tobacco. But despite its complete control of economic governance of the colony, the company collapsed in 1624. This was mainly due to a lack of investment by the City's merchant class. The plantations of Virginia were very new, and required constant infusions of money, goods and labor. "As was obvious to contemporaries, the great merchants of London were prepared neither to take the risk nor to wait [for profits]."[2] James had intended to reorganize the company, but died before it was carried out.

Rather than resurrect the company, Charles I administered the colony directly through an appointed royal governor. Suddenly, with the monopolists cut out, anyone with the means could trade in tobacco. Commerce across the Atlantic now took place under the rough-and-ready conditions of free trade, rather than the regulated monopoly companies trading to the East. This opened opportunities to entrepreneurs who had heretofore been excluded from the great trading routes. "Originally men of the 'middling sort,' they were mostly born outside London and were, in many cases, the younger sons of minor gentry or prosperous yeomen." Some also came from middling business families in the towns — shopkeepers, domestic traders, or mariners.[3]

Initially various arrangements were made. Some retailers entered into partnerships with planters, advancing capital and taking payment in a share of the crop. Or resident plantation owners partnered with ship captains who sold their crop in England. In 1616, a program to promote colonization granted fifty acres of land to anyone who paid his own or another person's way to the colony; this facilitated new-merchant land ownership. The Atlantic merchants were, therefore, from the beginning involved with promoting colonial production. Trendsetting merchants, men like Maurice Thomson, not only imported tobacco, but were also able to dominate the provisioning trade to the colony, to their great profit. As early as 1632 the Virginia

1 *Karl Marx and Frederick Engels Selected Works* (New York: International Publishers, 1848, 1970), 36

2 Brenner, *Merchants and Revolution*, 97

3 Brenner, *Merchants and Revolution*, 114, 685

Assembly voiced complaints about the planters' chronic and substantial indebtedness to "unconscionable merchants."[4]

> If there is a hero who can speak for his fellows in this mixed drama of careers open to the talents, colonization, City revolution and London merchants and shopkeeping tradesmen breaking into the protected, closed corporations of world commerce, it is Maurice Thomson, the "greatest colonial merchant of his day," a much neglected figure in our histories whom Brenner has rescued from near obscurity...[5]

As a leader "among the colonial merchants, freebooters and interlopers" Thomson supported government restrictions on Dutch merchants, building up the English navy, and founding new colonies in Africa and the Far East.[6]

Older overseas monopolists resisted the anarchic conditions of free trade. As contractual "mere merchants" their responsibility was to buy, ship and sell goods, plain and simple. Their companies "operated under restricted, corporately controlled conditions designed to regulate competition to minimize risk, and to ensure profits."[7] They were, in short, an early form of cartel. In 1634, 175 men engaged in the tobacco trade from America; in 1640 the number had risen to 330. In the same two years the Levant Company's large and lucrative currant trade had only 61.[8]

The new Atlantic merchants were thus able to make fortunes for themselves. Members of this class joined in new business ventures, and intermarried among each others' relatives, creating extended networks of family and business associates. Thomson and others were soon able to return to London, where they ran their affairs from an office. Not quite as wealthy as the monopoly oligarchs, they were close enough. They also traded with Bermuda and some Caribbean islands, reexported tobacco to Holland and the Continent, aggressively attacked Spanish ships and ports in the West Indies, and increasingly interloped on the established monopoly companies' preserves all the way to the East Indies.[9] As the European tobacco market became saturated circa 1640,[10] they turned to the English presence in Guyana and Barbados where they became "profoundly involved as capitalist entrepreneurs in colonial production...[of] sugar planting, while pioneering the Africa-West Indies-Virginia-New England trades in slaves, provisions, and staple crops."[11] Most essentially, unlike the older merchant princes, they were not beholden to the king for their wealth.

4 Brenner, *Merchants and Revolution*, 103-105, 129-130

5 Valerie Pearl, "Merchants and Revolution: Commercial Change, Political Conflict, and London's Overseas Traders, 1550-1653 by Robert Brenner," *Urban History* 22, no. 2 (August 1995): 290, https://www.jstor.org/stable/44613964 Accessed 27 October 2018

6 Pearl, "Merchants and Revolution...by Robert Brenner," 290

7 Brenner, *Merchants and Revolution*, 106; Manning, *Aristocrats, Plebeians*, 63

8 Brenner, *Merchants and Revolution*, 25, 27, 76, 105; Ashton, "Three Phases in the Role of the City," 47

9 Brenner, *Merchants and Revolution*, 125, 127, 148, 154-155, 169-170, 410-411

10 Brenner, *Merchants and Revolution*, 161

11 Brenner, *Merchants and Revolution*, 685-686

The aristocratic opposition to the Stuarts was led by a small group of Puritan nobles and knights who desired to establish colonies in the New World to which Puritans could escape from Laud's persecution. Principal among these were the same Lords Brooke, Saye and Sele, and the Earl of Warwick who actively opposed paying ship money to Charles, along with gentry connected to their families and party. Almost certainly through the offices of Puritan divines, such as the activist Hugh Peter, they came in contact with the Atlantic merchants who could provide experience, technical know-how, and additional financing. They collaborated on establishing new colonies in Massachusetts Bay, Providence Island (later moved to Central America), and Bermuda as refuges for Puritan expatriates.[12] By 1640, these two powerful groups had already been working together for a decade. The self-governing colonies became strongholds of Independency, as were some exile English communities in Holland. Leading Atlantic merchants "forged very intimate connections with the Independent militants who formed the lay and clerical leadership of the colonizing movement to New England..."[13] Cooperative activities between the aristocrats and Atlantic merchants in the 1630s also included privateering against Spain in the Caribbean; new colonizing efforts north of Virginia; and "joint political resistance in the City and Parliament."[14]

The Atlantic merchants and Independent ministers also had many close ties to the religious separatists of the less affluent middling class, that were indispensable to the former.[15] With their wide commercial and personal contacts among London "shopkeepers, mariners, and artisans," the aggressive, free-trading merchants, primarily religious and political Independents, would come to play a prominent role in the overthrow of the old regime in London. This gave them "powerful influence" in both Houses which they used to pursue their political demands, not infrequently against a reluctant Parliament.[16]

From the beginning of 1642 they and their supporters, including businessmen of the livery companies, would provide Parliament's financing and administrative organization. At the same time they democratized the London government; allied themselves with the war party in the Commons; attempted to reconquer Ireland; pursued the Independent reformation of religion; "and pushed ultimately for parliamentary supremacy, something like a republican settlement in the state."[17] The Atlantic merchants were, in short, the bourgeois vanguard of the English Revolution.[18]

12 Brenner, *Merchants and Revolution*, 275-276, 278-279, 684-685

13 Brenner, *Merchants and Revolution*, 416-417

14 Brenner, *Merchants and Revolution*, 281

15 Brenner, *Merchants and Revolution*, 426

16 Brenner, *Merchants and Revolution*, 395-396

17 Brenner, *Merchants and Revolution*, 396

18 It is curious that Brenner himself does not make this claim. To him the bourgeois revolution in England happened at an earlier time. For Brenner's views on this subject, see Brenner, *Merchants and Revolution*, 641-644, 648-656; Robert Brenner, "Agrarian Class Structure and Economic Development in Pre-industrial Europe," *Past & Present*, no. 70 (February 1976); Robert Brenner, "The Agrarian Roots of European Capitalism," *Past & Present*, no. 97 (November 1982). Both are reprinted in *The Brenner Debate*, eds. T.H. Aston and C.H.E. Philpin (Cambridge: Cambridge University Press, 2005)

9) RELIGION, REBELLION AND WAR (1637-1640)

All the weight of tradition, custom, inertia, laziness, communal village life, the influence of many powerful landlords, helped to prolong the old way of thought and behavior. From Elizabeth's reign onwards they were abetted by courageous and skillful Jesuit propaganda, with powerful lay backing. On a world scale two ideologies were in conflict, and it was by no means clear that Protestantism was not going to be driven under, as so many heresies had been before.

~Christopher Hill[1]

As the Atlantic merchants were making their fortunes and founding Puritan colonies, the crisis of the *ancien régime* was proceeding apace. From the time of Henry's Reformation, the Church of England had been subordinate to the monarchical state. Licensing of preachers was reinstated under Edward VI. Those who preached without licenses were persecuted under Elizabeth, and those who obtained them had to swear to "only read that which is appointed by public authority..."[2] Her government regularly interfered with preachers and sermons, the latter often widely distributed, at the preeminent St. Paul's Cross Church in London. In 1622, James I attempted to micromanage what church officials of different ranks could say in public, specifying sources and topics by time of day. This followed the 1614 torture and trial of one Edmond Peacham for merely possessing a sermon the government considered seditious. Censorship of sermons, like the press, only increased under Charles I. In 1640, the divine right of kings was ordered to be preached in every church four times a year.[3]

The Bishops' Wars Against Scotland

Charles was unwisely determined that his three kingdoms must all follow a single religion: his. To this end he had the Episcopal Book of Common Prayer rewritten to make it more Catholic.[4] In 1637 he ordered its use in Presbyterian Scotland in place of John Knox's liturgy. This followed several other steps to reintroduce Catholicized practices there, and to centralize power in the Kirk (church) under the bishops and the crown.[5] Such steps threatened to reduce Scotland, like Wales, to the status of a province of England, or a colony like Ireland.[6] The first reading of the Book in Edinburgh caused violent rioting. A significant faction of Scottish aristocrats were, unlike most of their English counterparts, orthodox Calvinists; they organized popular opposition at all levels of the Kirk based on the 1596 Confession of

1 *Society and Puritanism in Pre-revolutionary England*, 33

2 Hill, *Society*, 19

3 Hill, *Society*, 20-23.

4 MacCulloch, "Mumpsimus, Sumpsimus"

5 Green, *History of the English People* Vol. 5, 141-142. Charles simultaneously issued a manifesto appointing a general governor to take control of government and church in New England. Tyacke, "Revolutionary Puritanism," 758-759, 760-761

6 Manning, *Aristocrats, Plebeians*, 16-17

Faith. A new document, the National Covenant, was written and submitted for approval by parishes across Scotland in early 1638. In November, a National Assembly was held in Glasgow from which bishops were excluded. The National Assembly

> pushed new reforms to the Kirk without Royal approval. In the first week of December, the Assembly moved into legislative overdrive, removing the contentious prayer book, abolishing the office of archbishop and bishop and punishing those who refused to accept the National Covenant.[7]

At the same time, military preparations were made and an army to defend the Covenant was organized; strategic ports and arsenals around Scotland were seized, as well as Edinburgh Castle.[8] In the less developed realm of Scotland the aristocracy still retained its military function.[9]

Despite negotiations, Charles was intent on raising an army to subdue the Scots. His severe lack of funds, however, caused the government to make fresh demands on the City municipality. In an attempt to shore up his position, the king made concessions to the City and its merchants: he renewed London's charter which restored some of its privileges, and backtracked on decisions that had harmed various merchant companies' interests.[10] The London Board of Aldermen had agreed to raise money and supply 3,000 soldiers for the war, but instead, in March 1639 the Common Council drew up a petition of grievances, an unprecedented step known to be opposed by the king.

> It complained of the "extreme dearness of all things in so much that the poor householder had much ado to subsist," of the multitude of patents and monopolies, and of the infringement of the City charters in requiring that citizens should be compelled to march out and fight other than in the defense of London.[11]

It also protested "the decay of navigation, and clothing, and the manufactures of this kingdom;" arrests for nonpayment of ship money; and asked for a new parliament.[12] The aldermen refused to take the petition and the measly £5,000 raised to the king. The councillors resolved to do it themselves, but were prevented by the king's own command.[13]

The king went to York the same month in what became known as the First Bishops' War. The army he assembled was the largest military mobilization in

7 "The National Covenant, 1637-60," The Scottish History Society, https://scottishhistorysociety.com/learning-resources/the-national-covenant-1637-60/ Accessed 10 June 2016

8 "The First Bishops' War, 1639," BCW Project, http://bcw-project.org/military/bishops-wars/first-bishops-war Accessed 10 June 2016

9 Anderson, *Absolutist State*, 142

10 Brenner, *Merchants and Revolution*, 283-286, 288-290; Pearl, *London and the Outbreak*, 86-88; Ashton, "Three Phases in the Role of the City," 48, 50

11 Pearl, *London and the Outbreak*, 95

12 John Noorthouck, *A New History of London Including Westminster and Southwark* (London: R. Baldwin, 1773), Chapter 11 fn. 27, British History Online, https://www.british-history.ac.uk/no-series/new-history-london/pp154-174#p32 Accessed 7 June 2017

13 Pearl, *London and the Outbreak*, 95

England since the Spanish conflict in 1588. It was also a motley, ill-equipped, untrained, and resentful force, largely unpaid, led by inept noble commanders pessimistic about their chances of success. After a few skirmishes on the border, the English retired to Berwick in disarray, and an interim truce and inconclusive treaty were negotiated. The army was largely disbanded.[14]

The war against Scotland was unpopular in England, in part due to the economic cost during a downturn in trade, but also because of considerable sympathy for the Presbyterians in Puritan circles. "...opposition groups in England and Scotland now began to enter into active collaboration."[15] At least five unlicensed pro-Scottish pamphlets were surreptitiously printed and circulated in London during 1640.[16]

The commercial depression and Scottish events caused "a crisis of business confidence which had provoked a rapid flow of capital from the country." Charles' own record as a debtor was dismal for he rarely repaid his creditors.[17] Foreign merchants and banks, particularly the Dutch, were calling in their loans, and credit dried up except for the wealthiest. Customs farmers, who owed their positions to the king, did raise huge sums for the crown during 1639-1640; one farmer alone was reported to have made a loan of £100,000 in April 1639. But in June, the Privy Council was obliged to command the Lord Mayor and 24 aldermen to appear before it. The Council demanded they raise £30,000 within one month. By order of Charles, they were forbidden from submitting the loan to the Common Council for approval. The Lord Mayor and 15 aldermen refused (the only time they did so) in no small part because the securities offered by the crown were dubious. Four of these aldermen became staunch Parliamentarians.[18] The war and the economy inflamed the opposition and alarmed the highest levels of the bourgeois class. A few days later, John Lilburne distributed petitions against his imprisonment at an outdoor meeting of unemployed cloth workers, which turned into a demonstration against Archbishop Laud.[19]

Charles returned to London in July. By January 1640 he was ready to try again. He sent for his governor general of Ireland, Sir Thomas Wentworth, whom he made Earl of Strafford. The new earl then returned to Dublin where he forced the Irish Parliament to appropriate funds for an Irish army against the Scots. Once transported across the sea, there was nothing to prevent Charles from using it against English dissenters. Yet the situation was pressing.

14 David Cressy, *England on Edge: Crisis and Revolution 1640–1642* (Oxford: Oxford University Press, 2007), 70, https://oxford-universitypressscholarship-com.i.ezproxy.nypl.org/view/10.1093/acprof:oso/9780199237630.001.0001/acprof-9780199237630 Accessed 5 December 2020; Manning, *Aristocrats, Plebeians*, 23; "The First Bishops' War, 1639," BCW Project

15 Tyacke, "Revolutionary Puritanism," 762

16 Como, "Secret Printing," 41

17 Russell, "Parliament and the King's Finances," 110; Hill, *Century*, 46-47; Pearl, *London and the* Outbreak, 98; C. H. Firth, "London During the Civil War," *History* 11, no. 41 (April 1926): 25, http://www.jstor.com/stable/24399633 Accessed 29 December 2018

18 Pearl, *London and the Outbreak*, 96-98

19 Pearl, *London and the Outbreak*, 107

> English soldiers moving northward had already terrified the areas they passed through. If they were kept idle much longer, or disbanded without pay, there would be mutiny and plundering. Uncontrolled armies might associate with popular risings.[20]

From the Short to the Long Parliament: Breakdown of government

Still unable to raise new loans for the English army, Charles reluctantly called Parliament. Elections for the House of Commons were held, and Parliament duly convened on 13 April 1640 for the first time since 1629. Oliver Cromwell, now the owner of a small estate inherited from a maternal uncle, was elected for the borough of Cambridge. John Pym, influential leader of the opposition to the king, immediately called for reformation of church and state, a reduction on taxes in the colonial trade, and an anti-Spanish foreign policy before authorizing any funds.[21] Three weeks after Parliament opened, on 5 May, Charles dismissed it; hence it became known as the Short Parliament.

The king immediately attempted to again force loans from the City by demanding that London aldermen draw up lists of the richest men in their wards. Seven aldermen publicly refused in court to submit the names of wealthy commoners in their wards to the king. "Strafford, in exasperation, told Charles that he should make an example of some of the Aldermen and hang them for their refusal. The prosecution was to remind him of this ill-advised remark at his trial."[22] The king settled for imprisoning the four most senior alderman who had refused.

A few days after Parliament was dismissed a riot against Archbishop Laud broke out in London. "By 1640, London was a hotbed of discontent." Laud's persecution of Puritans caused him to be blamed for the war on Scotland. In addition, the economic depression was causing widespread unemployment, and there was plague in the city. Puritans made common cause with the Scots Covenanters whom Charles was fighting. There were fears of French invasion. Teenage apprentices, always volatile, were being drawn into political action. Following the quick dismissal of the Short Parliament "placards suddenly appeared throughout the City urging the apprentices to rise and free the land from the rule of Bishops."[23]

> At a great public meeting on St. George's Fields, Southwark, the City apprentices, and the glovers and tanners of Bermondsey and Southwark on holiday for the May Day celebrations, joined up with the sailors and dockhands, now idle through lack of trade, to hunt, as they put it, "Laud, the fox." The Trained Bands...could not prevent five hundred citizens from marching on [Laud's] Lambeth Palace...[24]

20 Pennington, "The Making of the War," 162; Cressy, *England on Edge*, 82-86

21 Brenner, *Merchants and Revolution*, 308-309

22 Pearl, *London and the Outbreak*, 100

23 Pearl, *London and the Outbreak*, 107

24 Pearl, *London and the Outbreak*, 107-108

Laud, who had to row himself to Whitehall to escape, provided the figure of 500. A newswriter, John Castle, estimated the "'unruly multitude'" carrying clubs and drums at 1,200. "The majority of the crowd may have been apprentices, but most of those identified as ringleaders were established tradesmen and craftsmen."[25] A few nights later the apprentices attacked the prisons, freeing those arrested at Lambeth Palace, and also a popular alderman, Thomas Atkins, one of the four Charles was holding for refusal to provide lists of wealthy men. Alderman Atkins addressed the crowd and declined to leave prison, but all four were released next day.[26]

In response to the anti-Laud disorders, the Privy Council brought in 6,000 men of the Trained Bands from outlying counties. A Southwark glover, John Archer, "said on the flimsiest evidence to be the ringleader, was brutally tortured" on the rack and executed. On 23 May, a wounded apprentice, Thomas Bensted, was hung and quartered for treason.[27] However new placards were posted calling for "the citizens to kill Rossetti, the Papal Ambassador, and defend the true faith." Two Puritan merchants, Richard Chambers and the recent MP Samuel Vassall, were arrested in June for "'seducing the King's people'" by circulating a petition to the king for the return of Parliament. A well-known Puritan clergyman was also arrested, and some Puritan leaders had their homes searched and papers confiscated. The arrests only provoked more resistance.[28] On 11 June the Common Council refused Charles' request for 4,000 troops.[29]

To get financing, in June the king seized £130,000 from the mint in the Tower. This seriously added to England's economic woes:

> Credit had been shaken by the breach with Scotland, and foreign merchants had been steadily reducing their commitments in England. The sudden diversion of this bullion prevented many, engaged in commerce abroad, from meeting bills of exchange they had accepted. The protestation of these bills led to a cessation of shipments of coin to London. This reacted on the exchange — "the only sinews and livelihood of all trade." The disorder of trade abroad affected the home market. The crisis was followed by failures, and the purchases of cloth and other goods for exportation were greatly reduced. Bankruptcies became numerous; and, with the suspension of credit, the amount of losses multiplied.[30]

The deteriorating economic picture added to discontent. During June

25 Cressy, *England on Edge*, 117-118

26 Pearl, *London and the Outbreak*, 108; Samuel R. Gardiner, *History of England* Vol. IX 1639-1641 (London: Longmans, Green, and Co., 1884), 135, Internet Archive, https://archive.org/details/historyofengland017044mbp/mode/2up Accessed 5 November 2018

27 Pearl, *London and the Outbreak*, 108 and fn. 7; Lindley, *Civil War London*, 8; Cressy, *England on Edge*, 122

28 Pearl, *London and the Outbreak*, 108-109; Brenner, *Merchants and Revolution*, 311

29 Pearl, *London and the Outbreak*, 102

30 William Robert Scott, *The Constitution and Finance of English, Scottish and Irish Joint-Stock Companies to 1720* Vol. 1 (London: Cambridge University Press, 1912), 224, Internet Archive, https://archive.org/details/constitutionfina01scotuoft Accessed 21 October 2016; Hill, *Century*, 91

and July mutinies broke out among the men conscripted to fight in Scotland. Several officers were beaten and at least two, both Catholics, killed.[31] Others were abandoned or driven off, and the number of desertions and refusals to march were high. "From south to north, in an unofficial crusade of reformation, they taunted conformist clerics, tore up surplices, ripped Books of Common Prayer, and pulled down communion rails." The recruits were often supported by local citizens.[32]

The lower classes among the population were beginning to test their strength amid the breakdown of governmental authority.

> But it was a mark of a changing world that "persons of quality" no longer monopolized the political arena. The events of May 1640 demonstrated that the political domain now encompassed the streets of the metropolis, suburban taverns, country churchyards, toll booths, and markets, where commoners took issue with the affairs of the kingdom.[33]

In August, the Scots army invaded England. To raise money for troops, the Pepper Loan, a financial scheme involving the crown's purchase from, and resale to, the same merchants, was forced through the East India Company general court by its leadership.[34] Charles' excuse for an army was routed in the Second Bishops' War, and he again went north to negotiate an interim treaty. It resulted in the Scots' Covenanter army remaining on English soil at England's expense. On 28 August, twelve peers petitioned the king for the recall of Parliament (written by Pym and Oliver St. John).[35] The Earl of Manchester, who was Lord Privy Seal and father of the later parliamentarian general, made a counterproposal in the Privy Council advising the king to call a Great Council of peers instead of a Parliament, which passed.[36] But in the cover letter sent to the king it became apparent just how much sympathy for the aristocratic "rebels" there was:

> ...that the ground and motive of it [the Council's advice] hath been the uniting of your Majesty and your subjects together, the want whereof the Lords conceive is the source of all the present troubles; ...if your Majesty should receive a blow...monies and forces will be raised very coldly and slowly...[37]

Indeed, "Every day more nobles were arriving in London to give their support to the petition."[38]

31 Cressy, *England on Edge*, 87-88; Robin Clifton, "The Popular Fear of Catholics during the English Revolution," *Past & Present*, no. 52 (August 1971): 26, https://www.jstor.org/stable/650394 Accessed 13 February 2019; Gardiner, *History of England* Vol. IX, 160

32 Cressy, *England on Edge*, 92, 155; Manning, *Aristocrats, Plebeians*, 18-19

33 Cressy, *England on Edge*, 126

34 Brenner, *Merchants and Revolution*, 311-312

35 Hexter, *King Pym*, 78; Gardiner, *History of England* Vol. IX, 199

36 Brian Manning, "The Aristocracy and the Downfall of Charles I," in *Politics, Religion and the English Civil War*, ed. Brian Manning (London: Edward Arnold, 1973), 43-44

37 Manning, "The Aristocracy and the Downfall of Charles I," 44-45; Manning, *Aristocrats, Plebeians*, 23-25

38 Manning, "The Aristocracy and the Downfall of Charles I," 43

Beginning on 10 September, a mass petition was also circulated in London with similar but more extensive demands against ship money, impositions, monopoly patents, innovations in religion (i.e., Arminianism), the war on the Scots, and the "sudden calling and dissolving of Parliaments without the redress of grievances."[39]

> A movement of these proportions could not fail to cause alarm in the Privy Council. In spite of repeated promptings from the Council, the Lord Mayor and Aldermen were unable to suppress the petition. ... On September 22nd, the Court of Aldermen officially disowned it. The Privy Council still had cause for alarm. Although only four Aldermen had signed, the manner of its circulation among the citizens and its wide support revealed the strength of popular feeling. The Council's fears were justified...[40]

As a result, the Privy Council changed its recommendation to the king for the calling of Parliament; even the queen was persuaded.[41] "...the aristocracy had virtually taken power out of the king's hands..."[42] The 10,000 signatures on the London petition were presented to Charles at York by the Atlantic merchant Maurice Thomson and his close associate, Richard Shute. Both men were to become leading figures in the radical parliamentary movement and London Common Council.[43] Charles, having lost the confidence and support of a large section of the peerage as well as the gentry, in the financial, political, and military crisis, was forced to call a new Parliament.

Opposition to the government by now also included well-off artisans and business men of the livery companies as well as those without property (such as wage workers and apprentices).[44] In September 1640, the annual election for Lord Mayor was held in Common Hall. Normally the most senior alderman acceded to the post, but this time the candidate, a close supporter of the royal court, was rejected. Instead, the two nominations were for aldermen who had been imprisoned by Charles for refusing to provide lists of citizens for the forced loan.[45]

This was a radical democratic break with feudal tradition, evidenced by the Secretary of State's panicked letter to the king. The Lord Mayor consulted the Privy Council about the unprecedented action, and a second, more controlled meeting was held a week later where a compromise candidate was chosen. "...the Privy Council thought it wise to accept this election..."[46] The parliamentary Puritan citizenry on the other hand was enraged, and retaliated by electing their preferred candidate, Alderman Thomas Soames,

39 Pearl, *London and the Outbreak*, 175; Brenner, *Merchants and Revolution*, 312-313

40 Pearl, *London and the Outbreak*, 174

41 Manning, "The Aristocracy and the Downfall of Charles I," 46

42 Manning, *Aristocrats, Plebeians*, 25

43 Brenner, *Merchants and Revolution*, 313

44 Pearl, *London and the Outbreak*, 109

45 Pearl, *London and the Outbreak*, 110-111

46 Pearl, *London and the Outbreak*, 111-112

along with three other oppositional Puritan merchants, again including Samuel Vassall, as MPs to the new Parliament.[47] The most important of these, however, was the Independent Puritan Alderman Isaac Pennington, owner of two breweries, and formerly a modest overseas merchant. Pennington was one of those who had refused the king a list of wealthy men in his ward. The new MPs were immediately presented by the citizens with their same petition of grievances to be submitted to the House of Commons. This was in violation of the tradition that petitions be approved by the Lord Mayor and Aldermen, who had only recently rejected it. In the debate that followed it was agreed to have the petition read in the House of Commons instead of Common Hall, which was done just a few days after Parliament opened. These merchant MPs would soon become the critical link between the citizens of London, and, as its left wing, the overall parliamentary opposition in the Commons, tying the two together.[48]

47 For biographies of these men see Pearl, *London and the Outbreak*, 176-193

48 Pearl, *London and the Outbreak*, 112-113

10) PARLIAMENT AND THE PEOPLE: THE ROAD TO REVOLUTION (1640-1641)

> *Much of England's world turned upside down before the outbreak of hostilities, between 1640 and 1642. It was a revolution that caused the war, not the war that brought about revolution. ...the spring of 1642 saw the Elizabethan confessional state disintegrate and the Stuart ancien régime fall apart. Though there would be further revolutions within the revolution...the fundamental shifts occurred in the sixteenth and seventeenth years of the reign of Charles I. This early dating of the revolution used to be more common, but was swamped by the revisionist tide. ... Seventeenth-century chronicles of England's troubles also dated the core of the crisis to 1641.*
>
> ~David Cressy[1]

On 3 November 1640 the members of what became known as the Long Parliament (it would govern until 1653) took their seats. The overwhelming majority of MPs in the House of Commons were well-to-do gentry, a consequence of the archaic electoral districts still in use, and the frequent ability of local gentlemen to assume the seats of nearby towns.[2] London in particular was insufficiently represented given its economic importance and large population.[3] Due to the piecemeal expansion of the franchise in the 1620s however, the election of 1640 returned a larger number of middle or lower gentry to the Commons, men such as Oliver Cromwell, who were more likely to be Puritan, and somewhat more radical in their views.[4] Pym and the Commons leadership were supported by, and worked closely with, the same minority of Puritan nobles in the Lords who had been active in establishing expatriate colonies during the 1630s. These Puritan nobles, particularly Saye and Sele, Warwick, and Brooke, were men with whom the Commons leadership had innumerable ties.[5] But "...the bond they shared was an intellectual one, of common ideas and political principles."[6] It was these men, but not them alone, who would eventually lead the nation into civil war, although at this time they had no inkling of the fact.

Reform vs. Revolution: The Root and Branch Petition

Shortly before Parliament opened, a meeting of the prerogative court of High Commission in St. Paul's Cathedral was disrupted on 22 October

1 "Revolutionary England 1640-1642," *Past & Present*, no. 181 (November 2003): 40-41, http://www.jstor.org/stable/3600785 Accessed 17 September 2016

2 Hill, *Reformation*, 68-69; *Century*, 37; Underdown, *Pride's Purge*, 25; Keith Thomas, "Just Say Yes," *New York Review of Books* 35, no. 18 (November 24, 1988), http://www.nybooks.com/articles/archives/1988/nov/24/just-say-yes/ Accessed September 15, 2013

3 Pearl, *London and the Outbreak*, 193

4 Underdown, *Pride's Purge*, 4; Manning, *English People*, 13-14. This was despite "unprecedented efforts" to interfere in the elections by the king and his allies. Cust, "Election and Selection in Stuart England," 344-345

5 Hexter, *King Pym*, 84-85; Brenner, *Merchants and Revolution*, 394

6 Thompson, "Parliamentary Middle Group," 72

by a hostile throng of perhaps 2,000 people. "Laymen crowded the court making 'a hemming, hooting and shouting,' and began to throw cushions at the commissioners." An unpopular senior judge of the court was forced to flee, his robes shredded. A week later, another crowd tore the Commission's paper records to bits.[7]

On 11 November, two days after the London citizens' petition was presented by Alderman Isaac Pennington, the Commons debated the rumors of military force to be used against the people or Parliament by Charles and Strafford, and a committee was established to bring charges against Strafford. On the 23rd, a hundred citizens with swords, identified by blue ribbons, offered via Pennington to protect the House, but their offer was declined.[8] Strafford and Archbishop Laud were impeached on 18 December. The entire political atmosphere had by now changed.

> With the meeting of the Long Parliament puritans and radical protestants came out into the open: puritans were able to preach publicly again, to gain adherents, and to organize pressure for the reform of the church; the more radical protestants no longer had to meet in secret, but held their assemblies openly, propagated their doctrines and won converts to a more fundamental reformation of religion.[9]

Pennington and the City MPs used their positions to advance the Puritan program of radical church reform. In late November, MPs refused communion at St. Margaret's Church until the altar rail was taken down, and the communion table moved to an acceptable space.[10] Parliament freed William Prynne and the religious martyrs of Star Chamber, imprisoned in 1637. They were greeted as heroes on 28 November 1640 when they re-entered London accompanied by a joyous crowd of 10,000, an unprecedented event which sent shock waves through the royal court and its supporters.[11]

> The part played by the City Members in the struggle for ecclesiastical reform was of crucial importance in the development of opposition to the crown and the growth of radicalism in the Long Parliament. …the ecclesiastical debates divided episcopalians from reformers, and helped to widen the gulf between what were shortly to become two contending parties. The religious issue also divided the moderate Puritan reformers from the supporters of Root and Branch, the radicals, and presaged some of the future divisions which were to split the Long Parliament.[12]

7 Cressy, *England on Edge*, 160-162; Anthony Fletcher, *The Outbreak of the English Civil War* (London: Edward Arnold, 1981, 1985), 110

8 Pearl, *London and the Outbreak*, 211

9 Manning, *English People*, 42-43; Cressy, *England on Edge*, 162-166; Keith Thomas, "Women and the Civil War Sects," *Past & Present*, no. 13 (April 1958): 44, https://www.jstor.org/stable/649868 Accessed 4 April 2020. Reprinted in *Crisis in Europe 1560-1660*, ed. Trevor Aston (New York: Anchor Books, 1967)

10 Fletcher, *Outbreak*, 109

11 Pearl, *London and the Outbreak*, 211-212; Manning, *English People*, 14-16

12 Pearl, *London and the Outbreak*, 212

It was Pennington, on 11 December 1640, who presented a new petition[13] with its 15,000 signatures to the Commons, calling for the abolition of the episcopal state church "root and branch," along with hundreds of "respectable, well-to-do citizens, 'a world of honest men in their best apparel'"[14] with another thousand waiting outside.[15] The mass petition demonstrated the existence of "a highly organized political machine among the parliamentary puritans of the City…"[16] Conservatives were shocked that the petition came, not from the City government, but ordinary people. Pennington defended them: "They were not 'mean rebellious' people, he said, but 'men of worth and known integrity.' … 'If there were any mean men's hands to it,' he said, 'yet if they were honest men, there was no reason but these hands should be received.'"[17] Had corrupt methods been used to get signatures as conservative opponents suggested, Pennington continued, "'instead of 15,000 they might have had fifteen times 15,000…'" Conservative attempts to bring evidence of fraud failed.[18]

The seating of the Long Parliament thus kicked off two simultaneous struggles.[19] One was an intra-ruling–class contest for power over the *existing* government of England, whose roots stretched back to the Parliaments of the 1620s, and even further. "…in 1641 speeches from as long ago as 1610 were published…"[20] The other was the Puritan-led revolutionary petty bourgeois movement in London which aimed at bringing down the feudal system in order to replace it with an unspecified godly kingdom. The two movements were in competition, yet their leaders were in a *de facto* partnership. With common enemies, they mutually reinforced each other, creating a duel for power with the king's government. When the crisis reached its height at the end of 1641, their respective leaderships and followers were politically as well as militarily united behind Parliament.

The House of Commons leadership, headed by the master politician John Pym, was determined to bring the king to heel. Its reform program was aimed at making the crown politically dependent on Parliament.[21] (Modern day bourgeois historians romantically refer to this as "the constitutional crisis.") They aimed to exclude bishops from the House of Lords and clergy from government posts, and wanted approval power over all major government appointments. In this way they believed they could control his majesty's government, and they naturally saw themselves as the proper candidates to hold

13 One of whose authors was Oliver Cromwell. Hill, *God's Englishman*, 73

14 Pearl, *London and the Outbreak*, 214

15 Manning, *English People*, 17

16 Pearl, *London and the Outbreak*, 214

17 Pearl, *London and the Outbreak*, 214-215

18 Pearl, *London and the Outbreak*, 215

19 Brenner, *Merchants and Revolution*, 393-394; Underdown, *Pride's Purge*, 7

20 Hill, "Parliament and People in 17th-Century England," 109

21 Hexter, *King Pym*, 199

the leading positions in it.[22] It was never their aim to overthrow the king, or to dissolve the old social order, but to "restore balance" in the feudal government by subordinating both state and church to the landowners in Parliament.[23]

There was only one fly in the ointment of this reform program: it required agreement by the king. During the 1620s, Pym and company had likewise promoted their fitness to lead through the blue water policy of attacking Spanish shipping and colonies in the New World to cut the legs out from under the Catholic empire, relieving the Palatinate and protecting Holland. This of course meant a degree of promotion for Puritanism at the expense of English Catholics, but it did not envision a dismemberment of the established Church or abolition of monarchy. The Commons pursued a fanciful strategy of seeking an accommodation with first James, and then Charles, on this program, primarily by having parliamentary leaders appointed as their counselors and ministers. But it had no more chance of success in 1640 than previously. All Charles had done since attaining the throne made it quite clear that he was committed to reinforcing every aspect of the feudal system, most especially his own power.

The Commons leadership disingenuously claimed to oppose, not the king, but only his "evil counselors," a hoary English tradition.[24]

> By arguing that the king's sacred power was inalienable, they urged that royal ministers like Laud and Strafford were encroaching upon his divinity; and since the king himself could do no wrong, it followed that the ministers were to blame for his policies and should be punished accordingly.[25]

No independent legal framework existed for parliamentary action however. Even on the rare occasions in history when the House of Commons had tried to curb a monarch's policies, it had lacked the power to do so unless backed by the nobles in the House of Lords.[26] (Only in the Tudor era did they have any success at all.)[27] Most often, whatever debates may have occurred, Parliament had acted as little more than a rubber stamp.[28] But now, having laid hold of the ready-made feudal Parliament, the reformers attempted to wield it for their own purposes.

Few MPs supported outright abolition of episcopacy, but most were opposed to the innovations of Arminianism. They were intent only on placing

22 Brenner, *Merchants and Revolution*, 319

23 Manning, "The Nobles, the People and the Constitution," 50-51; Brenner, *Merchants and Revolution*, 320; Hexter, *King Pym*, 176; Hill, "Parliament and People in 17th-Century England," 108, 109; Underdown, *Pride's Purge*, 58-59

24 "But the fiercest resentment was always against evil counselors, represented as sticky-fingered opportunists (sometimes, as in 1376, as scarlet women)... The legend of private favorites with sinister ends was a routine scapegoat of popular political movements from the songs and chronicles of the fourteenth century to the civil wars of the 1640s." Rollison, "The Specter of the Commonalty," 232

25 Thomas, "Just Say Yes"

26 Russell, "Parliament and the King's Finances," 92

27 Hill, *Reformation*, 32

28 Hill, *1640*, 41

limits on the power of the bishops and the king. But a month after convening, they were confronted by the mass Root and Branch petition from London's middling class. Led by militant Puritan preachers and radical Independent Atlantic merchants, they were intent on a wholesale frontal attack to smash the power of the church and court hierarchies so they could decide how to pursue their religious and economic lives on their own. Whatever their subjective beliefs and goals, which were not uniform, this sweeping program aimed to end the feudal system as it then existed. "...it is necessary to recall the importance of the Church in relation to the civil government at this period."[29] New religious canons were hastily promulgated by the government in a futile attempt to forestall the revolutionary attack on the religious hierarchy.[30] Abolition of the established church, as James I had foreseen, would lead to the collapse of the monarchy.

This put the popular movement at odds with those sitting in Westminster. "'Many of the nobility and gentry...were contented to serve his [the King's] arbitrary designs, if they might have leave to insult over such as were of a lower order,'" wrote the republican MP Edward Ludlow.[31] This second front by the large petty bourgeois and laboring classes was unlooked for by the gentlemen of the House, and made many of them uncomfortable, if not outright trepidatious. "'If by multiplying hands, and petitions, they prevail for an equality in things ecclesiastical, this next demand perhaps may be *Lex agraria*, the like equality in things temporal,'" argued the conservative Edmund Waller in 1641.[32]

Societal shifts

In the opening decades of the 17th century, it became more and more acceptable for lesser gentry to purchase apprenticeships for their younger sons with merchants or artisans,[33] which increased the economic and social overlap between them. By 1640 many businessmen in the livery companies came from gentry origins, and were viewed as an asset by their families.[34] A new prefix, "Mr.," was coming into use by shopkeepers, professionals, lesser gentry, upper yeomen.[35] "As early as 1635, there were nearly 1,200 persons resident in London who described themselves as gentlemen, the great majority of whom were engaged in trade or in some professional occupation."[36] Lawyers, doctors, clergymen and civil servants were becoming respectable professions in the 17th century, the social equals of lesser gentry, especially

29 Margaret James, "The Political Importance of the Tithes Controversy in the English Revolution 1640-60," *History* 26, no. 101 (June 1941): 4-5, http://www.jstor.org/stable/24401760 Accessed 2 February 2017

30 Como, "Secret Printing," 61-62

31 Hill, *Century*, 105 [Insert in original]

32 Manning, *English People*, 71; Fletcher, *Outbreak*, 123

33 Grassby, "Social Mobility and Business Enterprise," 356-357; Stone, "Social Mobility in England," 27-28

34 Grassby, "Social Mobility and Business Enterprise," 379

35 Stone, "Social Mobility in England," 54; Manning, *1649*, 58-59

36 Stone, "Social Mobility in England," 53

inasmuch as they catered to the upper classes.[37] "The Privy Council reported that from 1578 to 1633 the number of attorneys practicing in Common Pleas increased fourfold..."[38] Thus, an emergent middle class, totally unconnected to the monopoly company merchants, had already become a fact of social life. These trends helped to subvert the rigid status categories from earlier feudal society.

The nimbler, more thrifty Puritan gentry were now rather wealthier than the more staid but profligate nobility, whose incomes from rents, like the king's, had declined.[39] "In 1628 a peer observed, with disapproval at the way times were changing, that the Lower House could buy the Upper house three times over."[40] This made those nobles with court appointments more dependent on royal favoritism and the crown's largesse, and those not at court more resentful at their exclusion. Both provided Puritans with ammunition against idle parasites.[41]

The overarching contradiction of the privileged gentry in their dual roles as both peasant landlords, and agricultural or industrial principals, meant that very few MPs in the Long Parliament had any republican leanings.[42] Most would only support demands for reform of the existing system. This contradiction would be starkly revealed in the split in the House of Commons in 1641-2, when only a slim majority of MPs would ally itself with the Atlantic merchants, the middle and petty bourgeoisie. Gentry opposition to the crown, or support of Parliament during the Civil War, was a result of being caught between the growing capitalist economy and the decay of the feudal social system: insecurity of property and their own persons; arbitrary taxation and fines (such as for enclosure); the drag on improved estate management by the tangle of feudal land tenures; state limitations on manufacture and trade; as well as Laud's persecuting Arminianism. These violations of what they considered their rights were all the more galling since they themselves were still part of the feudal ruling class.

> The gentry were exempt from the servile punishment of flogging. ... The resentment which the Star Chamber sentences on Prynne [a lawyer], Burton [a clergyman], and Bastwick [a physician] aroused sprang not so much from their savagery as because this savagery was employed against gentlemen, members of the three learned professions.[43]

Gentlemen were not accustomed to being treated so roughly.

37 Manning, *1649*, 56-57

38 C. H. George, "The Making of the English Bourgeoisie, 1500-1750," *Science & Society* 35, no. 4 (Winter 1971): 409, http://www.jstor.org/stable/40401600 Accessed 7 January 2017

39 Hill, *Reformation*, 65-66

40 Hill, *Century*, 12; Stone, "Social Mobility in England," 50-51

41 Hill, *Reformation*, 67

42 Brenner, *Merchants and Revolution*, 320; Hill, *Reformation*, 128

43 Hill, *Century*, 38; *1640*, 48-49

The London Puritan Movement

In the urban feudal class designations of the time merchants were at the top. This category included the great overseas monopolists, domestic wholesalers and retail shopkeepers, all of whom sold goods. Below them were craftsmen who combined art with manual skills. On the bottom were laborers, porters, carters, and watermen (ferrymen on the Thames). In reality, however, shopkeepers were part of the middling stratum: they were nowhere near as wealthy as the larger wholesalers and traders, and they were in daily contact with, and directly dependent on, their middling-class neighbors. Craft apprentices, servants under the law, lived in their masters' homes, and were also actually part of the middling class, unlike maids or kitchen help. Nonetheless most of them, lacking the money to set up as masters, would end up as journeymen who worked for wages.[44] During periods of economic downturn, the middling craftspeople and small shopkeepers "had to sell their wares every week to live, and the labourers had to have work or starve,"[45] but rich merchants could live comfortably off their capital.

The Puritan leaders of the London movement, like those with whom they collaborated in Parliament, held a range of opinions on various aspects of religion, and the proper relationship between church and state. The Puritans' differences would come to the fore in the second half of the decade. At this early stage however, they saw the overriding need to confront the monarchy and church hierarchy as compelling them to act in a coalition, subordinating their disagreements, and directing all their efforts to the political defeat of the king.[46]

Despite being a minority within the London religious movement, Independent congregations were able to influence events due to being well-organized, tightly knit units in close communication. Because they rejected the Calvinist tenet of a controlling Church governance or discipline, they in fact had a great deal in common with the more radical separatist sects (in particular Anabaptists). Despite their attempts to play down the similarities, there was frequent cooperation between them. The Independents' major difference with the radical sects was their opposition to complete separation of church and state believing, with Presbyterians, that government support was necessary for an orderly and thorough reformation.[47] Independents, like the sectarian separatist groups, insisted

> that the sermon should be followed by discussion: that worship was not a matter of passively hearing the Word preached by a learned minister, but participation by the congregation after a gifted member had opened up a subject for discussion. … Meaningful discussion had hardly been possible

44 Manning, *English People*, 104-105

45 Manning, *English People*, 116-117

46 Pearl, *London and the Outbreak*, 278-279

47 Brenner, *Merchants and Revolution*, 418-419, 425-426; Underdown, *Pride's Purge*, 18

> in the pre-1640 parish church, with the parson safely in control,...with squire and churchwardens to enforce decency and order. Things were quite different in a gathered church, non-hierarchical in structure and social composition, with an elected minister who might himself be a mechanic, with no ritual, no squire or churchwardens.[48]

This was the actual practice of many gathered churches, meeting in people's homes or in fields outside of the city, which mushroomed with the coming of Parliament, and in which women as well as men participated.[49] These gathered churches, based on religious affinity, violated the existing geographical boundaries of the parish. This was a step too far for many, usually upper class, Independents. Isaac Pennington, for one, insisted on maintaining the traditional parish structure in conformance with the feudal past.[50]

The Presbyterians considered such discussion sinful, as it could easily result in a pluralist church, but English Presbyterianism was not exactly the same as the Scottish. Since the days of Elizabeth Puritan propaganda had promoted nationalist ideology intertwined with religious devotion.

> They were on their guard against the extremer pretensions of Calvinist clericalism, and meant to retain over the church the supremacy of the Parliament which represented property. But like the divines, they were bent on uniformity and stoutly rejected toleration.[51]

Unlike the English Reformation imposed by Henry VIII, Scotland's had been a popular movement led by Calvin's disciple John Knox from within the Kirk itself, making it the dominant institution.[52] As a result, nobles were as subject to church discipline as anyone else. In a 1606 speech before King James and Scottish Presbyterian clergy, the Kirk was assailed "as a 'world turned upside downe, where the people commandeth all.'"[53] To most English aristocrats this state of affairs was woefully democratic.[54]

Both Independents and Presbyterians regarded religious discipline as the glue that could hold society together, and replace the feudal hierarchy that they abhorred, "to create a new order through creating new men."[55] The question was how far the inner discipline of the "new men" could be trusted. Presbyterians saw the traditional need for outside compulsion; Independents

48 Hill, *World*, 104-105

49 Thomas, "Women and the Civil War Sects," 44-46, 46-48; Hill, *World*, 310-312

50 Brenner, *Merchants and Revolution*, 420-421

51 Brailsford, *The Levellers*, 24; Trinterud, "William Haller," 37-38. This view derived from Thomas Erastus (1524–1583) a Swiss theologian who argued that church governance, especially excommunication, should be exercised by the state and not the church.

52 Knox also traveled and preached in England, including in front of King Edward VI, until forced to leave by Mary Tudor's accession.

53 Tyacke, "Revolutionary Puritanism," 751

54 Hill, *Reformation*, 134; *Society*, 185-186; Manning, "The Godly People," 101

55 Hill, *World*, 47-48; John Field, a Puritan organizer, wrote in 1587, "'it is the multitude and people that must bring the discipline to pass which we desire.'" Hirst, *Representative?*, 12; Plumb, "Growth of the Electorate," 94

were willing to rely on men's consciences, which they held sacrosanct. "I had rather that Mahometanism was permitted among us, than that one of God's children should be persecuted," Cromwell declared in 1652.[56] It was not until after the decisive defeat of the Scots army at Dunbar in 1650 that the Elizabethan Act of Uniformity, imposing fines for absence from church on Sundays, was at last repealed.[57]

The appointment of approved ministers from above naturally flowed from Presbyterianism, just as voluntary election by the congregation did from Independency. What was worse to the former was the acceptance by the latter of "mechanik" preachers, i.e., ordinary people who had not attended university and had no need of tithes. The condemnation of lay mechanic preachers proceeded from its economic implications:

> The attack on tithes, common to all the radicals, undermined the whole concept of the state church, since if parishioners could not be legally compelled to pay tithes there would be no 'livings' for the clergy to occupy, no impropriated tithes for the gentry to collect in the forty per cent of livings which were lay fees. Disestablishment of the church would deprive the gentry of another property right — the right of presentation to a living, a right for which they or their ancestors had paid hard cash and which gave them useful opportunities of providing for a younger son or a poor relation.[58]

Impropriations, the transfer of tithes to a secular owner, was mostly a result of Henry VIII's dissolution of the monasteries. Like church lands, the right to local tithes was expropriated by the crown, which could then sell or gift them.[59] The fact that so many gentlemen drew income from the collection of tithes "goes far to explain the bitter opposition which proposals for tithe abolition were to arouse during the Revolution."[60] University financing depended on them, and these would lose their primary function of graduating religious ministers if they were abolished. Voluntary support by congregations of lay clergy, ordinary men who worked for a living, was not only far cheaper, but meant "the church as an organ for imposing and maintaining a single consistent outlook would cease to exist."[61] The more conservative arguments of Presbyterians did nothing to mollify the fears of the feudal ruling class on these grounds. In all these aspects, social, economic, and ideological, the London Puritan movement posed what the rulers correctly regarded as a mortal threat to the established order.

56 Hill, *God's Englishman*, 75; Brailsford, *The Levellers*, 394; Firth, *Oliver Cromwell and the Rule of the Puritans in England*, 307

57 Hill, *World*, 103; "September 1650: Act for the Repeal of several Clauses in Statutes imposing Penalties for not coming to Church," Acts and Ordinances of the Interregnum, 1642-1660, British History Online, http://www.british-history.ac.uk/no-series/acts-ordinances-interregnum/pp423-425 Accessed 18 November 2016

58 Hill, *World*, 99; *Century*, 65

59 James, "The Political Importance of the Tithes Controversy," 3

60 James, "The Political Importance of the Tithes Controversy," 4

61 Hill, *World*, 99

The struggle begins

To avoid a debate in the Commons, the Root and Branch petition was referred to committee, with the stipulation that the fate of episcopacy was off the table. However, a week later a subcommittee was given authority to "inquire into the causes of the decay of preaching and the increase of Popery and 'scandalous' ministers." The committee chairman, Member for Southwark, had been one of the Feoffees (trustees) of Impropriations[62] which, until its suppression in 1633 by Laud, had purchased lectureships for Puritan preachers. Isaac Pennington continued his campaign on the issue, backed by a steady flow of petitions both moderate and radical. This resulted in a bill to abolish superstition and idolatry in February 1641, but it was not passed until the following August.[63]

A week after the Root and Branch petition was received, the Commons impeached Archbishop Laud and the Earl of Strafford, Governor of Ireland. The fight against the king, through attacks on two of his closest and most powerful appointees, was on. The committee's recommendations to remove bishops from the House of Lords and bar clergy from holding secular offices was passed on 10-11 March 1641. The Commons leadership hoped this would appease the citizens' movement enough to focus on the trial of Strafford which had far more support in the House. It worked. Whether by prior agreement or not, the leaders of the City radical movement shifted gears and made the trial of Strafford the burning issue of the moment. Archbishop Laud was already safely in the Tower following his attempt on 1 March to secretly flee London, which had been thwarted by a crowd in Cheapside.[64]

Parliament also had to deal with the pressing and awkward financial situation. Under the interim Treaty of Ripon, signed by Charles in September 1640, England was required to pay £25,000 per month to the Scots, whose army remained on English soil. The Long Parliament was faced with either providing the money itself, or allowing the king to do so, which would likely mean Parliament's dismissal. The solution was to secure a loan. With individual MPs acting as guarantors, Alderman Pennington was able to extract a promise from the City government that would cover two months' payments. The Commons majority embraced the Scots army as their own because it was the only force they had available against the king. Without it, they were defenseless.[65]

> The policy of Pym and his supporters was to procure sufficient money to keep the Scottish army in the north, but not so much that it would be paid off before enough concessions had been wrung from Charles. ... The policy owed its success, very largely, to the City M.P.s, who...were quick

62 Pearl, *London and the Outbreak*, 213

63 Pearl, *London and the Outbreak*, 213, 219-220

64 Manning, *English People*, 20

65 Pearl, *London and the Outbreak*, 197-198

to establish themselves as financial intermediaries between the House of Commons and the City.[66]

Pennington and MP Alderman Thomas Soames shortly became treasurers for the loan, releasing funds or not as they saw fit. Future City loans were referred to Common Hall directly, where Pennington had a large following, giving him "a platform in the City from which to influence the liverymen to lend or withhold their money, as parliamentary tactics dictated."[67] By mid-March, 1641, the two armies together were owed the enormous sum of £278,000.[68] During this time Pennington and the parliamentary opposition stayed in close touch with the Scottish Commissioners in London.[69]

Pennington used his control of funding as leverage over the Commons majority for the radical Puritan program. Whenever a political matter was raised on the floor he would announce that loan money could not be secured, or if already collected, could not be paid, unless the House took acceptable action. This put significant pressure on Pym and the large and amorphous "middle group" in the Commons, and enjoined the right wing to push back, so that a more or less continual tug-of–war went on in the chamber over all major political and religious issues at stake.[70]

Both the extreme left (republican) and right (royalist) wings of the Commons were small, no more than 30-50 members. There was nothing called the middle group at the time; this is a 20th century designation.[71] Its members were not anti-monarchical, but insisted on limits being placed on the powers of the king. The 1628 Petition of Right may be said to be its founding document.[72] As there were no formal party organizations or discipline, factions were quite loose and often changing. Members "could vote as they deemed best on each issue as it emerged without being bound in advance,"[73] and it was not uncommon for MPs to move one way or the other depending on the business at hand.[74] Pennington's tactic of withholding funds was not always successful since Pym, the leader and epitome of the middle group, was cautious about pushing his members too hard, and was intent on preventing serious interruptions to supplies for the Scottish army in the north.[75]

Royalist MPs wanted to use the same tactic in order to pay off the Scottish army and send it back across the border, thereby depriving Parliament

66 Pearl, *London and the Outbreak*, 198

67 Pearl, *London and the Outbreak*, 199

68 Brenner, *Merchants and Revolution*, 336

69 Pearl, *London and the Outbreak*, 199-200

70 Brenner, *Merchants and Revolution*, 330-331

71 Hexter, *King Pym*, 47; Underdown, *Pride's Purge*, 1; William G. Palmer, "Oliver St. John and the Middle Group in the Long Parliament, 1643-1645: A Reappraisal," *Albion* 14, no. 1 (Spring 1982): 21, http://www.jstor.org/stable/4048483 Accessed 28 November 2016

72 Thompson, "Parliamentary Middle Group," 86

73 Hexter, *King Pym*, 66-67

74 Hexter, *King Pym*, 36-47; Palmer, "Oliver St. John," 20; Underdown, *Pride's Purge*, 2

75 Pearl, *London and the Outbreak*, 200-202

of its hold over the king. They attempted to go around Pennington by raising money from the old-line company merchants and the official City government, which they controlled. But they did not get far, although Pennington's inability to raise promised funds at one point hurt his credibility. Company merchants had no wish to finance the Scottish army against the king, and they objected to a leaked statement by the Scottish Commissioners stating their desire for the abolition of episcopacy, which scandalized the entire right wing. Moreover, the political situation was quite tense. The campaign against Strafford was reaching its height, and there was always the possibility that Charles could dismiss Parliament at any time. Worse, rumors were rife that the king and some army supporters were plotting to free Strafford, and use force against the people and Parliament.[76] Given the highly unsettled situation, potential lenders would doubtless have had grave qualms about getting their money back.[77]

The center-left coalition quickly used this last objection to strike a blow at the king: ostensibly to reassure potential lenders, a bill was unanimously passed and sent to the Lords declaring that Parliament would remain in session until it voted to dissolve itself. They then rejected a proposal for a £300,000 loan from the Customs Farmers against future customs duties. Such a scheme by the king's supporters was intended to make him financially independent. "There was to be no financial grant without the removal of 'that great stumbling block' Strafford."[78]

The trial of Strafford in the House of Lords had dragged on. The Commons had charged the earl with high treason for subverting the fundamental law of England, a difficult charge to prove. Militant Puritans began a petition and agitation for "justice" for Strafford to counteract eroding support in and out of Parliament, and so that reform of the church could go forward. They also feared the king's Catholic army in Ireland which Strafford had raised.[79] On 10 April 1641, the king ordered the anti-Strafford petition suppressed. On the same day, in response to the radicals' pressure, a Bill of Attainder was brought in the Commons "by which the earl would simply be declared guilty of treason and condemned to death by Act of Parliament." But the House was divided on the matter.[80]

To encourage them, on 21 April, up to 10,000 Londoners, led by three captains of the Trained Bands, presented a petition at the House of Commons with somewhere between 8,000 and 30,000 signatures. It cited the laxity shown to Catholics in violation of the law, and the "Irish popish army" still in existence, and called for church reform and the death of "'notorious

76 See the section "The First Army Plot and the Protestation" in Chapter 11 below.

77 Pearl, *London and the Outbreak*, 202-203; Brenner, *Merchants and Revolution*, 333-334

78 Pearl, *London and the Outbreak*, 205-206

79 Manning, *English People*, 21; William Palmer, "Catholic Plots and the English Revolution: Some Comments," *The Catholic Historical Review* 73, no. 1 (January 1987): 82-83, https://www.jstor.org/stable/25022454 Accessed February 25, 2019

80 Manning, *English People*, 21-22. Bills of Attainder are explicitly prohibited in the U.S. Constitution, Article I, Sections 9 and 10.

offenders.'" The presenters included John Venn (who would soon become an MP), John Fowke and Randall Mainwaring, radical Puritan merchants who had been politically active in the past, and who would become key players in the near future. The House passed the attainder the same day, and sent it to the Lords. MPs voting against were denounced as traitors, who "'should perish with Strafford'" in placards posted up in London and Westminster. In response, the king ordered the City magistrates to suppress all petitions.[81]

Due to the crisis over Strafford, in mid-February 1641, the king had appointed opposition nobles Bedford, Essex, Saye, Mandeville, and Warwick, among others, to the Privy Council. All of these had signed the Petition of Twelve Peers to call a new parliament six months previously, and all accepted their elevations. Oliver St. John, who was close to Bedford, had been made Solicitor-General the month before.[82] By late April to early May, Pym and the Earl of Bedford were negotiating with Charles to assume the offices of Chancellor of the Exchequer and Lord Treasurer respectively. In exchange, they offered to provide authorized revenue to replace nonparliamentary impositions, and to rationalize the crown's finances; preservation of episcopacy; and Strafford's life:[83] i.e., a complete sellout of the Puritans' revolutionary program. However Bedford died in May, and the agreement was never completed, at least in part due to lack of support in the Commons. Pym and Bedford's financial reforms would have raised taxes on the aristocracy,[84] and some MPs were suspicious that high offices were a sop that would fail to bring reforms in church and state. Shortly afterwards, Lord "Saye accepted the highly profitable office of Master of the Wards," a Tudor institution whereby the crown took over estate management from widows or orphans.[85] The unenthusiastic response may have been due to radical City influence in the Commons, but Charles then insisted that his demands be met before making any appointments. Even his advisor Lord Clarendon thought this position untenable.[86] But the real sticking point was that there was no way to reconcile the king's adamant demand for Strafford's life with the force of the London movement for his execution.[87]

81 Manning, *English People*, 22-23; Pearl, *London and the Outbreak*, 216-217; Brenner, *Merchants and Revolution*, 337-338

82 Manning, "The Aristocracy and the Downfall of Charles I," 55; Conrad Russell, "The First Army Plot of 1641," *Transactions of the Royal Historical Society* 38 (1988): 87, http://www.jstor.org/stable/3678968 Accessed December 26, 2016; Fletcher, *Outbreak*, 45

83 Brenner, *Merchants and Revolution*, 338-339; Russell, "Parliament and the King's Finances," 111; Pearl, *London and the Outbreak*, 205

84 Russell, "Parliament and the King's Finances," 112

85 Russell, "Parliament and the King's Finances," 113

86 Manning, "The Aristocracy and the Downfall of Charles I," 55-56; Brenner, *Merchants and Revolution*, 396-397

87 Brenner, *Merchants and Revolution*, 339

11) THE MAY DAYS (1641)

Modern histories have demonstrated that absolute monarchy appears in those transitional periods when the old feudal estates are in decline and the medieval estate of burghers is evolving into the modern bourgeois class, without one of the contending parties having as yet finally disposed of the other. ... The reaction of the rule of the princes, instead of proving that it creates the old society, proves rather that its day is over as soon as the material conditions of the old society have become obsolete. Its reaction is at the same time the reaction of the old society which is still the official society and therefore also still in official possession of power or in possession of official power.

~Karl Marx[1]

The First Army Plot and the Protestation

Charles told the Lords on 1 May that he would not agree to the execution of Strafford, but would accept his exclusion from office. The same day he sent one hundred armed men to the Tower (where Strafford was being held), but the officer in charge, Lieutenant Balfour, refused to admit them. News of the attempted rescue enraged the populace. They also learned of chilling discussions between the king and army officers to march the army in the north on London to suppress the citizens and release Strafford.[2]

Again some 10,000 people turned out on 3 May at Parliament and, as the Lords passed through the crowd to enter, shouted "Justice and Execution!" at them. Lieutenant "Balfour's resistance was supported by a petition to the House of Lords, from the citizens, who kept a very close watch on what happened at the Tower."[3] They briefly blocked the Earl of Arundel who presided over Strafford's trial, and demanded an answer to the petition on Strafford, which was immediately read. The king was to attend the session. Instead, he sent a message saying they should "'settle peace and prevent these tumults,'" but the Lords adjourned without taking action. A known supporter of the king, the Earl of Bristol, was threatened when he left as "'an apostate from the cause of Christ, and our mortal enemy...'"[4] At the same time, Pennington and another City MP announced in the Commons that the king was attempting to seize the Tower, using the subterfuge that it was necessary to guard munitions, and that armed men were being brought into the City. All of which was true. No one doubted that at least one plot was afoot, or that Charles was responsible, which he was.[5] "Leading members knew perfectly

1 "Moralising Criticism and Critical Morality," Marx and Engels, *Collected Works* Vol. 6 (London: Lawrence & Wishart, 1847, 1976), Marxists Internet Archive, https://marxists.architexturez.net/archive/marx/works/1847/10/31.htm Accessed 28 July 2019

2 Manning, *English People*, 23; Russell, "The First Army Plot of 1641," 95, 96

3 Russell, "The First Army Plot of 1641," 96

4 Manning, *English People*, 23-24

5 Russell, "The First Army Plot of 1641," 91-96, 98-99, 101; Pearl, *London and the Outbreak*, 218; Gardiner, *History of England* Vol. IX, 351

well, in the first week of May 1641, that what they were facing was a royal plot."[6] Clearly a response was required, but "...the real difficulty...lay in the fact that the danger came from the King himself." Pym, who already knew a good deal about what was going on, was not yet prepared to openly proclaim it.[7] Instead he proposed a Protestation, a direct pledge of loyalty to Parliament aimed at the London citizens, which passed next day.

With the demonstration of 3 May going outside, the House of Lords sent an inquiry to the king for information. In response, the king acknowledged authorizing the irregularly pulled-together troops to occupy the Tower, but when he refused their first request to withdraw the royalist soldiers, they sent their own officer, the Earl of Newport, and guards to take command.[8] The next day, the Protestation was taken by nearly all the Lords "in attendance, including, uneasily, the bishops."[9]

> Throughout the country, at quarter sessions and borough assemblies, the governing class met to subscribe the Protestation. The text was passed from magistrates to chief constables, to ministers and parochial officials, across the local matrix of command. It was not yet intended for ordinary people, though occasionally there was pressure to tender it lower down the social scale.[10]

Eight months down the road, in January 1642, the Commons would order local officials to administer it to all males age eighteen and over with specified dates to return the names of both subscribers and refusers to Parliament. In a few places women took it as well.[11]

The Protestation was a cautious document. In the realms of both religion and law its vague language could leave it open to interpretation.[12] "The importance of the Protestation lay far more in what was implied by it than in what it actually said."[13] It was not technically an oath, as the subscriber did not swear, but was only asked to "promise, vow and protest."[14] It upheld "his Majesty's Royal Person, Honour and Estate" as well as "the Power and Privilege of Parliament, the lawful Rights and Liberties of the Subjects..." But in the circumstances, the main thrust was to require the subscriber to "endeavour to bring to condign Punishment" anyone who attempted "by Force, Practice, Counsel, Plots, Conspiracies or otherwise" anything against "the true, reformed, Protestant Religion, expressed in the Doctrine of the

6 Russell, "The First Army Plot of 1641," 105

7 Gardiner, *History of England* Vol. IX, 352-353; Russell, "The First Army Plot of 1641," 92-93

8 Russell, "The First Army Plot of 1641," 96; Gardiner, *History of England* Vol. IX, 355

9 David Cressy, "The Protestation Protested, 1641 and 1642," *The Historical Journal* 45, no. 2 (June 2002): 254, https://www.jstor.org/stable/3133645 Accessed February 13, 2019

10 Cressy, "The Protestation Protested," 259

11 Cressy, "The Protestation Protested," 267, 272. "Returns from more than 3,200 parishes from thirty English counties survive in the House of Lords Record Office, and dozens more have been found in local archives." 252

12 Cressy, "The Protestation Protested," 257-258

13 Gardiner, *History of England* Vol. IX, 354

14 Cressy, "The Protestation Protested," 255-256

Church of England," specifically, "Popery, and Popish Innovations."[15]

In this respect, it was a pledge to defend Protestantism, and cast Parliament as the equal of the crown. Since the king was popularly reckoned to be pro-Catholic, its intent was easily perceived as "a declaration of readiness to resist a royal *coup d'état*."[16] But far from calming the situation as they'd hoped,

> ... the circulation of the Protestation in the summer of 1641 triggered hundreds of rancorous debates. ... Zealots in dozens of parishes attempted to put their vow against popery into immediate effect, sometimes with violent consequences. ...the Protestation could be used to justify not just the elimination of altar rails and surplices but the elimination of bishops and the book of common prayer.[17]

The crowd that had turned out at Parliament on the third of May was "'for the most part men of good fashion;' ... 'many thousand of the most substantial of the citizens;' '...some worth £30,000, some £40,000.' The most prominent leader was John Venn." John Lilburne, the future Leveller leader and past victim of the Star Chamber, said, "they came unarmed today but tomorrow they would bring their swords."[18] Ignoring the Lord Mayor's prohibition on tumults, the crowd that returned next day was predominantly lower-class in composition, "ordinary 'mechanic folk,'" who brought swords and staves with them.[19] "Swords traditionally were gentlemen's weapons... so their flaunting by artisans represented a social challenge as well as a risk of violence."[20] A new mass petition was brought to the Commons the same day by two City MPs, along with several Puritan ministers and captains of the Trained Bands. It sought the Parliament's authorization to administer the Protestation to all London citizens, which passed at once. The Commons directed "that it should be taken by all the [London] citizens in their parish churches,"[21] and in practice the names of subscribers were recorded, as well as the names of those who refused. This served to identify and isolate royalists or Catholics, although a few Puritans raised reservations as well.[22]

But the City government initially refused to authorize its administration; meanwhile Puritan radicals circulated it themselves. After receiving additional instructions from the House of Commons, the government had to allow parish congregations to begin subscribing on 30 May.[23]

15 "The Protestation," House of Commons Journal Volume 2: 03 May 1641, British History Online, https://www.british-history.ac.uk/commons-jrnl/vol2/pp131-133#p10 Accessed 13 February 2019; Cressy, "The Protestation Protested," 255; Gardiner, *History of England* Vol. IX, 354

16 Russell, "The First Army Plot of 1641," 104; Brenner, *Merchants and Revolution*, 340-341

17 Cressy, "The Protestation Protested," 262, 264

18 Manning, *English People*, 25; Pearl, *London and the Outbreak*, 216

19 Manning, *English People*, 26; Pearl, *London and the Outbreak*, 217

20 Cressy, *England on Edge*, 383

21 Pearl, *London and the Outbreak*, 218; Brenner, *Merchants and Revolution*, 341

22 Cressy, "The Protestation Protested," 260-261

23 Cressy, "The Protestation Protested," 261; Pearl, *London and the Outbreak*, 218; Brenner, *Merchants and Revolution*, 341

> On 5 May Pym revealed to the Commons what he knew of the conversations between army officers, courtiers and the king about the possibility of intervention by the army on the king's side. It was believed that the French king was sending an army to Portsmouth to help the queen, his sister; that the army which Strafford had built up in Ireland was about to invade; that the papists in England were about to rise and seize power.[24]

In fact, on 6 May the queen's confessor, Father Philip, did send a letter asking for French intervention, and the queen herself was planning to escape to Portsmouth on the southern coast the day after.[25]

Tensions and fears of a *coup d'état* were running very high. A loud noise sounding like a gunshot in the middle of the debate caused a panic. Members fell all over each other, drew their swords, or fled. Rumors immediately flew through London that the Commons had been attacked by papists. Shops were instantly closed, and a large group of armed citizens along with a regiment of the Trained Bands headed for Westminster. It was a false alarm; a chair had collapsed under a member. But the incident demonstrated on the one hand the willingness of the people to defend by arms what they regarded as "their" House, and on the other the dependence of the MPs on the radical movement for their security.[26]

Pym's exposure of the First Army Plot badly undermined the pro-Strafford party by publicly demonstrating their predisposition to use illegal force against the citizenry and/or Parliament. The following day four royalist gentlemen fled to the Continent "before anyone had accused them…;"[27] the Lords issued orders for their arrests.[28] The Plot alienated even some prominent supporters of the king, who feared that it entailed the dissolution of Parliament, or a move toward restoring Catholicism.[29] This backed the Lords into a corner. They could neither countenance the king's illegal efforts to free Strafford, or use force against Parliament, nor stop the rowdy demonstrations demanding Strafford's death which continued on their doorstep. To save face, they agreed to the Bill of Attainder, but requested the Commons to call off the demonstrations so as not to appear to be making concessions to the people.[30]

The people's victory

Three days after Pym's revelations, on 8 May, the House of Lords passed the Bill of Attainder, with many, including all of the Catholic members, absenting themselves out of fear of the people. The political victory was made complete by passage of the bill against dissolution of Parliament without its

24 Manning, *English People*, 26-27

25 Russell, "The First Army Plot of 1641," 97

26 Pearl, *London and the Outbreak*, 27-28; Brenner, *Merchants and Revolution*, 340

27 Russell, "The First Army Plot of 1641," 90

28 Gardiner, *History of England* Vol. IX, 361

29 Russell, "The First Army Plot of 1641," 103-104, 105

30 Gardiner, *History of England* Vol. IX, 355

consent on the same day. Armed demonstrations began next day at Whitehall palace, where Charles resided and held court, as the two Houses of Parliament made their case to the king. "All through the night panic reigned at Whitehall."[31] The next morning, the king was urged to approve the attainder by the Privy Council, judges and even some bishops. "All day long the street in front of Whitehall was blocked by a shouting multitude. Every minute it was expected that an attempt would be made to dash in the doors."[32] Late that evening, Charles, demoralized, tearfully gave his approval to the attainder, which was announced the following day. On 12 May Strafford was executed; the streets were filled with people rejoicing.[33]

The ruling class was now openly polarized. That the victory had been the people's was all too obvious. The idea that Parliament should be responsive to the people, indeed, that the people should play any role at all in the political life of the country, was antithetical to the entire construction of feudalism.[34] The attitude of aristocratic conservatives was not so different as those at the time of the Peasants' Rebellion who "had regarded the peasants as little more than laboring beasts of the land."[35] The specter of democracy to them was nothing less than the advent of anarchy, not to mention an appalling threat to their own positions.

Some army officers wrote a petition to the king with his permission. Also addressed to the Houses of Parliament, it offered to restore order and deliver up the ringleaders for punishment, but this was suppressed by senior officers. Nevertheless, a royalist party of order had begun to coalesce.[36]

The City government was rapidly losing the ability to rule in the old way. The Trained Bands were a citizens' militia and therefore unreliable for the purpose of keeping order. "When a member of the Company of Watermen was told that he ought to be obedient to law, order and the Lord Mayor, he answered that 'it was Parliament time now, and the Lord Mayor was but their slave.'"[37] This identification of the London populace with Parliament, and more especially the House of Commons, was a source of strength to the Puritan middling class movement, and the seed of its eventual betrayal. The large crowds mobilized by the London Puritan leaders against the king and his government brought a new urban power onto the scene. It was socially distinct from the market-agrarian landlords, and from the few well-off merchants and manufacturers in the Commons, with a far more radical program it intended to fight for. It was also "joined often enough by the labouring

31 Gardiner, *History of England* Vol. IX, 364

32 Gardiner, *History of England* Vol. IX, 366

33 Manning, *English People*, 30

34 Hill, *Reformation*, 55-57. As in earlier centuries, the idea of a commonweal, or common good, was widely understood by the masses to mean the good of all social classes, even as the ruling aristocracy used it to mean only themselves. Rollison, "The Specter of the Commonalty," 225-227, 244-245

35 O'Brien, *When Adam Delved*, 47

36 Manning, *The English People*, 31-32

37 Pearl, *London and the Outbreak*, 119-120; Hill, *World*, 22

classes of the City and suburbs."[38] The open conflict between the royal court and the Commons, backed by the mass artisan/workers movement, began a struggle for power, raising the question: which class would rule?

> A culture of obedience which had designated the people subjects for whom unconditional obedience was a divine duty was being challenged by the emergence, if only temporary and half-formed, of a citizenry of free-born Englishmen (and, for some, free-born women).[39]

The political development of the citizens' movement was blunted, however, by the wholesale support of the movement's leaders, the bourgeois Atlantic merchants and Puritan preachers, for the gentry in the Commons. During 1641 Pym

> struggled against the idea that the conflict with the King must be fought out by other than constitutional means. The King must be brought round by persuasion, not by force. In the end he must be surrounded by new counsellors, as a guarantee that he would conform to the new order of things. It was far too sanguine a view of what was possible with Charles.[40]

"'If he [Charles] understood the laws, he would not err,'" Pym had argued in 1628.[41] Within the anti-absolutist coalition, this blind moderation sabotaged the revolutionary process to the advantage of the reforming landowners and their pro-free trade merchant allies. The separate interests of the mass of small, more radical craftspeople in the end would be sacrificed to those far wealthier magnates of the new capitalist order.

Unlike the landowning gentlemen of the Long Parliament, the French Third Estate in 1789 was purely bourgeois: they were *not* in the main landowners, but mostly lawyers and civil servants. Unlike English landlords, French aristocrats "took no part in trade or industry."[42] There was thus no overlap of economic interests between aristocrat and bourgeois in France, and neither class had ever been able to share a significant portion of power during the absolute rule of the French monarchy. The defection of the French bourgeoisie from the feudal political system was therefore a hard split, one instantly made good by the establishment of a revolutionary democratic governing state authority, the National Assembly. A considerable number of MPs were also lawyers (including Pym), but they were not particularly distinguishable as common lawyers frequently came from gentry backgrounds.[43] (Some knowledge of law was considered to be part of gentlemen's general education, a help to them in administering their estates.)[44] In England, the

38 Pearl, *London and the Outbreak*, 228

39 Walter, "the English Revolution Revisited," 180

40 Gardiner, *History of England* Vol. IX, 352

41 Derek Hirst, "Parliament, Law and War in the 1620s," *The Historical Journal* 23, no. 2 (June 1980): 460, https://www.jstor.org/stable/2638680 Accessed February 23, 2019

42 Hill, *Century*, 86; Grassby, "Social Mobility and Business Enterprise," 355; Rabb, "Investment in English Overseas Enterprise, 74

43 Hill, "Land in the English Revolution," 28

44 Hill, "The Inns of Court," 543, 545-546; Porter, "Impact of the Civil War Upon London," 188

governmental evolution begun by Magna Carta had institutionalized the limited, but nonetheless real, powers of the lower House, and this made its members, mostly landed gentry, more conservative in their willingness to check the king's excesses.[45]

To the extent that the middling people, and especially their Puritan leadership, were aware of the MPs' reluctance to act — and when it came to religion they certainly were — the Puritans of whatever sort were unable, or unwilling, to put forward a comprehensive political program that reflected their demands for greater democracy and equality. The Commons would not have considered such a program in this early period, which therefore, to be effective, would have to have been asserted independently of its power struggle with the king. Not until the Levellers in the later 1640s, after the king's military defeat, would this be accomplished.

In the wake of the May Days

Not long after Strafford's execution a major public controversy broke out with the publication in June 1641 of Henry Burton's pamphlet *The Protestation protested.* Burton had been one of the radical Puritan martyrs of the Star Chamber in 1637, and although the pamphlet was published unsigned, his sermon on 20 June at St. Margaret's Church, next door to Westminster Abbey and Parliament, contained the same ideas. He

> insisted on a revolutionary interpretation of "that noble Protestation" of the previous month. ...the Protestation, in his view, also embraced "those that have been in the church of God ever since the apostles; whatsoever any man hath set up...that are in the sight of God idolatrous and against the scripture, that is popish innovation."[46]

This was to impugn the entire history of the bishops' rule going back to 1534. The sermon was not well received by the MPs in attendance. It was attacked by Presbyterians as well as Episcopalians as justifying Independency. A future bishop wrote it "would lead to 'schism and democracy.'" The pamphlet and the uproar it caused, however, stimulated more radical discussion on religion.[47]

The same month London Common Hall demanded the right to elect both sheriffs. One of the two had traditionally for the last 300 years been appointed by the Lord Mayor, or so a petition to the king and Privy Council by the Court of Aldermen claimed. Their petition was referred to the House of Lords, which attempted to have the matter negotiated between six elected citizens and the City magistrates, thereby establishing an equality between the two sides. The six elected were opponents of the Crown. Five were associates or relatives of Maurice Thomson, Isaac Pennington or other leading Puritan merchants, and included John Fowke and Randall Mainwaring, who would eventually serve on the City Militia Committee. The dispute dragged

45 Zaller, "The Concept of Opposition," 231-232

46 Cressy, "The Protestation Protested," 264

47 Cressy, "The Protestation Protested," 265

on for two months, the Lord Mayor being backed by a petition of "172 of the wealthiest and most prominent merchants in the City."[48] When negotiations failed, the Lords, to end the matter, reluctantly allowed the vote to proceed in Common Hall, but expressed the hope they would choose the Lord Mayor's candidate. They did, but the Mayor and aldermen, appearing before the Lords at the end of August, threatened to resign over the order claiming it would "'destroy and dissolve the ancient government of the City.'" The Lords however stood by their order as fair to both sides.[49]

Over 50 of the 172 "prominent" signatories to the Lord Mayor's petition were monopoly company members who obviously realized the threat the radical movement represented to their oligarchic rule. The petition organizers would go on to become the London nucleus of political reaction "that would grow in strength and audacity in the succeeding months."[50]

The House of Commons goes on the offensive

On 5 July 1641 an act passed at the end of 1640 came into force proclaiming "the said Court commonly called the Star Chamber...and the Power and Authoritie thereby given unto it be...repealed and absolutely revoked and made void." This act, which began by citing Magna Charta (sic), further prohibited any other court from obtaining "like jurisdiction," and specifically excluded the king or Privy Council from exercising any power over the lands, goods, or inheritances of subjects, reserving these matters to the Common Courts.[51] A similar act took effect the same day abolishing the Church High Commission.[52]

The king had been stripped of his main prerogative powers, ending the feudal government's judicial terror against the citizenry. Simultaneously the security, not to say sanctity, of property, an absolute essential for a stable bourgeois society, took a major step forward: no longer did merchants, tradesmen or gentry need fear that judgements awarded in the common courts might be summarily overturned by the crown. To a greater degree, the capitalist economy could now develop on its own terms without arbitrary interference by the government. The concurrent breakdown of church courts freed the people from prosecution for sin, or excommunication for offenses of conduct. These acts alone would have the most enduring effects: the prerogative courts would remain in the dustbin of history through the 1660 Restoration, and, despite a brief attempt by James II to resurrect the High Commission, all the way to the revolution of 1688 and ever after. The Act

48 Pearl, *London and the Outbreak*, 120-121

49 Pearl, *London and the Outbreak*, 121-122; Brenner, *Merchants and Revolution*, 343-345

50 Brenner, *Merchants and Revolution,* 344

51 "Charles I, 1640: An Act for the Regulating the Privie Councell and for taking away the Court commonly called the Star Chamber," Statutes of the Realm: Volume 5, 1628-80, British History Online, http://www.british-history.ac.uk/statutes-realm/vol5/pp110-112 Accessed June 10, 2016

52 "The Act for the Abolition of the Court of High Commission," July 5, 1641 Statutes of the Realm, v. 112, Online Library of Liberty, http://oll.libertyfund.org/pages/1641-the-act-for-the-abolition-of-the-court-of-high-commission Accessed June 13, 2016

of 1641 also "insisted that a writ of *habeas corpus* should be issued 'without delay upon any pretence whatsoever' when demanded on behalf of anyone arrested on warrant from the King or Privy Council."[53]

The events of the spring had opened up the political situation, but it remained unsettled. Matters were complicated early in the summer when the House of Lords rejected expulsion of bishops from their chamber,[54] and soon after the bill barring Catholics from holding state offices. The Commons majority made renewed approaches to Charles, but the king left for Scotland in August after making clear his disinterest in negotiating with Parliament, an ominous sign. Before leaving, he appointed several royalists to high offices.[55] This made the Commons more susceptible to pressure from radical City leaders to advance on several of the most glaring grievances of the City movement. In mid-1641, the House addressed issues of monopolies, trade and religion.

As a tactical move to pressure the Lords, the Commons reintroduced a new root and branch bill that would give Parliament substantial control over the church. This was quite different from the popular demand to abolish episcopacy in favor of more local control by congregations. MPs "were, for the most part, repelled by both the Presbyterian and Independent alternatives" advocated by each in their own way.[56] Nonetheless, the Commons bill encouraged renewed activity by Puritans who saw it as a renewed attack on the established church hierarchy.[57]

As indicated by the 1639 Common Council petition of grievances, monopolies were an oppressive sore point and regular complaint of the middling people.

> The period before the Civil War was one of extensive economic controls. First imposed as a deliberate system of regulation of economic life for socially desirable ends, these degenerated fairly rapidly into a ramshackle bunch of monopoly patents, either sold for ready cash or more often given away as rewards to importunate courtiers.[58]

Monopolies retarded production, inflated prices to consumers and wage workers, and provided only a minimum of funds to the government.[59] These feudal patents drove already existing small craftsmen out of business to the benefit of upper class gentlemen. They were so extensively used that there were monopolies on bricks, glass, coal, iron, tapestries, feathers, brushes and combs, soap, starch, lace, linen, leather, belts, buttons, pins, dyes, butter, currants, salmon, lobsters, salt, pepper, vinegar, wine, tin,

53 Hill, *Century*, 196

54 Pearl, *London and the Outbreak*, 219

55 Manning, "The Aristocracy and the Downfall of Charles I," 69, 71; Fletcher, *Outbreak*, 44, 45

56 Brenner, *Merchants and Revolution*, 412

57 Brenner, *Merchants and Revolution*, 342

58 Stone, *Crisis of the Aristocracy*, 162

59 Hill, *Reformation*, 96

hops, tobacco, pipes, playing cards, pens, writing paper, candles, books, alum, gunpowder, saltpeter, hay, and mouse traps, among many hundreds of other goods.[60]

One of the Commons' first acts had been to expel twelve elected MPs for being monopoly merchants.[61] Beginning in December 1640, the House of Commons sent shock waves through the overseas monopoly trading companies by public investigations into how they were operated pending renewal of their charters. The Committee on Trade first demanded all of the "'books, letters, etc.'" of the East India Company. In January 1641, it required the Merchant Adventurers to provide all of the company's patents and books. The Adventurers offered the committee an enormous loan of £200,000 in the spring, but the Commons as a body rejected it. By the end of 1641 however, desperate for funds as the political situation was reaching its critical point, the House renewed the Levant and East India Company charters in exchange for loans. The Merchant Adventurers' charter was also approved; over the next two years Parliament received £140,000 from the company.[62]

Many individual London magistrates came under attack by Parliament. "Complaints about the municipality poured in to the [Commons'] Committee for Grievances from London citizens." The Committee held that imprisonment of those who refused to pay ship money or other taxes, or had their goods or papers seized at the behest of City governors, was a violation of the law. Their property was ordered restored to them. They even ordered reparations paid to two collectors of ship money who had been jailed for failure to raise the required funds. Not a few aldermen who were merchants or manufacturing monopolists, or customs farmers, were heavily fined or even imprisoned for their actions in previous years.[63]

In August, the House voted to return to colonial merchants tobacco shipments which had been seized by the government in a dispute over customs duties. They slashed the customs tax on tobacco, setting a uniform rate, and ordered any fines or other charges repaid. The MPs also acted in a dispute between London wine sellers and the monopoly French Company. An economic settlement imposed by the king in 1638 had hurt the retailers in favor of the wholesalers' profits. The Commons took the side of the middling-class shopkeepers, and imprisoned several of the monopoly importers, supporters of the City oligarchy.[64] The same month, in response to a petition by the Atlantic merchants, a joint committee of Lords and Commons was set up to consider forming a West India Company to advance against the Spanish in the Caribbean.[65]

60 Hill, *Century*, 25-26; Manning, *English People*, 168-170

61 Hill, *Century*, 102

62 Brenner, *Merchants and Revolution*, 346-347

63 Pearl, *London and the Outbreak*, 118-119

64 Brenner, *Merchants and Revolution*, 347-349

65 Brenner, *Merchants and Revolution*, 350-351

The Commons lastly moved on reform of religion, although this topic caused fierce debates. On Pennington's initiative, they authorized altar rails to be removed from local churches, and communion tables to be repositioned by churchwardens, while upholding the "Government of the Church established by Law."[66] Just before recessing in September they further reversed Laud's innovations by ordering the removal of crucifixes, candles, images, etc.; elimination of superstitious rituals; and banned sports and dancing on Sundays. On a motion by Oliver Cromwell, they also upheld the right of parishioners to hire lecturers at their own expense to preach when regular ministers were not scheduled.[67] Both orders were rejected in the Lords, who repeated their order of eight months earlier, "That the Divine Service be performed as it is appointed by the Acts of Parliament of this Realm; and that all such as shall disturb that wholesome Order shall be severely punished..." But the Commons' orders were widely circulated, resulting in violent conflicts around the country.[68]

Thus the House of Commons, urged on by its left wing, the radical Puritan leadership of the London citizens' movement, took up a host of issues near and dear to the middling class and liverymen, the Atlantic merchants and many gentry. The outcomes were decidedly mixed. The signal failure was the persistence of monopolies by overseas merchant companies. The collaborative activity between the Commons and the City forces, however, was in sharp contrast to the split between the two Houses of Parliament, each of which contained minorities in sympathy with the other.

Settlement in Scotland and its effects

Meanwhile, Charles had been busy negotiating in Scotland, and signed the Treaty of London in August 1641. Although the Scottish army was ordered to disband, "it required the Crown to pay the Scottish army's arrears of pay and, critically, demanded that the changes ordered by the Glasgow Assembly be given royal assent."[69] Under the circumstances, the abolition of episcopacy in Scotland may have seemed a small price to pay for getting rid of the only armed force the English Parliament could look to. But in reality, Charles, as was his custom, was only feigning. He had no intention of back-

66 Pearl, *London and the Outbreak*, 220; "Abolishing Superstition," House of Commons Journal Volume 2: 08 August 1641, British History Online, https://www.british-history.ac.uk/commons-jrnl/vol2/pp245-246#p44 Accessed 10 January 2021

67 Brenner, *Merchants and Revolution*, 351-352; Manning, *English People*, 46-47; Fletcher, *Outbreak*, 114-116; "Innovations in Religion," House of Commons Journal Volume 2: 01 September 1641, British History Online, https://www.british-history.ac.uk/commons-jrnl/vol2/pp278-280#p8; "Innovations in the Church," House of Commons Journal Volume 2: 08 September 1641, https://www.british-history.ac.uk/commons-jrnl/vol2/pp281-284#p56; https://www.british-history.ac.uk/commons-jrnl/vol2/pp281-284#p75 Accessed January 10, 2021

68 Pearl, *London and the Outbreak*, 124; Brenner, *Merchants and Revolution*, 352; Manning, *English People*, 47-49; Fletcher, *Outbreak*, 117-119; "Order about Common Prayer and Service in the Church," House of Lords Journal Volume 4: 16 January 1641, British History Online, https://www.british-history.ac.uk/lords-jrnl/vol4/pp133-134#p27; "Order concerning Divine Service," House of Lords Journal Volume 4: 9 September 1641, https://www.british-history.ac.uk/lords-jrnl/vol4/pp393-396#p50 Accessed 15 February 2012

69 "The National Covenant, 1637-60," The Scottish History Society, http://scottishhistorysociety.com/wp-content/uploads/2016/07/the-national-covenant.pdf Accessed June 10, 2016

ing off from imposing rule by the bishops in all his domains. The apparent settlement of the war allowed the London oligarchs, at the end of September, to ram their nominations for Lord Mayor through Common Hall. The names of a royalist and a popular alderman were carried by the sheriff to the Court of Aldermen, who promptly elected the former.[70]

When the House of Commons reconvened in October, the leadership "conscious of the dubious legality of the Orders [on religion], deliberately shelved them…[and] quashed further discussion on a measure that was alienating moderate opinion and dividing the House…"[71] Nevertheless, encouragement given to radical Puritans by the Commons' actions spurred the creation of new gathered congregations and spread of lay preaching.[72]

Charles remained in Scotland plotting with conservative Scottish nobles against those who had put themselves at the head of the Presbyterian Covenanters, the Earls of Argyl and Lanark and the Marquis of Hamilton, who in early October, forewarned, fled Edinburgh. "The Incident," as it came to be called, failed, but the story was recounted in the Commons by Pym as the horrible example of what had nearly happened. He specifically cited the Catholic Earl of Crawford in Scotland as a prime conspirator. Such an attack was considered still possible as new royalist army plots were being hatched in England. The situation was made more volatile by angry demonstrations at Parliament of disbanded English soldiers from the Scottish campaign demanding back pay. At the request of both Houses, one hundred men from the Trained Bands were placed on guard around Parliament by the Earl of Essex (son of the rebel executed by Elizabeth, and later first head of Parliament's army).[73]

With the Scots army removed from England, Pym and company found themselves in a quandary. The Commons' middle group of gentry was beginning to react negatively to the unruly participation of the London citizens' movement, and its revolutionary religious program which appeared to them seditious. The king could obviously not be trusted with the safety of MPs, much less to carry out reforms. "From the time of the Petition of Right, Charles showed with what ease he could ignore parliamentary enactments that he himself had approved."[74] The only way to compel the king was to rely on the Puritan middling class movement, but this risked alienating many of Pym's own supporters.[75] For all its independence, the historic impotency of the House of Commons was here starkly revealed by its inability to effect changes to the feudal political system. To do so required either the backing of

70 Pearl, *London and the Outbreak*, 124-125

71 Pearl, *London and the Outbreak*, 220

72 Brenner, *Merchants and Revolution*, 354

73 Manning, *English People*, 34-35; Vernon F. Snow, "Essex and the Aristocratic Opposition to the Early Stuarts," *The Journal of Modern History* 32, no. 3 (September 1960): 224, 231, http://www.jstor.org/stable/1872425 Accessed November 29, 2016

74 Brenner, *Merchants and Revolution*, 352

75 Brenner, *Merchants and Revolution*, 353

the Lords (which, as usual, it did not have), or calling in extra-parliamentary forces. Uniquely, for the first time, these social forces existed in England; moreover, they were organized and militant.

The threat from the right was quite real. "If Charles had the military power to dissolve Parliament, the Act against Dissolution would not restrain him. …they could expect to be tried and convicted for treason."[76] Playing to the conservatizing fear of the City population, the king "placed the protection of order and social hierarchy at the core of his program, making the defense of a non-Laudian episcopacy and of the prayer book the central plank on which to build a royalist party."[77] In these circumstances, Pym sought to draw back from religious reform in order to concentrate on winning control of the House of Lords by excluding bishops and lay Catholics, who constituted a reliable monarchist voting bloc. Once again Puritan leaders in London met and agreed to prioritize the campaign against bishops over reform of religion.[78]

76 Russell, "Introduction," 29

77 Brenner, *Merchants and Revolution*, 355

78 Brenner, *Merchants and Revolution*, 355-357; Manning, *Aristocrats, Plebeians*, 33-34

12) THE DECEMBER DAYS AND THE END OF FEUDAL POWER (1641-1642)

> *It so happens that the "social questions" which have been "dealt with in our own day" increase in importance in proportion as we leave behind us the realm of absolute monarchy. Socialism and communism did not emanate from Germany but from England, France and North America. The first manifestation of a truly active communist party is contained within the bourgeois revolution...*
>
> ~Karl Marx[1]

Rebellion in Ireland

On 1 November the Privy Council informed Parliament of a rebellion in Ireland and a massacre of Protestants, including women and children, in Ulster. That the Irish lords and people were retaking their lands forcibly confiscated from them cut no ice in England.[2] Hearsay evidence, sketchy reports and speculation, from Ireland and in England itself, pointed to the possibility of Catholic uprisings or terrorist acts on English soil. "The people had been brought up on stories of their cruelty and bloodthirstiness... All this seemed to be confirmed and given immediacy by the massacre of the protestants in Ireland..."[3] The burning days of Queen Mary were still very well remembered thanks to Foxe's popular *Book of Martyrs*, as were the Gunpowder Plot of 1605, massacres of French Huguenots, and the Spanish Inquisition.[4] Panic over "popish plots" raced around the country. Armed watches were set, provisions laid up, prayers offered. A list of 65 leading papists including most Catholic peers was drawn up in the Commons. The Marquis of Winchester was found to have arms for some 1500 men, which were seized.[5]

The popular fear of papists fed into anti-government fervor. A report from Ireland claimed "that the rebels had friends in England, amongst the king's councillors, amongst the bishops, and amongst the aldermen of London."[6] As these three groups had been the strongest opponents of religious reform, and the most ready to countenance popish innovations in the church, they were easily amalgamated with the imputed hostility of English Catholics, and the real hostility of the Irish. Conversely, the radical Puritans, who had been the chief agitators for a thoroughgoing Protestantism, and tireless denouncers of popery and the old order, now found their authority significantly enhanced.[7]

1 "Moralising Criticism and Critical Morality"

2 Harris, "Revisiting the Causes of the English Civil War," 634

3 Manning, *English People*, 181

4 Hill, *Century*, 47; Trinterud, "William Haller," 51; Caroline M. Hibbard, "Early Stuart Catholicism: Revisions and Re-Revisions," *The Journal of Modern History* 52, no. 1 (March, 1980): 30, https://www.jstor.org/stable/1877953 Accessed October 31, 2018

5 Manning, *English People*, 36-40; Clifton, "The Popular Fear of Catholics during the English Revolution," 29, 49-50

6 Manning, *English People*, 35

7 Manning, *English People*, 42; Lindley, *Civil War London*, 77

The ruling-class split and the triumph of the Puritans

The Irish uprising forced Pym's hand. All sides agreed on the necessity to raise a new army to subdue the Irish and relieve the Protestants; the question was, who would control it? On 8 November, by only 151-110, the Commons voted that Parliament had to approve all royal officers appointed by the king. "'If his Majesty should not be graciously pleased' to grant the request to remove his evil counsellors, then 'we should take such a course for the securing of Ireland as might likewise secure ourselves.'"[8] If Charles refused, it could only mean the members had reason to feel endangered, and must take further steps.

Two days earlier, Oliver Cromwell had spoken on the floor in favor of putting all Trained Bands in southern and middle England under the command of the Earl of Essex.[9] This would have made them responsible to Parliament, removing them from the king's command. One month later, the first Militia Bill to carry this out was presented in the Commons, "and a long, lively debate ensued in which 'verie violent expressions' were used." It would have put the militia "under a Lord-General who was not named and who was given extraordinary powers to raise and command the militia, levy money for their pay, and execute martial law, all for an unlimited time." Such a bald centralization of military power would have immediately brought the question of supremacy to a head. No vote was taken on the bill, but a motion to throw it out failed 158-125.[10]

The anti-absolutist opposition in the Commons was being pushed towards revolution by events. With the fate of the entire reform program at stake, Pym finalized the Grand Remonstrance, an indictment containing a litany of over 200 grievances against Charles I's 17-year reign. Ostensibly it was a petition to the king against the bad advice of his evil counselors. It passed the Commons by an even closer vote of 159-148 on 22 November, and was presented to the king on 1 December without submitting it to the House of Lords.[11] Oliver Cromwell said that "'if the Remonstrance had been rejected he would have sold all he had the next morning, and never have seen England more…'"[12] In reality, the Remonstrance was a thinly disguised appeal to the people, a revolutionary act in itself, as demonstrated by the fact that swords were drawn in the House on 15 December during a fierce debate

8 D.H. Pennington, "The Rebels of 1642," in *The English Civil War and After 1642-1658*, ed. R. H. Parry (Berkeley: University of California Press, 1970), 33; Brenner, *Merchants and Revolution*, 357; Samuel R. Gardiner, *History of England* Vol. X 1641-1642 (London: Longmans, Green, and Co. 1884), 56-57, Internet Archive, https://archive.org/details/in.ernet.dli.2015.275096/page/n3/mode/2up Accessed 5 November, 2018

9 Snow, "Essex and the Aristocratic Opposition," 231-232; Lois G. Schwoerer, "'The Fittest Subject for a King's Quarrel': An Essay on the Militia Controversy 1641-1642," *Journal of British Studies* 11, no. 1 (November 1971): 50-51, http://www.jstor.org/stable/175037 Accessed November 29, 2016

10 Schwoerer, "the Militia Controversy," 54; Gardiner, *History of England* Vol. X, 95-96

11 Hill, *Century*, 94, 102; "The Civil War," UK Parliament, http://www.parliament.uk/about/living-heritage/evolutionofparliament/parliamentaryauthority/civilwar/overview/the-breakdown/ Accessed June 3, 2017

12 Fraser, *Cromwell*, 77

over whether to publish it.[13] Like all important speeches by opposition MPs it was widely circulated in the country.[14]

The growing split among the MPs had little to do with any specifics regarding government, or even religion. The bulk of the gentry MPs were largely in agreement on the reform program Pym had shepherded through the House during the last year. But a large minority recoiled from the necessity of allying with the movement of London citizens to achieve it, because this "risked further political and especially religious radicalization." They chose instead to place their trust in Charles for the fate of their reforms, thereby preserving their elite status as the sole arbiters of political authority in the nation.[15] "The breach was only made irreparable by the association of the parliamentary cause with popular agitation."[16] The fact that a majority of the Commons and a minority of the Lords were willing to seek the people's support demonstrated their determination to overawe the king, and prevent the triumph of an intolerable absolutism, even at the cost of a political break with a large section of their own class. Control of armed forces would be a key question in any country let alone one where a royal standing army had been a fraught issue between the aristocracy and monarchy for centuries. For Parliament, it was rely on the people or surrender and go home. The alliance of a substantial section of the landed aristocracy with the bourgeois class leadership of Atlantic merchants and Puritan ministers was critical, for it gave them good reason to believe they could control the citizens' movement. But it was a step full of risk.[17]

On 25 November, three days after the Remonstrance passed, the king returned from Scotland. He re-entered London with great pomp, and was given a public banquet by the aldermen and major City officials. The Recorder gave a speech on behalf of the City government pledging "their loyalty and affection, and of their devotion to 'our established religion,'" a backhanded denigration of the Puritan opposition. The king was then presented with £20,000 in a golden cup, and the queen with £5,000 in a golden basin. In return, Charles made promises of prosperity and the City's liberties, pledged to uphold the Protestantism of Elizabeth and James, knighted the Recorder, and made the Lord Mayor a baronet.[18]

With the king's return, Essex's commission in charge of the Trained Bands expired, and Charles immediately dismissed the men guarding the two Houses. His Majesty was here asserting his power over the militia, and, indirectly, Parliament. A request from Parliament that the guard be restored was granted, but Charles gave the command to the Earl of Dorset, Lord Lieutenant of Middlesex, and a member of the royal court. When, a few days later, demonstrators

13 Hill, *Century*, 106; "Parliament and People in 17th Century England," 118

14 Hill, *World*, 22

15 Brenner, *Merchants and Revolution*, 358

16 Pennington, "The Rebels of 1642," 34

17 Brenner, *Merchants and Revolution*, 358-359, 393-394; Hill, *Reformation*, 128; "Lord Clarendon and the Puritan Revolution," 192-193

18 Pearl, *London and the Outbreak*, 126-128

carrying swords and staves and chanting "No bishops!" massed outside the House of Lords Dorset gave orders to fire at the crowd, and run them through with pikes. There is some question whether the guards' guns were loaded with bullets or only powder, but a clash which might have proved very bloody nonetheless ensued.[19] The House of Commons could obviously not have their supporters treated in this manner on their own turf, and informed Charles:

> ...it is fit the Guard should be continued under the same Command, or such other as they should choose: But, to have it under the Command of any other, not chosen by themselves, they can by no means consent to; and will rather run any Hazard, than admit of a Precedent so dangerous, both to this and future Parliaments.[20]

Either they got to choose the officer for the guard, or they would do without.

Rather than submit to the king the Commons dismissed the Band from duty. Conservatives in the Commons accused Pennington's fellow radical London MP John Venn of having summoned the armed people in the first place. Venn denied this, and Pym saw to it that the matter was dropped.[21] On 10 December a "'strong guard'" from outside the City (not actually part of the Trained Bands), sent to Parliament by a JP on the king's orders, was questioned by the Commons and again dismissed. They then sent the JP to the Tower.[22]

The struggle reached its crescendo during December 1641 and January 1642, a period characteristic of dual power leading to insurrection. One aspect were the bold assertions by the House of Commons of its authority and legality against that of the crown, most especially over the militia, but also the House of Lords. Early in December the

> ...Commons attacked the Lords as disrespectful and described the Commons as "the Representative Body of the whole Kingdom" while the Lords were but "particular Persons, and coming to Parliament in a particular Capacity." ...before the end of the month John Pym informed the Lords that the House would be glad of their help in saving the kingdom, but if it were not forthcoming the Commons would "save the Kingdom alone."[23]

What gave the orders of the Commons teeth was the backing of the London citizens movement. It was the symbiotic actions of the Puritan middling class in the city that would bring down the Stuart regime.

19 Nagel, "The Militia of London," 26-30; Schwoerer, "the Militia Controversy," 50-51; Manning, *English People*, 65-66; Lindley, *Civil War London*, 96-97; Pearl, *London and the Outbreak*, 221

20 "Parliament Guard," House of Commons Journal Volume 2: 30 November 1641, British History Online, https://www.british-history.ac.uk/commons-jrnl/vol2/pp327-328#p28 Accessed 10 January 2021

21 Pearl, *London and the Outbreak*, 221

22 Nagel, "The Militia of London," 31; Manning, *English People*, 97; Schwoerer, "the Militia Controversy," 54

23 Barbara Taft, "That Lusty Puss, The Good Old Cause," *History of Political Thought* 5, no. 3 (Winter 1984): 451, https://www.jstor.org/stable/26212381 Accessed June 10, 2019; "Reminding Lords of Bills," House of Commons Journal Volume 2: 03 December 1641, British History Online, https://www.british-history.ac.uk/commons-jrnl/vol2/pp330-332#p7 Accessed 28 February 2021

A new petition with 20,000 signatures was presented to the Commons on 11 December by 400 "grave" men "of great rank and fashion," including Common Councilmen. The timing was kept strictly secret to avoid a large multitude that would have alienated moderate MPs. The petition supported Pym's policy for expulsion of bishops from the House of Lords, and Parliament's control of the militia. It rejected the City government's evident siding with the crown against Parliament: they "'should always be ready to spend their estates and lives for our [Parliament's] safety.'"[24] It also attacked undemocratic practices in the City government. The well-known Puritan merchant John Fowke reported the magistrates' attempts to take punitive measures against the petitioners, and a committee to investigate was appointed by the House.[25]

The demonstrations against bishops that began the first week of December 1641 revealed, contrary to the hopes of the king's court, that only the City's official leadership and some very wealthy citizens were pro-royalist. A contemporary lamented "'that the power of the City magnates… was already broken.'"[26]

The primary conduit for political propaganda and agitation in London was the Puritan ministers and lecturers. The rector of St. Antholin's, a Puritan stronghold, had previously "organized house-to-house collections and canvassed support to augment the lecturers' stipends." This experience, and the contact lists it produced, were surely of benefit during the upheavals of 1641-1642. From the end of 1640, the Scottish High Commissioners resided next door to St. Antholin's, with their own private entrance. So popular were the lectures that from morning to night on Sundays, the royalist historian Lord Clarendon wrote, "'the church was never empty.'"[27]

The arrest of Archbishop Laud in mid-December 1640 rendered moot the restrictions on preaching and printing. The church courts were no longer able to function, relieving the populace from prosecution for sin,[28] and unleashing a flood of cheap pamphlets for people to read and discuss.

> The author of *Persecutio Undecima* tells us that the Puritan clergy of the City used to meet in Edmund Calamy's house in Aldermanbury to discuss ways of propagating the godly cause in Parliament and among the citizens… The citizens, he says, could learn from their sermons and lectures "not only what was done the week before [in Parliament] but also what was to be done in Parliament the week following; besides the information, which their pulpits gave the people, for coming in tumults to the House for justice."[29] [Insert in original]

24 Pearl, *London and the Outbreak*, 128, 222-223 [Insert in original]

25 Pearl, *London and the Outbreak*, 130-131; Manning, *English People*, 79-80

26 Pearl, *London and the Outbreak*, 130 [Ellipsis in original]

27 Pearl, *London and the Outbreak*, 230-231

28 Hill, *World*, 98

29 Pearl, *London and the Outbreak*, 232

Calamy, a protégé of Warwick,[30] also appears to have made his house available for discussions between Presbyterians and Independents where they agreed not to pursue their differences in public until episcopacy had been abolished.[31]

For some time Puritans had been getting themselves elected to the various minor posts of the City districts, and organizing thus also took place in the electoral wards as well as parish churches. Throughout the early 17th century, literary and political clubs had met in taverns, as the Levellers would do later in the decade. Taverns were where "the country carriers brought their messages and took away pamphlets and news-sheets...which suddenly proliferated in 1641, [and] were circulated and read aloud..." The mass petition of 11 December 1641 against bishops and episcopacy could be found at the White Lion Tavern, and City shopkeepers habitually displayed petitions for their customers to sign. Some private homes of well-established liverymen were known meeting places for Puritan leaders. Mass meetings were held in places such as St. George's Fields in Southwark or the piazza at Covent Garden.[32]

On 17 December 1641, the House of Lords reaffirmed the Episcopal Church as the only legitimate religion. Three days later Puritan ministers petitioned the Commons "asking that they might not be forced to use prayers which their consciences could not accept, and calling for a national synod."[33] It was introduced by radical London MP John Venn, who, along with Alderman John Warner, and other members of their parish, separately petitioned the Commons for the removal of their "scandalous" minister.[34] They were not the first — nine hundred such petitions were received during all of 1641.[35] These often cited "particular 'innovations, usurpations, vexations, and wrongs' that mirrored the oppressions of the kingdom."[36] The social fracturing over religion clearly promoted revolutionary sympathies.

On 23 December Charles rejected the Grand Remonstrance and, even more threatening, replaced the Lieutenant of the Tower, an opposition sympathizer who had prevented Strafford's rescue. The king appointed Colonel Thomas Lunsford, a royalist, and "a debauched ruffian, who was believed to be capable of any villany."[37] This obvious attack on the opposition in London and the Commons had to be met. A petition against Lunsford, with 83 signa-

30 Brenner, *Merchants and Revolution*, 356

31 Pearl, *London and the Outbreak*, 232 fn. 129

32 Pearl, *London and the Outbreak*, 232-235; Manning, *English People*, 75-76

33 Pearl, *London and the Outbreak*, 223

34 Brenner, *Merchants and Revolution*, 366

35 Hill, *World*, 30

36 David Cressy, "Remembrancers of the Revolution: Histories and Historiographies of the 1640s," *Huntington Library Quarterly* 68, no. 1-2 (March 2005): 260, http://www.jstor.org/stable/10.1525/hlq.2005.68.1-2.257 Accessed January 7, 2017

37 Gardiner, *History of England* Vol. X, 108

tures, was brought the same day by two captains of the Trained Bands, some newly elected Common Councilmen (including Richard Overton, future Leveller leader),[38] and at least fifteen Atlantic merchants including Randall Mainwaring and Maurice Thomson's brother George. It was introduced by Pym himself.[39]

The same day Alderman Pennington presented another petition organized by apprentices, with 30,000 signatures again calling for root and branch reform of the church, and opposing Colonel Lunsford's appointment to the Tower. The apprentices declared they would fight against a "'royal coup,'" and complained of harassment from City officials. The Commons deferred on the petition, but voted the apprentices their sanction.[40] The Lords refused to join the MPs in a petition to the king to recall Lunsford, so the latter passed a Declaration next day. It disclaimed responsibility for any "'blood which is like to be spilt, and of the confusions which may overwhelm this state'" if Lunsford, whom they deemed "'not fit,'" remained in the post. They also blamed bishops and papists for the obstruction in the Lords which encouraged the "'malignant party.'" The Lords postponed consideration of the Declaration over the heated protests of 22 peers.[41]

These steps by the members reflected the results two days earlier of the annual Common Council elections. Many longtime members who served on important committees were defeated, and so many royalist oligarchs were routed by parliamentary Puritans that the Council's leadership was replaced. The victory was due to the mix of opposition against episcopacy and the revised Book of Common Prayer, and the old City leadership's support for and enforcement of loans and taxes to the king.[42] The Irish situation and fears about dangerous popish plots were still fresh as well. The sweep represented a culmination of the Puritan political goals that had begun back in the 1580s.

The day after the Lunsford petition to the Commons, a new petition was presented to the House of Lords by 108 Atlantic and domestic traders demanding that the Lords stop obstructing the reform program, and especially the legislation for an army in Ireland.

> Among the signers are found, once again, Maurice Thomson and his brother William, William Thomson's father-in-law Samuel Warner, Maurice Thomson's long time trading partner Thomas Stone, Randall Mainwaring… Company merchants were once again conspicuous by their absence. The petition's signers were overwhelmingly domestic traders, a good many of them already established leaders of the City opposition…[43]

38 Brenner, *Merchants and Revolution*, 398

39 Brenner, *Merchants and Revolution*, 364-365

40 Brenner, *Merchants and Revolution*, 366; Manning, *Aristocrats, Plebeians*, 34-35; Pearl, *London and the Outbreak*, 223

41 Manning, *English People*, 87-88; Brenner, *Merchants and Revolution*, 363

42 Pearl, *London and the Outbreak*, 132-134, 136-138

43 Brenner, *Merchants and Revolution*, 367

The appointment of Lunsford inflamed the populace. "By the end of the month it was reported that 'the Trained Bands keep watch everywhere' and that 'the citizens for the most part shut up their shops, and all gentlemen provide themselves with arms as in a time of open hostility.'"[44] Disturbances in the City by apprentices and others forced the Lord Mayor to inform the king on the 26th that unless Colonel Lunsford was replaced as Lieutenant of the Tower he could not keep order in the city. The king was compelled to dismiss Lunsford, but prepared a proclamation banning assemblies in London and Westminster.[45]

The next day, the 27th, a crowd of several hundred citizens chanting "No bishops!" went to the House of Lords. They formed a cordon letting sympathetic lords through with approval, but chanting and jostling bishops, some of whose gowns were torn. As it happened, Lunsford and other officers were inside the hall seeking back pay and new commissions in Ireland. Six or eight of them drew their swords and attacked the crowd, injuring many. The crowd defended themselves with bricks and tiles, and took refuge in a Commons committee room. Pennington brought some of the citizens to the floor of the Commons as evidence of what was occurring. John Lilburne led a group with some cudgels, a half-dozen swords, and some sailors with truncheons, and, backed by the crowd with stones, drove the attackers off. This was the first actual combat between the two sides.[46]

When news of the fight reached the City, hundreds of armed people, mainly apprentices, went directly to Parliament where some were arrested and held in the Mermaid Tavern. The remaining apprentices attacked the tavern and freed their comrades. The House of Lords ordered the crowd to go home, forbid them to assemble at Parliament, and asked the Commons to join in a petition to the king for a guard. The king issued his own proclamation to the same effect, written the previous evening.

> The king commanded the trained bands of Westminster and Middlesex to be raised and sent to guard the Palace of Whitehall night and day. The lord mayor and sheriffs of London rode about all evening trying "to appease the tumults": they ordered the gates of the City to be shut and strong watches to be set in every place, "as well men in arms as otherwise." The king instructed the lord mayor to raise the trained bands of London to help him restore order, by shooting to kill if the crowds resisted them or refused to disperse...[47]

This the Lord Mayor did the next day, but as night fell the House of Lords was still surrounded by 10,000 people with halberds and staves, carrying torches and chanting, "No bishops, no papist lords!" Some bishops left secretly, others passed the entire night in the House in fear of their lives. The crowd searched the Lords' carriages as they left to see if bishops were hiding in them.[48]

44 Nagel, "The Militia of London," 32; Manning, *English People*, 108-109

45 Manning, *English People*, 89; Pearl, *London and the Outbreak*, 131

46 Manning, *English People*, 89-91

47 Manning, *English People*, 91-92; Gardiner, *History of England* Vol. X, 134

48 Manning, *English People*, 92-93

An even larger crowd, equally hostile, appeared the next day, 28 December, and prevented bishops from landing at Westminster by river. Only one or two bishops made it into the House that day, and they did not stay long.[49] Some apprentices were arrested and taken to Westminster Abbey to be questioned by the Archbishop of York. A large group, led by John Lilburne and Sir Richard Wiseman, went to secure their release, but were attacked by forty gentlemen with swords and pistols. Lilburne was wounded, and Wiseman was killed, becoming a martyr, and further enraging the crowd. Only the presence of the Trained Band posted all night inside Westminster Abbey prevented the people from entering the church.[50]

Royalist reaction proceeded. The king entertained 120 officers, including Lunsford, who had offered him their services. The Archbishop of York met with bishops at his house to discuss how to blame the opposition for mob violence. Lord Digby made a motion in the upper House that, due to the actions of the "'rabble,'" "'this is no free parliament,'" which would have invalidated the act of Parliament to remain in session until it voted to dissolve, setting it up for the king to do so legally. With the bishops absent, Digby's motion was defeated by only four votes.[51]

Few gentlemen in the Commons were comfortable with the protests at Westminster, but they could not do without the support of the London populace. To call for a restoration of order, as the Lords wanted them to, would be to side with the king, who was only too likely not to stop with repression of the masses, but to use force against the MPs themselves. The City's trained bands and constables were primarily made up by members of the middling class. Since the time of Elizabeth, participation in these militias was considered a civic duty in case of need; it was not a permanent professional force. The petty bourgeois artisans and shopowners, the mainstay of the radical Puritan movement, supported the demonstrations in which they or their sons, employees, and apprentices, with their permission, were often participants. The lower classes generally followed the lead of these small employers. As a result, many refused the Lord Mayor's orders to muster for duty.[52]

A royalist report of 9 December named William Hobson and Deputy Daniel Taylor as dangerous men who gathered parishioners and exhorted them to sign radical petitions. Both had close family connections to the Atlantic merchant leadership.[53]

The economic interests of the small and middle bourgeois class, as well as a portion of the aristocracy, required the freedom to invest capital in trade and manufacture. The monopoly oligarchs steadfastly adhered to

49 Lindley, *Civil War London*, 109

50 Manning, *English People*, 93-94

51 Manning, *English People*, 94

52 Manning, *English People*, 96-97; Pearl, *London and the Outbreak*, 104-105, 228-229

53 Brenner, *Merchants and Revolution*, 369; Lindley, *Civil War London*, 153

the royal court, and thereby enforced the laws that constrained the expansion of business, so uncomfortably accommodated within feudal society. The Puritan radicals sought to replace the interconnected oppression of the aldermanic court and monopoly trading companies, and the Episcopal hierarchy. They were aided in this by the Independent ministers' experience of radical Puritan experiments in government and religion in the exile communities of Holland and America. Crucially, the Atlantic merchants' "continuing participation in domestic commercial activities gave them strong and extensive ties to that broad layer of City shopkeepers, mariners, and artisans who largely made up the City radical movement."[54] They were thus in a novel position to assume leadership of the middling class movement.

The day after the fight at Westminster Abbey where Richard Wiseman was killed, 29 December, an armed demonstration including "men of quality," shouting "No bishops! No popish lords!" appeared early at Parliament. They then went to the palace at Whitehall (where the king resided and held court). A clump of dirt was thrown at the gentlemen guards who attacked the crowd with swords. The famous derogatory epithets Cavaliers (from the Spanish *caballero* or French *cavalier*, implying a Catholic mercenary) and Roundheads (i.e., short-haired commoners, as gentlemen usually wore their hair long) were exchanged for the first time.[55] Fifty to sixty demonstrators were hurt, and nine arrested. The Commons had them released, and defended the citizens. The alarming reports of armed men being gathered by the king at Whitehall and the Archbishop of York at Westminster Abbey could no longer be ignored. It all pointed directly to a military coup.[56] They asked the Lords for a joint petition to the king to appoint a guard under the Earl of Essex. The Lords debated at length, but voted against it, so the MPs ordered a guard around Westminster themselves, and provided halberds for the safety of the House.[57] An observer noted that

> "Both factions look very big, and it is a wonder there is no more blood yet spilt, seeing how earnest both sides are. There is no doubt but if the King do not comply with the Commons in all thing they desire a civil war must ensue, which every day we see approaches nearer."[58]

The undisciplined crowds were becoming a problem for the Commons leadership. While the members of the House were dependent on the people for their protection, and to achieve their aims, they did not want to provoke the king and his party to violence. The parliamentary leaders "were anxious to maintain law and order, and the security of property, and did not want to release radical forces that they could not control." The London MP, Captain John Venn, used his authority on the evening of 29 December to disperse a

54 Brenner, *Merchants and Revolution*, 395

55 Manning, *English People*, 98

56 Lindley, *Civil War London*, 113-114; Manning, *English People*, 98-99

57 Manning, *English People*, 99; Lindley, *Civil War London*, 115

58 Gardiner, *History of England* Vol. X, 124; Lindley, *Civil War London*, 114

crowd of 2,000 armed apprentices, but a minority continued to clash with officers and search the prisons for any apprentices to free.[59]

With the king's connivance, twelve bishops complained of their treatment at the hands of the crowds, and their *de facto* exclusion from the House of Lords. Charles declared all laws passed in their absence, including "this is a free Parliament," null and void. This was yet another attempt by the crown to find an excuse to legally dissolve Parliament. The king sent the bishops' protest to the Lords, who forwarded it to the Commons as "being a Thing of high and dangerous Consequence."[60] "The Commons promptly impeached the twelve bishops and the Lords sent them to prison on 30 December 1641."[61] Coming two days after the defeat of Digby's motion, the Lords apparently felt provoked by the king's maneuver to dismiss them. There was public rejoicing in London.[62]

Nonetheless, the people had been put on the defensive as they were "'more tongue than soldier.'"[63] Hundreds of young gentlemen of the nobility and gentry rallied to the king and the Party of Order. "That very day drums were beating in the streets for the levy of the volunteers who were to form the army which was to be commanded by Lunsford and his comrades."[64] The guard at Whitehall was increased and defenses strengthened. Clearly a new army plot was in the offing. Following a message from the king on 31 December, the Common Council issued resolutions threatening punishment to anyone causing tumults or shirking their duty in the Trained Bands. Householders were ordered to keep their apprentices and servants indoors and be answerable for their conduct. The king again authorized the use of force against disorders, and a new royal nominee had taken charge at the Tower of London.[65]

59 Manning, *English People*, 99-100

60 "Sent to the House of Commons," House of Lords Journal Volume 4: 30 December 1641, British History Online, https://www.british-history.ac.uk/lords-jrnl/vol4/pp496-499#p14 Accessed 28 April 2021; Gardiner, *History of England* Vol. X, 123

61 Manning, *English People*, 100-101

62 Brenner, *Merchants and Revolution*, 368; Manning, *English People*, 101

63 Manning, *English People*, 101

64 Gardiner, *History of England* Vol. X, 125

65 Manning, *English People*, 101-103; Pearl, *London and the Outbreak*, 131-132. Manning points out that this "was not the old Common Council, but, contrary to custom, the newly elected and more radical Councilmen attended this meeting..." His explicit claim, however, that they "presumably approved these resolutions" is speculation. Fifteen years earlier Pearl had explained: "There is some evidence to suggest that the newly elected Common Councilmen took up their seats before Plough Monday (the first Monday after Twelfth Night) [5 or 6 January], which was the traditional date for their swearing into office. ... That this was probably so is suggested by Common Council's election of a Committee of Safety on January 4th, having been directed to take this step *by order of the House of Commons*. Such a Committee was without precedent in the history of the City and proved to be as revolutionary as its name suggests." 139-140 [Emphasis added]. Some royalists objected to the presence of the new councilors on 31 December, but they were allowed to stay. Nagel, "The Militia of London," 35. Since all three historians refer to the same source, exactly how many of the "new men" there were is unknown: "...the extant evidence makes it impossible to generalize accurately on the changes in the total membership of Common Council..." Pearl, *London and the Outbreak*, 136. While it is true that the House of Commons was trying to dissuade uncontrolled disorders by the people at this time, this does not automatically mean the new Puritan Council members supported the repressive resolutions. Not all of the new men may have been present, or they may not have participated in the vote since they were not yet sworn in. They may have voted against the resolutions; that no recorded

The revolution in London

On 3 January 1642, the king charged five reform leaders of the House of Commons with treason, claiming they were the organizers of tumults ever ready at their call, and, more accurately, "that they indirectly encouraged the tumults by obstructing efforts to suppress them."[66] The Commons and the king sent conflicting messages to the Lord Mayor regarding disposition of the Trained Bands (the king again authorizing them to shoot to kill), but the Commons also sent their orders to the Aldermen and Common Council.[67] On 4 January, Charles personally led a retinue of 100 royal officers to arrest John Pym and four other leading MPs on the floor of the Commons. No monarch had ever before even entered the House, much less with the intent to arrest sitting members. To add insult to injury, he arrogantly took the Speaker's chair.[68]

Warned in advance, the intended prisoners hid in a radical district of London. The king was forced to retreat empty-handed, making him look much the fool, if ever a more dangerous one. "...with the sense that they had but just escaped a massacre" and fearing a *coup d'état*, the Commons then voted 170-86 to adjourn to the Guildhall in the City, thereby throwing themselves on the mercy of the ordinary citizens.[69] (It was later moved to Grocers' Hall.)[70] Sir Simonds D'Ewes "went home and made his will."[71] While Colonel Lunsford had been removed, Whitehall continued to be stocked with arms and the Tower with artillerymen. "With a sense of impending danger, the whole City shut shop and provided themselves with weapons." Aldermen and sheriffs closed the gates to the City, and placed chains across streets to impede horses. "'...knocking at the doors for men to stand upon their guard,...every man his halberd and weapons in a readiness, and it was much feared that that night would have been a bloody night, but God of his mercy kept us.'"[72]

opposition exists is negative evidence, and not conclusive. Whatever the case, the diametrically opposite viewpoints and actions of the Council before and after 1 January, just as the political crisis was cresting, makes Manning's assumption implausible.

66 Manning, *English People*, 105-106

67 Nagel, "The Militia of London," 35; "Trained Bands," House of Commons Journal Volume 2: 03 January 1642, British History Online, https://www.british-history.ac.uk/commons-jrnl/vol2/pp366-367#p11 Accessed 27 February 2021

68 Gardiner, *History of England* Vol. X, 139

69 Gardiner, *History of England* Vol. X, 141; Manning, *English People*, 110; Nagel, "The Militia of London," 36; "Guildhall Committee" and "Vindicating Privilege-Committee to meet at Guildhall," House of Commons Journal Volume 2: 05 January 1642, British History Online, https://www.british-history.ac.uk/commons-jrnl/vol2/pp368-369#h3-0005 Accessed October 24, 2019. The Commons had taken the precaution on 3 January of voting to constitute the whole House as a committee. Brenner, *Merchants and Revolution*, 368. (Brenner gives the date in old style as 31 December.) "Privilege-King's Message to be considered," House of Commons Journal Volume 2: 03 January 1642, British History Online, https://www.british-history.ac.uk/commons-jrnl/vol2/pp366-367#p40 Accessed 27 February 2021. This subterfuge was necessary because "The House could not adjourn itself to any place but Westminster." Gardiner, *History of England* Vol. X, 126

70 Lindley, *Civil War London*, 123

71 Fletcher, *Outbreak*, 181

72 Pearl, *London and the Outbreak*, 141; Manning, *English People*, 109-110; Cressy, *England on Edge*, 394

The streets were filled by the armed citizens.[73] The same day Charles appeared at Parliament, 4 January, the London Common Council set up its own Committee of Safety by order of the House of Commons. All of the Common Councilors elected to the Committee of Safety were supporters of Parliament. Of the six aldermen elected, three were Puritans; of the other three, one resigned almost immediately and was replaced by a parliamentary Puritan who had signed the Root and Branch petition, and the other two, neutralists, were removed in the fall of 1642.[74] The Common Council was now in position to fight for Parliament against the king, led by its most radical and dedicated men who did not shrink from an armed struggle.[75]

The next day, 5 January, with the shopkeepers still on strike, and the armed people "'standing in their doors,'" the king appeared in front of the Common Council to demand the five "dangerous" Members be turned over. The Council, apparently now consisting of a shifting mix of both old and new members,[76] split between the king and Commons. As the king left, a large group of "ruder" people unanimously chanted "Privileges of Parliament!" (i.e., MPs could only be tried by the House itself). Thousands besieged him at the house of the City sheriff where he had gone for dinner, and followed his carriage with the same cry "Privileges of Parliament!" After escorting the king safely home, the Lord Mayor and some aldermen were knocked off their horses; women called him traitor and pulled his chain of office off his neck. The officials had to walk home being taunted all the way. On the same day, the Council approved a petition to the king drafted by the Committee of Safety implicitly criticizing his actions and outright defying his ban on petitions.[77]

> Offers of support to defend the Five Members poured into the committee sitting at Guildhall – from the apprentices of London; from the trained bands of Southwark; from over 1,000 mariners and seamen, including "the masters and inferior officers as well as the king's own ships as of merchants"... A crowd of several thousand assembled in Buckinghamshire and resolved to march to London to defend their member, John Hampden.[78]

The following night, 6 January, a rumor quickly spread that soldiers on foot and horse were approaching the city. The citizens again went on alert. Tens of thousands of armed men went into the streets while women built barricades and prepared pots of boiling water to use against the enemy.[79] The Trained Bands "were assembled without the authority of the Lord Mayor," who had refused to call them out.[80] The attack never came, but the widespread

73 Manning, *English People*, 110

74 Pearl, *London and the Outbreak*, 140-141 and fn. 135

75 Nagel, "The Militia of London," 37; Brenner, *Merchants and Revolution*, 400

76 Nagel, "The Militia of London," 37

77 Manning, *English People*, 110-111; Pearl, *London and the Outbreak*, 141-142, 143-144

78 Manning, *English People*, 112; Lindley, *Civil War London*, 124-125

79 Manning, *English People*, 111-112; Lindley, *Civil War London*, 123-124; Pearl, *London and the Outbreak*, 142, 143; Nagel, "The Militia of London," 38-39

80 Pearl, *London and the Outbreak*, 142; Nagel, "The Militia of London," 38-39

and determined action of the armed populace and Trained Bands made it impossible for the Court of Aldermen or the House of Lords to attempt any move against the Council.[81]

The House of Commons passed a series of measures on 8 January retroactively legitimating the actions taken in the city. The most important transferred the king's control, via the Lord Mayor, over London's Trained Bands to the majority of the Lord Mayor, the aldermen and Common Council together.[82] The Common Council endorsed it and removed the Lord Mayor's power to call them out on his own authority. Serjeant Major Philip Skippon, a militant Puritan and seasoned professional soldier, was entrusted with this authority, and the House of Commons promoted him to Serjeant Major General. The Council and its Committee followed up by reorganizing, expanding, and supplying the Bands. They were placed "on a war footing" under the command of leading parliamentary Puritans, and ammunition was moved to a secure location.[83] With the Trained Bands behind it, the Committee of Safety on behalf of the Common Council was in command of the city. A small cavalry force of royalists at Kingston-on-Thames, led by Lord Digby and Colonel Lunsford, was broken up some days later.[84] Under the new City government, Parliament developed a reliable armed force.[85]

The London Trained Bands were charged with protecting the Five Members, the Southwark Bands with holding the south bank of the Thames, and the apprentices with guarding the City.[86] Claiming that his life and the lives of his family were in danger, Charles fled London on the night of 10 January. The five MPs returned the next day "on a barge accompanied by flotillas of seamen from the Port of London to return amidst cheering crowds of supporters to Westminster," where they were met by the assembled Trained Bands "in full military regalia, each soldier waving a copy of the Protestation."[87] The anti-absolutist alliance between the people of London in arms, with the majorities and leaderships of the Puritan merchants on the Common Council, and the reform gentry in the House of Commons, had now been sealed.

The Committee of Public Safety was composed of sixteen members, nine of whom were Atlantic merchants, including Maurice Thomson, now a councilman. Four of these men had been selected by Common Hall at the instigation of the House of Lords in the dispute over sheriffs six months earlier. There were no company merchants. One member, Richard Shute, Maurice Thomson's trading partner, was appointed treasurer, and to coordinate be-

81 Pearl, *London and the Outbreak*, 144

82 Nagel, "The Militia of London," 39-40; Pearl, *London and the Outbreak*, 144

83 Pearl, *London and the Outbreak*, 144

84 Pennington, "The Making of the War, 1640-1642," 183; Nagel, "The Militia of London," 47

85 Pearl, *London and the Outbreak*, 224-225; Nagel, "The Militia of London," 41-42

86 Manning, *English People*, 112; Lindley, *Civil War London*, 124-125; Gardiner, *History of England* Vol. X, 148-149

87 Pearl, *London and the Outbreak*, 145

tween the Committee and Parliament. In effect, the unofficial leadership of the London Puritan movement was now the official City government.[88]

On 19 January all disputed elections were referred to the Committee of Public Safety (aka Militia Committee), a function previously performed by the Lord Mayor and aldermen. Following the Committee's report in early March, the Mayor was ordered to have aldermen promptly hold new elections in the disputed wards. They also carried out reforms in local electoral procedures restoring power to democratic wardmotes (local councils that held town hall meetings) against oligarchic cliques.[89] The Committee

> assumed broad powers of initiating legislation in London, took the authority to call and dissolve the common council, and put itself in command of the City's militia. During the critical days of the winter and early spring of 1642, this committee guided the consolidation of the City revolution. London's militant mass movement, having provided both the indispensable instrument for defending Parliament's program and the underlying cause of Parliament's dividing against itself, had thus saved Parliament from the King's coup d'état…[90]

On 20 January, Parliament ordered the administration of the Protestation to all males 18 years of age and older.[91] The Common Council, on 24 January, sent to the two Houses a petition urging Parliament to take up arms to relieve the Protestants in Ireland, disarm papists, take control of all forts and ports, and for the exclusion of bishops from the Lords.[92]

A new flood of petitions to Parliament arrived, but now they were coming from the provinces. For the next six weeks thousands of people arrived in London in organized contingents to petition and pressure the House of Lords. On the same day the Commons returned to Westminster, between 5,000 and 6,000 men from Buckinghamshire marched into London, of which 3,000 were mounted on horseback, and "'every man with his protestation in his hand…'"

> On 20 January 6,000 came from Essex, and on 25 January three or four thousand from Hertfordshire. On 8 February petitioners marched in from Kent…"many hundred of them…first the knights, and gentlemen, then about twenty ministers, then the other horse and footmen." On 10 February a petition was brought in from Northhamptonshire, "the best attended by gentlemen of quality of any petition that hath been yet delivered." "Near a thousand" people arrived in London on 15 February with a petition from Leicestershire, and two days later between fifteen hundred and three thousand from Sussex, led by their sheriff…[93]

88 Brenner, *Merchants and Revolution*, 370-371

89 Pearl, *London and the Outbreak*, 138-139; Brenner, *Merchants and Revolution*, 399-400

90 Brenner, *Merchants and Revolution*, 368

91 "The Protestation," House of Commons Journal Volume 2: 20 January 1642, British History Online, https://www.british-history.ac.uk/commons-jrnl/vol2/pp387-390#p66 Accessed March 1, 2020

92 Pearl, *London and the Outbreak*, 145, 225-226

93 Manning, *English People*, 118-119

Many if not most of the petitions complained about the continuing economic depression in the country. The "decay of trade" directly affected thousands of workers, manufacturers and retailers engaged in the cloth industry, and indirectly nearly the whole population including farmers, mariners and seamen. The solution to the economic crisis was popularly seen to be political action. If the House of Lords passed the reforms championed by the Commons, trade and the economy would be restored. The country was almost at a standstill and the spread of want, petitioners warned, had reached the point where threats of rebellion by the desperate poor might become reality. The economic crisis was made more acute by the strike of merchants and tradesmen against the actions of the king during the first quarter of 1642. The loss of customs duties in London totaled 600,000 ducats (the common coinage used in European trade).[94]

The coalition of the colonizing nobles, liberal gentry, Puritan ministers, and Atlantic merchants, supported by the middle and petty bourgeoisie, and wage workers, had fought through to the popular democratic movement's victory. It "forestalled a successful counter-revolution in London."[95] The leading reformers, gentlemen and ministers, were quite aware that legislative action would be needed to stay in the citizens' good graces. The problem which still lay ahead was that the gentry rulers merely wanted to adjust the powers of the king and Parliament, whereas the revolutionary Puritan movement was demanding a thoroughly anti-feudal program, especially in religion which was its major prop. The strain between Parliament and the people caused by these differences was indicated by a report that "sixteen or seventeen thousand people had assembled in the depressed cloth-manufacturing districts of Essex and Suffolk, to march with their petition to London." The discomfited gentlemen MPs "asked them to send no more than a thousand and for the rest to disperse, and [were] profusely grateful when this request was obeyed."[96]

The struggle to purge the House of Lords

Despite the abundance of petitions and demonstrators from near and far, the Lords still resisted. The day after the official 24 January petition to exclude bishops and Catholics from the House of Lords was sent by the London government, Alderman Atkins told the Commons that loans from the City were contingent on this.[97] By a vote of 40-32 the same day, however, the upper house refused to join the Commons in a petition to the king to subject top military officers to Parliamentary approval.[98] This action unleashed new demonstrations against them. A petition from apprentices and seamen of London on 26 January threatened "'that, if present remedy be not afforded,... multitudes will be ready to take hold upon that remedy which is next at

94 Manning, *English People*, 120-121; Lindley, *Civil War London*, 124

95 Pearl, *London and the Outbreak*, 277

96 Manning, *English People*, 120

97 Pearl, *London and the Outbreak*, 226

98 Manning, *English People*, 122

hand..."' Five days later, hundreds of poor people marched on the House of Commons with a petition blaming bishops and papists for their poverty, and demanding the names of those in the House of Lords who were obstructing the resolution of the crisis. Their petition likewise admonished that

> "...your petitioners shall not rest in quietness, but shall be enforced to lay hold on the next remedy which is to hand, to remove the disturbers of our peace, want and necessity...rather than your petitioners will suffer themselves and their families to perish through hunger and misery..."[99]

They also proposed that the minority of the Lords join in a single body with the House of Commons.[100]

A separate petition from women decrying their poverty "'by reason of the great decay of trading'" was received on the same day. This was followed the next day, 1 February, by hundreds of women at Parliament demanding bread. A tussle ensued when the women were rebuked by the Duke of Richmond, whose staff was seized and broken.[101] The Commons made full use of the campaign to privately stoke "their Lordships' fear of a popular uprising."[102] On 2 February the Commons received a petition from 15,000 unemployed porters "'and the lowest members of the city.'" "Soon they would be forced 'to extremities, not fit to be named, and to make good that saying, "That necessity hath no law;" it is true, that we have nothing to lose but our lives.'"[103] The Commons invited those Lords in agreement with them "to declare themselves with this House, that we may know them from the rest; and to protest ourselves innocent of whatever mischief or inconveniency may fall out..." This was, they added, their last offer.[104]

Fearing the people's wrath in new disorders, the conservatives in the upper House caved, and on 2 February joined in a petition to the king to put the Tower and all forts and militia under individuals selected by Parliament. On 5 February the Lords finally voted to exclude bishops from their House. Some Lords and MPs had already begun to leave Westminster for their country homes rather than risk the violence of the London population, and more now joined them.[105] Merely the willingness of the Commons majority and some nobles to stomach an alliance with the likes of "apprentices, handicraftsmen, porters and labourers" was sufficient to drive them into the royalist party of order.[106]

The repeated actions of the middle and working classes had polarized English society, and irrevocably split the ruling class. The London citizens'

99 Manning, *English People*, 123

100 Manning, *English People*, 123-124

101 Manning, *English People*, 124-125; Pearl, *London and the Outbreak*, 226

102 Pearl, *London and the Outbreak*, 227; Manning, *English People*, 124

103 Manning, *English People*, 125

104 Manning, *English People*, 125

105 Manning, *English People*, 125-126

106 Manning, *English People*, 127

election of a progressive Puritan government removed a critical mass of monopoly merchant oligarchs from the Common Council, and their armed defense of Parliament forced the impotent Charles Stuart to abandon his capital. Political power passed to the alliance of the gentry in the Commons and the Puritan leadership in London, most critically with the radical Atlantic merchants. In the aftermath, the purge of bishops from the House of Lords by the citizens' siege of the nobility was another nail in the coffin of the established church, already rendered moot. It confirmed the more languid, traditionalist upper house as subordinate to the lower. The feudal political system was shattered, and England would never be the same again.

13) THE LONDON REVOLUTION IN POWER (1642)

Anyone who is seeking an explanation of the internal logic of the historical process certainly must understand that the industrial revolution of the eighteenth century, which re-created Great Britain from top to bottom, would have been impossible without the political revolution in the seventeenth century.

~Leon Trotsky[1]

The Militia Ordinance and the lead-up to civil war

On the heels of their victory, 15 March 1642, Parliament took a fateful step: the implementation of the previously passed Militia Bill "for the safety and defence of the kingdom" despite the king's refusal to approve it. The bill gave Parliament, instead of Charles, the right to appoint the county Lords Lieutenant who controlled the Trained Bands. From now on, Parliamentary Ordinances had the force of law.[2] "The militia issue, more than any other, propelled men along a path of radicalism, prompting the strongest attack on the King and the strongest assertion of Parliamentary supremacy that had been made."[3] Having succeeded in taking power in London, Parliament now had to establish control over the rest of the country.

The Ordinance was an escalation of the tense intra-ruling–class struggle, one that could not help but subvert the feudal political system, thereby advancing the goals of the London Puritan movement. Parliament here asserted itself as the dominant power in the land, even as it still defensively and absurdly postured as being merely opposed to the crown's "evil counselors."[4] By this action it completed the long process of converting the 1215 Article 61 security clause,

> that the barons choose five and twenty barons of the kingdom, whomsoever they will, who shall be bound with all their might, to observe and hold, and cause to be observed, the peace and liberties we [King John] have granted and confirmed to them by this our present Charter,[5]

into a bourgeois political institution. What had made this development possible were the unique conditions that existed in England: the historically evolved semi-independence of parliament; the secular reformation of religion by Henry VIII and Thomas Cromwell; and most organically, the long, uninterrupted growth of capitalist market relations. These factors

1 "Mr. Baldwin and 'Gradualness,'" in *Leon Trotsky on Britain*, 51

2 "The Militia Ordinance, 1642," BCW Project, http://bcw-project.org/church-and-state/first-civil-war/militia-ordinance Accessed June 20, 2016; "Declaration concerning the Militia," House of Commons Journal Volume 2: 15 March 1642, British History Online, https://www.british-history.ac.uk/commons-jrnl/vol2/pp478-479#h3-0010 Accessed November 7, 2019; "That the People are bound by the Ordinance for the Militia, though it has not received the Royal Assent," House of Lords Journal Volume 4: 15 March 1642, British History Online, https://www.british-history.ac.uk/lords-jrnl/vol4/pp645-646#p39 Accessed February 18, 2020

3 Schwoerer, "the Militia Controversy," 75

4 Pennington, "The Making of the War, 1640-1642," 184

5 "Magna Carta 1215," http://avalon.law.yale.edu/medieval/magframe.asp Accessed June 1, 2017

resulted in the peculiar incongruity that gave a section of the aristocracy a leading, and limiting, role in the revolution. This accounts for the retention and partnership of the monarchy and aristocracy in the bourgeois order after 1688; indeed, down to the ludicrous but still reactionary role they play in Britain today.

Despite the revolutionary effect of some of their actions, the political conceptions of most MPs remained entangled with the feudal inheritance. Their aims were limited to redressing the "imbalance" between the king's prerogative and Parliament's "ancient liberties." The sharpening effect of events forced those MPs and Lords who were determined to resist the king's absolute power to counterpose their own power against it. Two months after the Militia Ordinance was proclaimed law,

> ...with war just weeks away, Lords and Commons agreed that the King was bound "to pass such Bills as shall be presented to him by both Houses." Perceived need and the King's intransigence brought both Houses to the position articulated by [Sir Henry] Marten alone less than nine months before.[6]

The contradiction in gentry politics, stemming from their twofold social position, here becomes glaring:

> While it is imperative that the conservatism of most M.P.s, *even after 1642*, be recognized, it should not be forgotten that however moderate Pym and his followers seem in retrospect, the members of the House of Commons who remained at Westminster after the spring of 1642 were in many respects a revolutionary group. They were not consciously revolutionary like the Levellers. But they were revolutionary enough to contest the king's religion and policy, execute his most trusted advisor, and take up arms against him.[7] [Emphasis added]

It is this contradiction that so many historians have stumbled over, one way or the other. Pym's position as leader of the opposition, a role he almost single-handedly invented, was predicated on his personal faithfulness to the institution of the monarchy.[8] For Pym it was necessary to be, in effect, a *loyal* oppositionist (a concept that did not exist at that time).[9] He "had been repeating since 1628, that the subversion of the fundamental laws was being attempted because the fundamental laws were an obstacle to the introduction of popery."[10] He did not try to force his program when there was serious opposition in the Commons, but waited until events favored a particular bill. By playing off the more extreme factions on the left and right against each other, providing justifications to placate reluctant MPs and peers, or proposing tactical compromises as events demanded, he continued to main-

6 Taft, "The Good Old Cause," 450

7 Palmer, "Oliver St. John," 21

8 Hexter, *King Pym*, 201-202

9 Zaller, "The Concept of Opposition," 232

10 Russell, "The First Army Plot of 1641," 104-105

tain a precarious unity in the Commons.[11] Just how precarious would be revealed in the summer of 1643 when the House would very nearly vote to surrender to Charles.[12]

For his part, Charles marched his entourage to take control of the city of Hull with its large store of munitions, but was refused entrance by the governor. The Commons support for the governor's action caused a general decampment of royalists: 32 noblemen and 60 MPs left London to join the king at York at the end of May.[13] But during the spring and summer of 1642 Charles had little success in recruiting soldiers. "The crown had lost control over local government, over collection of taxes, over the army. 'The King did not have the physical power to force the major part of his subjects to perform actions that they did not want to perform.'"[14] Charles had no army or bureaucracy, no immediate rewards to offer potential supporters, no ability to make anyone fight for him, or to penalize any who opposed him. "The monarchy was reduced to its bare essence — the sentiment of loyalty to the person of the king."[15]

Charles could only turn to the nobility and greater gentry. On 22 August, in the quaint, time-honored feudal manner, he "raised his standard" in Nottingham, formally calling on his nobles to come to his aid with their vassals. He called them to York, and announced "his intention of taking no important decisions without their agreement." The parliamentary reform program was a threat to the ruling class of landowners, he argued. Destruction of the monarchy would lead to "'a parity and confusion of all degrees and conditions.'"[16] In a word, equality.

"In September 1642 Charles…could not trust the loyalty of the trained bands, even in counties which he controlled."[17] As in London, middling class artisans and yeomen were far from pro-royalist in many parts of the country.

The revolution in government

The drive and organization that made the citizens' victory in January possible came from the London Committee of Safety.[18] "In the first few months after its election, it drew up practically every petition of the munic-

11 Hexter, *King Pym*, 19-22, 31-35, 59-61, 135; Lotte Glow, "Pym and Parliament: The Methods of Moderation," *Journal of Modern History* 36, no. 4 (December 1964): 373, http://www.jstor.org/stable/1875246 Accessed November 28, 2016

12 See Chapter 16 below.

13 Green, *History of the English People* Vol. 5, 164

14 Hill, "Parliament and People in 17th-Century England" [revised], in *The Collected Essays of Christopher Hill* Vol. 3, 52, quoting Conrad Russell.

15 Manning, *English People*, 249

16 Manning, *English People*, 250-251

17 Hill, "Parliament and People in 17th-Century England" [revised], 52

18 Not to be confused with the jointly-appointed Committee of Safety in Parliament, composed of MPs and Lords, which was far less important and is not discussed here. For the Parliamentary committee, see Lotte Glow, "The Committee of Safety," *English Historical Review* 80, no. 315 (April 1965), http://www.jstor.org/stable/560134 Accessed November 28, 2016.

ipality, and all important business was referred to it." A special tax for the defense of the City provided its funding, which was spent as the Committee saw fit, and it brought to the Council a plan to build watch-houses at strategic sites. The Committee worked closely with the House of Commons which, on 13 January, required the Lord Mayor to convene a Common Council meeting whenever the Committee of Safety requested one. He was also instructed to pass on to the Committee any orders from either House of Parliament. This overthrew the Mayor's centuries-old traditional right to call the Council according to his judgment. In addition to overseeing disputed elections, on 22 January, the Committee was put in charge of the militia.[19] A royalist attacked it for

> "being armed with as much power as will serve the most desperate treasonable designes which either Saye or Pym should suggest, they now goe on without checke or controule, and beate downe all before them that stand in their way."[20]

The enhanced power and independence of the Common Council and its Committee left the mayor and aldermen little choice but to carry out their decisions. To the same hostile contemporary, the City revolution seemed complete, "'...my Lord Mayor having no more sway than Perkins the tailor, Rily the bodicemaker, or Nicholson the chandler, they may dispose of the wealth and power of the City as they please.'"[21] This was not simply hyperbole; these were real men who now sat in the Common Council.[22]

But the old guard attempted to fight back. A majority of aldermen, a minority of Common Councilmen, and many officials were still royalists.[23] On 16 February, thirteen aldermen and the Lord Mayor introduced a petition in the Lords contesting sole control of the militia by the Committee of Safety, a power they claimed had been their's since "time out of mind." Known as "Benyon's petition," it was brought a few days later to the Commons, which was alarmed by the more than 330 signatures that included some of the wealthiest and most prominent monopolists and Common Councilmen in London. Forty-six were from the Levant Company alone. The House impeached the City Recorder, Sir Thomas Gardiner, and Sir George Benyon, silk mercer, who were held to be the authors of the petition, on charges some of which dated back to 1639. Parliament found both men guilty and they were imprisoned. Charles however managed to get Benyon freed from the Tower, and he joined the king at Oxford. Almost two hundred signers of Benyon's petition then prudently retracted their support in a 2 March petition to the Commons.[24]

19 Pearl, *London and the Outbreak*, 146-147; Nagel, "The Militia of London," 43

20 Nagel, "The Militia of London," 45

21 Pearl, *London and the Outbreak*, 148

22 Pearl, *London and the Outbreak*, 137, 148 fn. 163, 164

23 Pearl, *London and the Outbreak*, 145

24 Pearl, *London and the Outbreak*, 149-151; Lindley, *Civil War London*, 201-202, 204-205; Brenner, *Merchants and Revolution*, 371-372. Pearl lists him as Benion.

Meanwhile, an attempt to have this counter-revolutionary militia petition read in the Common Council, in which the aldermen still sat, was defeated, despite the aldermen splitting 8 to 5 in favor. This was the first time that the aldermanic veto was suppressed. To remedy this and regain what they viewed as their rights, on 10 March the Court of Aldermen ordered that all petitions had to be approved by themselves before being submitted to the Common Council. Three days later, when the Committee of Safety requested a Council meeting, the Mayor refused on the grounds that he was ill. The Committee went to the House of Commons, which ordered him to appoint a replacement. A new petition addressed to Parliament was read at the Council meeting next day, but no vote was taken due to opposition from the majority of aldermen. The Council again took the matter to the Commons, which appointed a committee to investigate. The committee heard testimony from both sides and judged that the aldermen, at least in this case, had violated the Council's rights.[25]

The issue did not end there, but dragged on into July 1642, with the royalist Mayor and aldermen obstructing the Council every way they could. On 22 July, Parliament put the Mayor on trial. Among the charges were his obstruction of Parliament's order for war preparations, and his 10 June proclamation of the king's Commission of Array, an antique feudal device Charles had resurrected in an attempt to raise troops. "Such commissions were first issued in 1324 but had last been employed in 1557…"[26] The Mayor was found guilty on 12 August of these openly counter-revolutionary acts, and "'imprisoned during the pleasure of the two Houses of Parliament.'"[27]

When Common Hall assembled to nominate a new mayor shortly afterward, Independent Alderman and MP Isaac Pennington was selected over several more senior members. The colonial trader Randall Mainwaring, a relative of Pennington's, was made his deputy. The tight grip over the City of the monopoly merchant oligarchy, wedded to the royal court, had been broken. The powerful movement of the middling class — small producers and craft workers, domestic traders, sailors and shopkeepers — with the poor often in their train, led by radical Puritans and Atlantic merchants, and working in tandem with the House of Commons leadership, had carried out a political revolution in the capital. As if to underline the point, the royalist party refused to recognize Pennington, calling him "'the pretended Lord Mayor.'" The outgoing Mayor refused to hand over the insignias of office which had to be taken from his house by force.[28]

The social groupings that had made up the old feudal ruling class, while not yet eliminated, had suffered a devastating setback. This enabled the pro-free trade bourgeois merchants, with the support of the bourgeoisified

25 Pearl, *London and the Outbreak*, 151-154

26 Joyce L. Malcolm, "A King in Search of Soldiers: Charles I in 1642," *The Historical Journal* 21, no. 2 (June 1978): 256, https://www.jstor.org/stable/2638260 Accessed June 15, 2019

27 Pearl, *London and the Outbreak*, 155-157

28 Pearl, *London and the Outbreak*, 157-158; Brenner, *Merchants and Revolution*, 373

gentry, to come to power in London, the single most important center, not only in England, but in all three kingdoms. The deep division in the overseas merchant community during this entire period is emphasized by the fact that

> of some four hundred or more different citizens who associated themselves with the constitutional royalists' petitions of July 1641 [over nominees for Sheriff] and February 1642 [over control of the militia], only about ten can be found to have been active in the colonial trades.[29]

Of those who signed three key petitions – one against Colonel Lunsford; one favoring passage of the 1643 Impressment bill; and one in opposition to Benyon's petition decrying the Militia Committee — twice as many became political Independents as political Presbyterians. Of those who initially served on the London Committee of Safety only one became a future Presbyterian, and two others wavered ("trimmers"). The other fourteen all became political Independents.[30] This picture also distinctly contrasts with the pre-revolutionary aldermanic bench: "only five [out of twenty-four] Aldermen who were members of the Bench in September 1640 became energetic supporters of the parliamentary opposition…"[31] The most revolutionary section of the capitalist class now ruled London.

Parliament's Puritan supporters

The most pressing need of Parliament was money. The City government was already heavily indebted, and until the revolution in January 1642, hostile to the Commons' requests for loans. So too were the royalist leaderships of most livery companies whose positions remained untouched by the City revolution. Atlantic merchants and their aristocratic Puritan partners offered Parliament one million pounds against confiscated lands for a private expedition to Ireland.[32] Authorized by Parliament in June, 1642, an initial investment scheme raised 5,000 infantry and 500 cavalry by July, but these were redirected to meet Parliament's needs for the Civil War. Despite this, the Irish committee contributed £100,000 to Parliament's war effort against the king.[33]

A smaller project known as the Additional Sea Adventure to Ireland was arranged with the Puritan Lord Brooke in overall command of arrangements, Hugh Peter as chaplain, his brother Benjamin as Admiral, the future Leveller Thomas Rainsborough as vice admiral, and Robert Thomson, Maurice's brother, as rear admiral. The sixteen-member commission overseeing the project included Maurice and eight of his relatives and business associates. Many of the non-merchant investors were or would become leaders in the City radical movement and officials in the Commonwealth of 1649-1653. Other backers were the MPs Sir Arthur Hasilrig, Lord Brooke's brother-in-

29 Brenner, *Merchants and Revolution*, 388, Table 7.1

30 Brenner, *Merchants and Revolution*, 398-399

31 Pearl, *London and the Outbreak*, 114

32 Pearl, *London and the Outbreak*, 94, 207-208

33 Brenner, *Merchants and Revolution*, 402

law, and Oliver Cromwell. This brought Independent radicals in Parliament and London together in joint activity at an early date. Their expenses were to be recompensed with land in Ireland by grant of Parliament. The Sea Adventurers spent six months fighting and plundering in Ireland before running out of money.[34]

The political composition of the Sea Adventure anticipated the New Model Army.

> Linking new-merchant and nonmerchant radicals, future political independents, and a few future Levellers, the Additional Sea Adventure may be considered in some respects the first autonomous project of that City militant Puritan party, or alliance of forces, buoyed up by new recruits from New England and very much religiously Independent in character, that was to form the hard core of City radicalism, political independency, and republicanism throughout the 1640s.[35]

During this same period the Atlantic merchants were ramping up their interloping activities in the East Indies.[36] In the Caribbean, Maurice Thomson's extended group invested in sugar plantations, and entered the triangular trade of sugar, slaves and provisions needed to support them. They also carried out extensive raids against Spanish possessions throughout the region. These private pursuits were the forerunners of future governmental territorial conquests which "these traders would be closely involved with and profit from each." Their aggressive economic program made them all the more determined to prevent any compromise between Parliament and the king.[37]

The leadership position of the colonizing merchants was due both to their ability to advance money to Parliament, and their ability to mobilize the city's citizens through their strong connections to the middling class. The revolutionary overthrow of the London oligarchy by the armed people had been all that stood between the survival of the Commons, and its crushing by the royal court. The Independent radicals were subsequently the most active in establishing and administering the financial apparatus to fund the army. This gave them "a leverage on the course of affairs far out of proportion" to their size over the Commons, or their weight in the City government.[38]

With the sizable desertion of royalists from both Houses in late May, Parliament passed the Nineteen Propositions on 1 June, 1642, and sent them to the king the next day. This was a concise programmatic list of Parliament's demands written by Pym. Presented by him as a basis for negotiations, it was an obvious ultimatum. The demands included Parliament's approval of all leading government and military officials, and official policies; approval of the education and marriage proposals of the king's children; strict enforce-

34 Brenner, *Merchants and Revolution*, 403-407, 409

35 Brenner, *Merchants and Revolution*, 409-410

36 Brenner, *Merchants and Revolution*, 169-170, 174-175

37 Brenner, *Merchants and Revolution*, 410-411

38 Brenner, *Merchants and Revolution*, 397, 429

ment of recusancy laws against Catholics, and the elimination of Catholic votes in the House of Lords; the king's approval for "assistance" to "preaching ministers," and for laws against "innovations and superstition;" his approval of the Militia Ordinance; restoration to office of sitting Members and Lords; an oath for judges and Privy Councilors to support the Petition of Right; that the positions of judges and officers depend only on their good behavior, rather than the king's pleasure; acceptance of Parliament's justice against "delinquents" (i.e., royalists who refused to pay taxes authorized by Parliament); the disbandment of the king's army; foreign alliance with Protestant states; withdrawal of the charges against the Five Members; and that membership in the House of Lords be subject to approval of both Houses. They offered, once again, to take over the royal finances, promising to provide "sufficient to support your Royal Dignity in Honour and Plenty..."[39] The king's lengthy rejection came little more than two weeks later.

Also in June, the House of Commons passed an ordinance, based on a proposal by Pennington, "calling on everyone to make voluntary contributions of money, plate or horse for the country's service."[40] Four Puritan Aldermen who were members of the Militia Committee (and two of whom were Atlantic merchants) were chosen to administer the collections from the Haberdashers' Hall. They would become "Parliament's leading financiers and financial administrators between 1643 and 1645."[41] Thirty Atlantic merchants sat on local ward committees for receiving voluntary contributions.[42] This interim measure prepared the way, the following November, for a full-blown tax called a weekly assessment. Until then, however, "...Parliament had no source of regular revenue, nor did it have any administrative machinery for the collection of taxes."[43] And by early 1643 the assessment would prove inadequate by itself; events would force Parliament to raise more taxes for its defense. Thus in the long run, this was only a major first step in establishing an income to prosecute the war against the king.[44] Parliament also had recourse to loans from its wealthy bourgeois supporters in the City.

Along with money, the rank-and-file of Parliament's army under the command of the Earl of Essex was also largely supplied by Londoners. "It was claimed that 8,000 apprentices of London joined the Army in the summer of 1642."[45] "The tradesmen of London gave mass support to Parliament...and the first to enlist were 71 dyers, 88 butchers, 186 weavers, 157

39 "The Nineteen Propositions," Rushworth Historical Collections: June 1642, British History Online, https://www.british-history.ac.uk/rushworth-papers/vol4/pp722-751#h3-0002 Accessed February 19, 2020

40 Pearl, *London and the Outbreak*, 209; "Ordinance of both Houses, for bringing in Plate, Money, and Horses," House of Lords Journal Volume 5: 9 June 1642, British History Online, https://www.british-history.ac.uk/lords-jrnl/vol5/pp120-123#h3-0031 Accessed October 23, 2020

41 Pearl, *London and the Outbreak*, 210

42 Brenner, *Merchants and Revolution*, 429-430

43 Hexter, *King Pym*, 15

44 Pearl, *London and the Outbreak*, 210; Johnson, "Disintegration of the Parliamentarian War Effort," 87-89

45 Manning, *English People*, 216

tailors, 124 shoemakers, 88 brokers and 49 sadlers."[46] Apprenticeships could cost £100-£200 or even more; they were generally filled by younger sons of gentlemen, or sons of yeoman, husbandmen, or clergy, in addition to those of the urban bourgeois class.[47]

The middling people and rural yeomen Parliament depended on largely saw the conflict as one for godly reformation, a cause they were most militant about.[48]

> ...parliament was pledged to the reform of the church and to the reformation of men's lives; it was supported by the leading reforming preachers; and so those who looked for reform of the church in a more protestant direction and for vigorous efforts to suppress vice and promote godliness, inevitably gravitated towards the parliamentary side.[49]

For many Puritans, Parliament was a means to an end.[50] Even those less religiously passionate were often driven into Parliament's arms (and army) by the hostility and low ways of Cavalier mercenary or impressed troops. "...Clarendon criticized 'the license, disorder, and impiety' of the king's soldiers."[51] Despite some lackluster admonitions from Charles,[52] "in mid-October 1642 [he] authoris[ed] Yorkshire royalists to 'plunder the estates, to kill and destroy all those that are well affected to the parliament.'"[53]

By the early autumn of 1642, 12,000 infantry volunteers, along with a large number of horsemen, were enrolled specifically to fight outside of London under the Earl of Essex. This was in addition to the militia, which by now had nine regiments for a total of about 10,000 men to defend the City. The commanding officers were mostly Militia Committee members, and the 40 captains were overwhelmingly livery company men or merchants.[54] In October, the Trained Bands took a significant step, resolving to join Essex's forces in the field, where they played a leading role in the battle at Edgehill.[55] A contemporary witness wrote:

> "The Trained Bands of the City of London endured the chief heat of the day, and had the honour to win it, for being now upon the brow of the hill, they lay not only open to the horse, but the canon of the enemy, yet they stood undaunted." [56]

46 Manning, *English People*, 262-263

47 Grassby, "Social Mobility and Business Enterprise," 356-357, 364-365

48 Manning, *English People*, 264-265

49 Manning, *English People*, 265-266

50 Manning, "The Godly People," 87

51 Manning, "The Godly People," 91; Fletcher, *Outbreak*, 327, 328

52 Fletcher, *Outbreak*, 328, 333

53 Johnson, "Disintegration of the Parliamentarian War Effort," 49

54 Nagel, "The Militia of London," 57

55 Pearl, *London and the Outbreak*, 251; Gardiner, *Great Civil War* Vol. I, 44; Brenner, *Merchants and Revolution*, 428

56 Johnson, "Disintegration of the Parliamentarian War Effort," 196

Traditionally, militias were for defense, and not expected to go beyond the boundaries of their counties, which contemporaries often referred to as their "countries." Peasants and artisans fought bravely in defense of their homes. However they would not fight very far from their localities, and returned to them as soon as the danger was past to pursue their livelihoods.[57] The difficulties with the king's armies during the Bishops' Wars at the Scottish border were in part due to the resentment of men recruited or impressed in London or elsewhere being sent so far away. This same issue would affect both armies during the Civil War,[58] but especially the king's; chronically short of men the Cavaliers resorted to impromptu impressment to a great extent. The London Trained Bands would again join the army in August of 1643 to relieve the siege of Gloucester in the west, a Parliamentary garrison town. Once again they distinguished themselves a few weeks later in the First Battle of Newbury.

Aristocrats were contemptuous of the new "citizen army" in London, but when the king's nephew, Prince Rupert, was about to invade in November 1642, it was the Trained Bands and the Auxiliary volunteers recruited under Warwick who were crucial in blocking his attempt at a quick victory.[59] Recruitment was encouraged through an October appeal by John Goodwin, Puritan minister of St. Stephen's, Coleman Street, in support of Parliament and "a war for religion."[60]

Other towns

In some towns, such as Gloucester, Nottingham and Manchester, parliamentarians were sizable minorities, but in these and many others, such as Portsmouth, Bristol, Worcester, and Chichester it was the middling class who were strongest for Parliament.[61] Birmingham and nearby Coventry were staunchly Parliamentarian: when the king tried to enter the latter in August 1642, he was refused entrance by between one and two thousand armed citizens from the city and vicinity, organized under John Barker, "a prosperous draper, alderman and MP for the city." Not just the towns, but areas around them took Parliament's side. The four to five thousand people of Birmingham and surrounding villages, who manufactured metal goods, sent 15,000 swords to the Parliamentary army. They not only refused to supply the royalists, but they arrested anyone suspected of buying arms for the king. Prior to the inconclusive October 1642 battle of Edgehill in the Midlands, the local people around Birmingham hid their provisions from the Cavaliers, "'and the very smiths hid themselves, that they might not be compelled to shoe the horses'" of the pro-feudal army. By contrast the Earl of Essex's army

57 Manning, *English People*, 246-247; Fletcher, *Outbreak*, 327

58 Johnson, "Disintegration of the Parliamentarian War Effort," 183; Underdown, *Pride's Purge*, 26-27; Brailsford, *The Levellers*, 13, 147

59 Manning, *English People*, 216; Brenner, *Merchants and Revolution*, 428

60 Manning, "The Godly People," 88

61 Manning, *English People*, 262

had no trouble obtaining provisions.[62] Again at Birmingham, in April 1643, it was the "'middle and inferior sort of people'" who opposed Prince Rupert, over the heads of the "'better sort.'"[63] Rupert took his revenge: "The royalists plundered the town, and took some £1,000 in money and goods... They fired the town, destroying 87 houses and leaving 340 people homeless."[64]

In the West Riding of Yorkshire, a cloth-making area, the parliamentarian Lord Fairfax and his son Sir Thomas were highly popular with the people. Nonetheless the Fairfaxes signed a treaty with local royalist gentry to keep the Riding neutral. The peace collapsed within a month, not least because Parliament rejected it in no uncertain language.[65] Sir Thomas raised an army from the clothing towns which drove back royalist assaults at Leeds and Bradford.[66] With Fairfax's army away in December 1642, Bradford was again saved by a remnant of determined men with reinforcements from Halifax. Less than a hundred men with no organization or officers drove off a royalist force of 1,000, to the latter's great surprise.[67] But by the early spring of 1643 the Fairfaxes were in desperate straits; repeated appeals to Parliament for money and men had brought neither. All the more striking then was Sir Thomas' victory at Wakefield against a force twice the size of his own in May.[68]

The year 1642 saw substantial gains in the consolidation of the Revolution in London and Parliament, the two closely connected and interdependent. The Common Council, composed of bourgeois merchants and business men from the livery companies, led by its Militia Committee, took over the municipal power in London, just as Parliament, led by improving gentry and noble investors, emerged as a fully independent central state power committed to the new capitalist order. Enthusiasm for the cause of Parliament in London solidified the revolutionary militia, and recruited a volunteer army against the king. But the hold of the revolution in London remained incomplete. The reasons why and the consequences will be examined in Chapter 15.

First we must look at the spontaneous support for Parliament that existed among much of the peasantry and rural artisans in the countryside.

62 Manning, *English People*, 218-220

63 Manning, *English People*, 262

64 Manning, *Aristocrats, Plebeians*, 61

65 Johnson, "Disintegration of the Parliamentarian War Effort," 49; Gardiner, *Great Civil War* Vol. I, 38-39; Keith Lindley, "The Part Played by the Catholics," in *Politics, Religion and the English Civil War*, ed. Brian Manning (London: Edward Arnold, 1973), 165. Johnson suggests that this may have been a delaying tactic to forestall an invasion of Yorkshire by royalist forces, though he admits that Lord Fairfax's initial concerns "were for peace, order and security." 49-50

66 Manning, *English People*, 231-232

67 Manning, *English People*, 232-233

68 Johnson, "Disintegration of the Parliamentarian War Effort," 55

14) THE REVOLUTION IN THE COUNTRYSIDE (1642)

> *The third class of landowners was that of the yeomen who owned small plots of land which they worked themselves, usually in the good old careless manner of their forebears; this class too has disappeared from the face of England, the social revolution has expropriated it...the parcels [of land] were being attracted by the large landed estates and swallowed up by them. Alongside the yeomen there were small tenant farmers who were usually engaged in weaving as well as farming; they too are no longer to be found in modern England; almost all the land belongs now to a small number of large estates and is thus let on lease. The competition of the large tenant farmers drove the small tenant farmers and yeomen out of the market and impoverished them; they became agricultural day-labourers and weavers dependent on wages and supplied the masses whose influx caused the towns to grow with such amazing rapidity.*
>
> ~Frederick Engels[1]

The social class divide

Only five of the twenty-three wealthiest peers in the land were consistent parliamentarians. Out of "700 gentry with estates of £1,000 a year or more...parliamentarians numbered 197 in 1643, falling to 172 two years later due to defections." Many of the rest were neutral, but overall, within the ruling landowning class, there were likely twice as many royalists as parliamentarians.[2] The extraordinary events of 1381 still haunted the aristocracy, and the menace of peasant unrest remained.[3] Outbreaks had recurred in England in the mid-15th and 16th centuries, and the years around 1630.[4] "...the German peasants' rebellion of a hundred years earlier was a nightmare spectre lurking behind all the extreme religious and social movements of the age."[5] During the spring and summer of 1642, the king's proclamations regularly equated the Parliamentary leadership with peasant rebel leaders of yore, Wat Tyler, Jack Cade and Robert Kett.[6]

As those with great stake in the feudal system could naturally be expected to rally to the king, Parliament had no alternative but to look to those middle sectors who viewed feudal social relations as an obstacle, if not outright oppression: "lesser gentry, greater yeomanry, middling

1 "The Condition of England, Part I The Eighteenth Century"

2 Manning, *Aristocrats, Plebeians*, 41

3 Hill, *Century*, 21; Rollison, "The Specter of the Commonalty," 242, 249-250

4 Hill, *Reformation*, 70

5 James, "The Political Importance of the Tithes Controversy," 6

6 Fletcher, *Outbreak*, 296

merchants and larger manufacturers."[7] To pursue profits these groups all needed to throw off feudal restrictions. As time went on therefore, the war broadened into a struggle for freedom from aristocratic oppression as well as the tyranny of the king.[8] This was reinforced by the accepted Puritan view "...that the common people had a very special role to play in this crisis, that they were somehow more chosen than the rich and the powerful" to fight the Antichrist.[9]

The contemporary "John Corbet saw the civil war of 1642-45 as having been fought between two classes, the 'middle rank' who 'keepe their owne' and the nobles and gentlemen who lived 'in the sweat of other men.'"[10] As early as the spring of 1640, the Hertfordshire trained band, in a petition regarded as scandalous by the Privy Council, gave as its reason for refusing to engage in the war with Scotland that "'We, the yeomanry, are as freeborn as any of the gentry of this kingdom, and in this respect we know no privilege they have above us.'"[11] When the king summoned the gentry of Yorkshire with their arms to the town of York in the spring of 1642, "'thousands of freeholders'" showed up and protested their exclusion from the meeting.[12] During the summer of 1642, the royalist gentry began to exclude landowning yeoman from grand juries on which they had historically sat.[13]

The greater gentry and nobles hated the new economic power of the middling people, and their claims to "social esteem and political rights" in both state and church. They wanted, in fact, what their French counterparts had — a guarantee of their privileges. The Puritans, well aware of this, denounced the misery of the French peasantry as villeinage and slavery.[14]

> The 1640s certainly saw a sharp increase in many forms of protest, some new, some old. In the case of agrarian protest there was a significant increase in crowd actions against enclosure — mainly the continuation of earlier disputes in which commoners took advantage of political breakdown to resume earlier opposition. This was notably so in those areas of forest and fen which had experienced recent Crown-sponsored large-scale enclosure.[15]

7 Manning, *English People*, 254; Underdown, *Pride's Purge*, 11

8 Tyacke, "Revolutionary Puritanism," 764-766; Manning, *English People*, 255

9 Hill, *World*, 33; Como, "Secret Printing," 63; Manning, *Aristocrats, Plebeians*, 73-74

10 Rollison, "The Specter of the Commonalty," 250. This was the Puritan theologian and preacher John Corbet (1620-1680), not to be confused with the Scottish anti-presbyterian minister of the same name (1603–1641), or Sir John Corbet (1594-1662), MP in the Long Parliament.

11 Cressy, *England on Edge*, 74-75

12 Manning, *English People*, 257; Malcolm, "A King in Search of Soldiers," 254

13 Manning, *English People*, 257

14 Manning, *English People*, 255-256; Hill, *Reformation*, 133-134

15 Walter, "the English Revolution Revisited," 177

The peasantry

Early modern rural England was a site of marked social change, conflict and inequality."[16] One purpose for the demand to abolish episcopacy was to eliminate tithes, particularly oppressive to the rural population.

> ...though townsmen generally tended to get off lightly, the burden of tithes fell disproportionately on yeomen and farmers. Furthermore, since many tithes went into the pockets of lay landowners who had impropriated them, this amounted to a tax for support of the nobility and gentry.[17]

The revolution gave the peasantry opportunities to fight back. By 1642 rural tenants were withholding rents. In part this was due to high taxes to pay for the war, and to losses suffered from billeted or pillaging soldiers. But the landlords' authority was weakened during the war, and tenants took the opportunity to escape the higher rents imposed on them in recent years. Many paid only what they wished, or stopped paying altogether. Tenants abandoned their leases for cheaper ones, and new tenants could only be found at much reduced rents, if at all.[18] In the Commons debate over the Lords' peace proposals to the king at the end of December, 1642, Sir Simonds D'Ewes, now a Peace party opponent of taxation, sarcastically suggested they should pass an ordinance "to compel tenants to pay their rents."[19]

Copyhold tenure was thus a burning issue in the countryside. In addition to rack rents, landlords in many places had been attempting to deny peasant families the right of inheritance to their lands, which they had often held for generations. Others imposed fines at higher levels, and/or at the landlord's pleasure, rather than the customary duties on the death of the head of household.

> A [Leveller] manifesto of 1648, claiming to speak for "many thousands" in London and the counties round about, demanded "that the ancient and almost antiquated badge of slavery, viz. all base tenures by copies, oaths of fealty, homage, fines at the will of the lord, etc...may be taken away; and to that end...all possessors of lands so holden may purchase themselves freeholders... [20]

The peasants' hostility to landlords as a result made recruitment to the Cavalier army extremely difficult in many areas. "Royalist and parliamentarian observers agreed that during the summer of 1642 the commoners of Yorkshire remained neutral or opposed to the king's party."[21] Peasants in the West Riding of Yorkshire in the north of England, parts of

16 Blomley, "Making Private Property," 1

17 Manning, "The Godly People," 109

18 Manning, *English People*, 212-215

19 Gardiner, *Great Civil War* Vol. I, 92

20 Manning, *English People*, 316

21 Malcolm, "A King in Search of Soldiers," 258

Somerset in the southwest, and Cheshire and Lancashire in the northwest, refused to follow their landlords in the royalist cause, and enrolled in the parliamentary army.[22] In Lincolnshire, Cambridgeshire and Huntingdonshire counties stretching north of London, armed peasants opened or destroyed sluices installed to drain the Fens, which had deprived them of the larger share of the commons land,[23] and the fish and waterfowl they supplemented their diets with.[24] "The inhabitants of Epworth threw down the banks, filled in ditches, destroyed crops and put their cattle back on the whole of their old commons, driving off the settlers, demolishing their houses and burning their ploughs."[25]

Killing deer for food in the king's protected deer park southwest of London had already begun in September 1641.[26] It was copied elsewhere, including by Parliament's soldiers later on.[27] In Essex and Suffolk to the east of London, there were antiroyalist riots in mid-1642 which plundered gentlemen's manors, pulled down fences, and killed deer and farm animals.[28]

> ...the attacks represented the pre-existing depth of a political popular culture to whose values of anti-popery and protestant patriotism Parliament was able to appeal. It was this more general fear of the threat posed to religious and political liberties that mobilized the crowds in the summer of 1642. Thus, a classed reading of...a political crisis which brought mass unemployment helps to explain the presence of clothworkers in the attacks...[29]

The peasants also destroyed records and estate documents relating to rents, payments, fines, etc.[30] These areas were in the main strongly Puritan.[31]

Even in many areas where the people rose to fight they were unable to do so for lack of weapons and leaders — few gentry would lead them. "In March 1643 multitudes came to Cambridge to serve parliament but they were thanked and sent away again..."[32] Many gentry were, of course, against raising the peasantry, craftsmen, and poor to battle for fear they'd be unable to put the genie back in the bottle. They advocated limited and defensive strategies, or neutrality, and in a few places signed treaties with the local royalist gentry.[33]

22 Manning, *English People*, 203-206

23 Manning, *English People*, 206-207; Malcolm, "A King in Search of Soldiers," 259-260

24 Sharp, "The Place of the People in the English Revolution," 107

25 Manning, *English People*, 206; Hill, *Reformation*, 134

26 Manning, *English People*, 207-210

27 Manning, *English People*, 210-212

28 Manning, *English People*, 189-196, 209-210

29 Walter, "the English Revolution Revisited," 178

30 Manning, *English People*, 205-206

31 Manning, *English People*, 266

32 Manning, *English People*, 244

33 Manning, *English People*, 242-243; Hill, *Reformation*, 133-134

The town artisans

In the outlying industrial areas it was the craftspeople and independent farmers, yeomen large and small, who were the most ardent parliamentarians.

> They were part-farmers and part-manufacturers, not wholly dependent on the gentry, nor wholly dependent on the merchants or larger manufacturers; men not rich, nor yet impoverished, independent in their economic life and in their opinions. The clothiers of Halifax and Bradford, the weavers of the Manchester area, the metal-workers of the Birmingham district, exhibited a close resemblance in their attitudes and actions during the civil war.[34]

Popular support for Parliament in the Midlands included important parts of Gloucestershire, Oxfordshire, Northamptonshire, Warwickshire, Worcestershire, and Staffordshire.[35] In many parts of the country during 1642-1643, crowds of armed townsmen and/or peasants ran off royalists attempting to raise troops or seize local stores of weapons and gunpowder. They were sometimes led by a parliamentary gentleman, but more often acted on their own initiative. Where local authorities sided with the "great men" the people revolted against them as well. Several nobles and high gentry were arrested and sent to London as prisoners.[36] Houses of the wealthy were sacked, especially in cloth manufacturing areas and most violently in the Eastern counties. Trained bands either refused to discourage the insurrections or, more often, joined them.[37] "The popular movement of resistance to the royalists was decisive in gaining parliament time in which to gather forces and mobilize resources to encounter the king's army, and territory in which to maneuver."[38] In this way the middling people of town and country, acting as watchdogs and enforcers, suppressed royalist activities and secured large areas and substantial weaponry for Parliament.

Anyone who declared for the king instantly lost all influence with the populace in these areas, who rightly feared for their property and liberties at the hands of the Cavaliers. But the alliance between Parliament and the people was an uneasy one, as neither fully trusted the other. The latter's power could make or break any leader, and they sometimes went further than the former, forced to accept them, liked.[39] "The fact that some of the ruling class took the side of the people rather than of their own class was welcome and gratifying, if somewhat suspect."[40] Thus, to a considerable

34 Manning, *English People*, 235

35 Manning, *English People*, 221-222

36 Manning, *English People*, 196-197

37 Manning, *English People*, 184-196

38 Manning, *English People*, 198

39 Manning, *English People*, 197-199

40 Manning, *English People*, 201

extent, middling people, acting out of fear and hostility to the ruling aristocracy, took the opportunity to settle accounts with them.

Land and class relations

The king relied on feudal ties for recruits, but landlords who responded to the king were often no longer able to command much loyalty from their cash-paying rural tenants. The peasants' grievances made it difficult to enlist them as troops on the king's behalf.[41] In much of the country the traditional loyalty and deferential respect of the tenantry had been undermined by high rents and enclosures. By 1640, "deference and obedience were no longer sufficient to command popular allegiance."[42] Large numbers of peasants thus either refused any support to the royalists, or actively supported Parliament. Tenants of royalist landlords requested the government to order that their rents be paid to London "'to save us harmless from our landlords hereafter.'" This began the process of Parliament sequestering royalists' estates.[43]

Parliamentary committees in each county took over and administered the estates, collecting rents and fines, leasing, etc., until the land could be sold. In the meantime they stripped them of assets for the benefit of Parliament, being careful to first pay off creditors. Appointees to the commission in charge of sequestration in London included Maurice Thomson, his brother Robert, Pennington's deputy Randall Mainwaring, Richard Shute, and the "dangerous Deputy," Daniel Taylor. "Of the commission's twenty-three citizen members, eight had taken part in the Additional Sea Adventure to Ireland and twelve were later political independents (while three were later political presbyterians)."[44] The result was a massive redistribution of wealth from the aristocracy to the business class, as Parliament gave contracts to meet the needs of the war.[45]

After the war, through a complicated process called compounding or composition, former landlords (but not bishops or churches) were given the opportunity to buy back their lands. They were required to forfeit a chunk of acreage, and had to pay whatever punitive prices and fines were imposed. Many royalist aristocrats did not have the cash to do so, and their lands were sold to whoever did, often for speculation. In either case, the customary tenants who worked the land by copyhold had no recourse if they were thrown out by the old or new owners. This helped accelerate

41 Manning, *English People*, 202-203

42 Walter, "the English Revolution Revisited" 178

43 Manning, *English People*, 203; "March 1643: An Ordinance for sequestring (sic) notorious Delinquents Estates," Acts and Ordinances of the Interregnum, 1642-1660, British History Online http://www.british-history.ac.uk/no-series/acts-ordinances-interregnum/pp106-117 Accessed May 23, 2017

44 Brenner, *Merchants and Revolution*, 435

45 Christopher Hill, "The Agrarian Legislation of the Revolution," in *Puritanism and Revolution* (London: Pimlico, 1958, 2001), 141, 146; "Land in the English Revolution," 34-35

the amalgamation of land into large estates, and the conversion to purely capitalist farming.[46]

Taking sides

In September 1642, Charles began to confiscate the arms of those trained bandsmen who appeared at musters he himself had ordered.[47] "…a cavalier confessed: 'our Maxime is not to trust the trained bands, but we will make the best use of them we can, and that is of their arms.'"[48] Midlands gentry and commoners alike opposed giving up their weaponry to the king because it would leave their areas defenseless. "The decision to disarm the trained bands was disastrous for the king's reputation. … The arbitrary way the king seized men's arms belied all his protestations of constitutionalism."[49] The action was denounced as tyrannical by Parliament and its supporters.[50]

The king claimed to be fighting for the Protestant religion, but he and his party were associated in the popular mind with papists,[51] for good reason. Flouting his own previous proclamations, at the end of September 1642 Charles ordered that armed Catholics be enrolled in his army.[52] Even some of the king's partisans were shocked by this move.[53] "There are no exact figures of the numbers of catholics who fought for Charles but of the 500 officers who fell in his cause during the Civil War, 198 were catholic."[54] The welding together, if any was needed, of royalism with popery was permanently fixed with the arrival in England, between September 1643 and June 1644, of some 20,000 Irish Catholics to fight for the king.[55]

The court believed all Puritans to be parliamentarians, and parliamentarians believed all Catholics to be royalists. The armies of each attacked

46 Hill, "The Agrarian Legislation of the Revolution," 170-171; "Land in the English Revolution," 35-36; *Century*, 125-126; *Reformation*, 148-149; "February 1647: An Ordinance for establishing Commissioners of Lords and Commons to sit at Goldsmith Hall to Compound with Delinquents…," Acts and Ordinances of the Interregnum, 1642-1660, British History Online, https://www.british-history.ac.uk/no-series/acts-ordinances-interregnum/pp914-915 Accessed June 5, 2017

47 Malcolm, "A King in Search of Soldiers," 268; Fletcher, *Outbreak*, 327

48 Malcolm, "A King in Search of Soldiers," 267

49 Fletcher, *Outbreak*, 327-328; Malcolm, "A King in Search of Soldiers," 267

50 Manning, *Aristocrats, Plebeians*, 69

51 Manning, *English People*, 181

52 Malcolm, "A King in Search of Soldiers," 270-271; Fletcher, *Outbreak*, 332-333; "The King's Order for Papists to provide Arms," Rushworth Historical Collections: October 1642, British History Online, https://www.british-history.ac.uk/rushworth-papers/vol5/pp25-52#h2-0010 Accessed January 14, 2020

53 Gardiner, *Great Civil War* Vol. I, 29; Malcolm, "A King in Search of Soldiers," 259; Clifton, "The Popular Fear of Catholics during the English Revolution," 25. Different sources are given in the similar essay by Robin Clifton, "Fear of Popery," in *The Origins of the English Civil War*, ed. Conrad Russell (Basingstoke, Hampshire: Macmillan Education, 1973), 145 fn. 3

54 Malcolm, "A King in Search of Soldiers," 271. See the study in Lindley, "The Part Played by the Catholics," which found the majority of English Catholic gentry remained neutral during the war.

55 Malcolm, "A King in Search of Soldiers," 272

and plundered the homes of the other's wealthy supporters, although some parliamentary officers attempted to curb this.[56] In predominantly royalist areas, Puritans were subject to attack by mobs, as well as soldiers, causing them to seek safety in Parliament's garrison towns, or enroll in the Parliamentary army.[57] Catholics, perennially suspected, faced similar threats in some Puritan areas. Puritans in the army fought for the cause, unlike many of the poor who were only interested in the money and plunder.[58]

Nobles who responded to the king's appeal called, in good feudal fashion, on their tenants, kinsman, servants, neighboring gentry, *their* tenants, and any others in their vicinity that they might influence. Semi-feudal gentry in outlying regions in the north and Wales defended the old order all the more fiercely as their positions were undermined.

> Once money became the measure of all things their local omnipotence would be ended. For the same reason it was perfectly logical for some at least of the tenants of this type of old-fashioned landlord to fight against the introduction of market rents.[59]

Still, many copyholders were blackmailed into fighting for the royalists, as crossing their landlords meant running the risk their leases might not be renewed or the rents increased. "Fear and force lay in the background, if loyalty and deference failed."[60] The Earl of Derby, Lord Lieutenant, used his position to overawe men on the king's behalf. "Derby deftly confiscated most of the county magazines and then marched bandsmen of Cheshire, Lancashire and North Wales to Shrewsbury to join the royal army."[61] Other nobles provided money, horses, men, and equipment.

Parliamentarians generally wanted a wider franchise, and royalists a narrower one. This reflected both sides' desire to control social policy, especially taxation. All sides were aware that the middling classes were overtaxed, and the landlords undertaxed.[62] The former looked to Parliament for redress of this grievance, knowing full well they would not receive any from the royalists. The issue would become a part of the Levellers' political arsenal after the war.[63]

Social trends are hardly ever absolute, and "it is true there were many yeomen and handicraftsmen in the king ranks,"[64] just as there were upper

56 Manning, *English People*, 183-184; "The Godly People," 93; Fletcher, *Outbreak*, 328

57 Manning, "The Godly People," 94

58 Manning, "The Godly People," 95-99

59 Hill, "Land in the English Revolution," 30-31

60 Manning, *English People*, 254

61 Malcolm, "A King in Search of Soldiers," 268; Christopher Hill, "Puritans and 'the Dark Corners of the Land,'" *Transactions of the Royal Historical Society* 13 (1963): 101, https://www.jstor.org/stable/3678730 Accessed April 29, 2020. Reprinted in Christopher Hill, *Change and Continuity in 17th-Century England* (New Haven: Yale University Press, 1974, 1991)

62 Manning, *English People*, 257-258

63 Manning, "The Godly People," 108-109

64 Manning, *English People*, 264

class aristocrats, and even a very few Catholics,[65] who backed Parliament. Exactly how many of the middling sort voluntarily joined Charles cannot be determined, but the king's army was initially filled by rural tenants from the north and west, Cornwall and Wales, many of whom willingly or unthinkingly followed their landlords. This does not, however, change the qualitative class nature represented on either side, and their corresponding political programs, as not a few contemporaries noted.[66] "At the start of the war popular support was crucial to the parliamentarians' strength."[67] As we have seen, it was the urban middling people who were Parliament's chief adherents at the outbreak.[68] In the windup for war, the discrepancies between the intentions of the parliamentarian leadership, and the demands of their petty bourgeois supporters, were tacitly submerged.

The polarization that drove people of all social classes to take sides, based on what they perceived to be their interests, need not obscure the fact that a majority of the gentry and peasantry, including Catholics, opted to remain defensively neutral if they could.[69] They often couldn't: preference for a neutral stance by peasants or gentry was rendered moot when the troops of one side or the other occupied their areas. This argument, however, was grossly overstated by some Revisionist historians:

> Indeed so great has been the stress on neutrals and neutralism and on the general reluctance to take sides and to begin fighting at all in 1642, that we are in danger of having to explain how a mere handful of obstinate or fanatical extremists on each side contrived to drag the country down into the abyss of Civil War.[70]

The privations imposed on the agricultural population by the several armies (including the Scots'), forced to live off the land as they criss-crossed England, would become increasingly devastating as the war dragged on.[71] Peasants often received little if any compensation for the produce carried off by hungry soldiers, sometimes in the form of well-meaning but worthless IOUs from parliamentarians. The resentment of "free quarter" would become clamorous after the end of the first civil war, when the Presbyterian Parliament, for political reasons, refused to pay the New Model Army unless it disbanded; and the soldiers refused to disband unless they were

65 Lindley, "The Part Played by the Catholics," 173-174

66 Underdown, *Pride's Purge*, 11-13

67 Fletcher, *Outbreak*, 417

68 Brian Manning, "Introduction," *The English People and the English Revolution* (London: Bookmarks, July 1991), 32-37; Hill, "Parliament and People in 17th-Century England," 101-102; Christopher Hill, "Parliament and People in Seventeenth-Century England - A Rejoinder," *Past & Present*, no. 98 (February, 1983): 156 and fn. 3, http://www.jstor.org/stable/650692 Accessed 15 December 2016

69 Manning, *English People*, 181, 247; Brailsford, *The Levellers*, 13; Hill, *Century*, 102; Lindley, "The Part Played by the Catholics," 174-175

70 G. E. Aylmer, "Presidential Address: Collective Mentalities in Mid Seventeenth-Century England: IV. Cross Currents: Neutrals, Trimmers and Others," *Transactions of the Royal Historical Society* 39 (1989): 1, https://www.jstor.org/stable/3678975 Accessed June 16, 2019

71 Brailsford, *The Levellers*, 166-167

paid, and their political demands satisfied.[72] The hard political core of the Army ranks came from those same middling yeomen and artisans,[73] many of them recruited by Cromwell himself.

72 Brailsford, *The Levellers*, 147, 173-175, 257; Hill, *1640*, 62-64; *Century*, 96; Manning, *Aristocrats, Plebeians*, 79, 81

73 Brailsford, *The Levellers*, 146-147

15) THE POLITICAL STRUGGLE INTENSIFIES (1642-1643)

> *...Cromwell and the English people had borrowed speech, passions and illusions from the Old Testament for their bourgeois revolution. When the real aim had been achieved, when the transformation of English society had been accomplished, Locke supplanted Habakkuk.*
>
> ~Karl Marx[1]

With such extensive support in town and country it seemed the Parliamentary cause in London should have been assured. But this was far from the case. The complex of reasons can be boiled down to the moderate, partial nature of the Parliamentary program, and the gentry/merchant alliance which kept the revolutionary Puritan movement bound to the House of Commons.

Up to this point, the Puritan bourgeois leadership, now in power in London, had been united in its opposition to the crown and church, just as the Common's leadership, personified by Pym, had mainly acted in concert with its left wing led by Pennington. With the success of the revolution, political differences began to emerge between the more moderate and more radical forces in each arena, reflecting their different goals. The civil war, begun by the king in the autumn of 1642, intensified this political struggle. The war brought the revolution to a grinding halt in the face of a conservative trend inside London, and the consequent need for military defense against internal and external enemies of the revolution. The full depth, configuration and consequences of the political split in the bourgeois leadership would not reach finality until several years into the future, but its origins were set here.

The bourgeois government of London

Between January 1642 and the summer of 1643, twelve London aldermen were elected to replace those who died, defected to the king, were imprisoned for non-payments, or otherwise left office. Only two of these newly elected aldermen had previously held office in a monopoly company; one was thrown out some months later. Richard Chambers, however, was famous for his public refusal to pay ship money and other illegal taxes to Charles. Collectively these twelve men were more moderate than those who served on the Militia Committee, the leaders of the City revolution. The majority of these later aldermen became political Presbyterians, whereas six of the eight aldermen on the Militia Committee became Independents.[2]

The Militia Committee, in addition to its political tasks of directing the defense of the City, also organized the financing of Parliament's army. Four aldermen on the Militia Committee — Sir John Wollaston, John Warner,

1 *The Eighteenth Brumaire of Louis Bonaparte*, in *Karl Marx and Frederick Engels Selected Works*, 98

2 Pearl, *London and the Outbreak*, 244-245

John Towse, and Thomas Andrewes — had been responsible for the voluntary contributions of plates, money and horses in June 1642; had been in charge of collecting loans and assessments earlier that year; and had also been treasurers for the Irish subscriptions in March as well. In September these same four would again be appointed to receive the subscriptions for raising troops. Three of the four became Treasurers for War.

These men did not come from great merchant families: they were liverymen who had started out in business and accumulated fortunes. Thomas Andrewes, a wholesale linen-draper and money-lender, was a business partner of Maurice Thomson and had subscribed to the Massachusetts Bay Colony. Unusually, he had participated in the private customs farming syndicate under Charles I and, along with John Fowke (by this time also an alderman) and three other Militia Committee members, he was appointed Commissioner of Customs in January 1643. Andrewes and John Towse, a member of the Grocers' Company who was elected Sheriff in 1640, were appointed Excise Commissioners, along with another Independent, John Kendricke, also of the Grocers' Company, who later served as Lord Mayor during the Commonwealth. Five members of the Militia Committee in 1642 would be named as Trustees to sell bishops' lands in 1646: Aldermen Andrewes, Fowke, and Thomas Atkins, Councilmen Stephen Estwicke, and Francis Peck. Estwicke and Peck, along with Alderman Atkins, "were the main suppliers of clothing and provisions to parliamentary armies"[3] which thereby gave these businessmen substantial trade and profit. (It has been estimated that from 1642 to 1646 tradesmen of London, small and large, were collectively paid £500,000 for equipment and supplies, though some still had to be acquired elsewhere in England or on the Continent.)[4]

Sir John Wollaston had been a Common Councilor in the 1630s, and Sheriff from 1638-1639 (along with Isaac Pennington). A member of the Goldsmiths' Company, he refused to loan money to the king in 1638, or to supply a list of wealthy men as alderman in 1639. Despite leaning towards moderation and Presbyterianism, he consistently lent money to Parliament during the Civil War, and accepted the Army in 1647. John Warner, a druggist and colonial merchant, and like Towse a member of the Grocers' Company, was elected Sheriff in 1639-1640 and Alderman in 1640. As an Independent and Lord Mayor in 1647 he would work to suppress Presbyterian and royalist riots before dying in office in 1648.[5]

Nearly all of the twelve commissioners appointed to oversee implementation of the weekly assessment, begun in November 1642, were Atlantic merchants or their allies. They included the same four treasurers above along with Maurice Thomson, Isaac Pennington, John Fowke, Richard Chambers, and the London MPs John Venn, Samuel Vassal, and Thomas Soames. Seven of these assessment commissioners were overseas traders, and eight also sat

3 Pearl, *London and the Outbreak*, 240-243, 321

4 Porter, "Impact of the Civil War Upon London," 178-179

5 Pearl, *London and the Outbreak*, 325-327, 328-331

on the City's Militia Committee. Many local ward assessors were drawn from the Atlantic merchant grouping.[6]

Thus, major elements of the bourgeois class, exclusive of the oligarchic company merchants, were firmly in control of organizing Parliament's war effort, sometimes to their own benefit.[7] In terms of public service these were all "new men" who had not been appointed to (and would not have been considered for) royal commissions or offices, high office in London's government, or directorates of monopoly trading companies. Some had held, at most, minor posts in the City before, such as Sheriff, or been Assistant in a livery company; but most were Puritans or Puritan sympathizers who had mainly declined to accept local offices prior to 1640.[8]

> These men were clearly not among the great merchant princes who monopolized office and enjoyed the greatest fortunes before 1640. They were wealthy, but not the wealthiest men in the City, merchants of middle and occasionally upper middle rank, unwilling to take office in the sixteen-thirties for political or conscientious reasons...[9]

or sometimes because of the time and money it took away from their business affairs. The Common Councilors who sat on the Militia Committee were of very similar backgrounds.[10] The livery company members were more broadly representative of the domestic bourgeoisie than the overseas merchants, old or new, and they engaged their "business acumen and organisational skills" in Parliament's service.[11] Most critically, they formed the pinnacle of the Atlantic merchants' base.

Formation of war and peace parties

As has been shown, the people in many areas were quite ready to rise: fear of papists and royalists; the destruction of their livelihoods due to depression and plunder; conscription of men by force to fight for the king; confiscation of arms; and Cavalier demands for money and supplies were sufficient provocations. They also hoped for a redress of their grievances by Parliament through religious reform and a wider democracy, while being "fearful and suspicious of the intentions of all superiors, whether royalists or parliamentarians or what."[12]

Thousands traveled to London to volunteer, but were sent home by Parliament. Those who spontaneously rose against the royalists were more motivated than soldiers for pay, but less disciplined, experienced and well-

6 Pearl, *London and the Outbreak*, 240-243, 309-311, 325; Brenner, *Merchants and Revolution*, 431-432

7 John Fowke had engaged in overseas trade with the Levant and East India Companies prior to 1641, but he was a loose cannon, as often at serious odds with their directorates and/or the king's government as not. Pearl, *London and the Outbreak*, 316-318

8 Pearl, *London and the Outbreak*, 241-243

9 Pearl, *London and the Outbreak*, 243; Manning, *Aristocrats, Plebeians*, 63

10 Pearl, *London and the Outbreak*, 243-244

11 Porter, "Impact of the Civil War Upon London," 177-178

12 Manning, *English People*, 235, 237-240

equipped. As a result of their lack of training they tended to collapse or run away in the midst of battle. The first major engagement of the war was the inconclusive battle of Edgehill in October 1642. It convinced Cromwell that the war could not be won by irregular volunteers from the lower classes, "'decayed servingmen and tapsters and such kind of fellows,'" facing sons of gentlemen trained in arms and to command, for whom honor was the highest virtue. What was needed were new regiments, particularly cavalry, composed of "'men of spirit,'" godly men who would be as dedicated to the fight as gentlemen.[13] Denzil Holles, another parliamentary leader, made the same observation, but his "contempt for his own soldiers"[14] led him and others to a different political conclusion.

> So they became leaders of the Peace Party, advocating negotiations with the king and peace at almost any price. Experiences with untrained and cowardly, disorderly and mutinous soldiers persuaded many parliamentarian leaders that they would be beaten, and defeatism led them to seek peace with the king on any terms he would accept.[15]

Cromwell, on the other hand, understood that military victory was essential to religious reform, and he believed, erroneously as it turned out, that it would force the king to make an agreement.[16] He became a leader of the war party in the Commons, but it would be two and a half years before reform of the army via the Self-Denying Ordinance was passed by Parliament, and the creation of the New Model Army.[17] Meanwhile, for the next nine months, Parliament was politically stalemated until the military situation was almost completely lost.

> Radicalism appeared almost as soon as the war began, not because…it was a logical consequence of Parliament's claims, but because in practice it became doubtful whether Parliament was prepared to stand firm, and the choice appeared to lie between the adoption of more radical principles or rapid defeat. … In December [1642] negotiations were taking place, and many feared that Parliament would cut its losses, hand the Five Members over to the King, and settle on his terms.[18]

From September 1642 on, the City government, with its new Lord Mayor Isaac Pennington and the Militia Committee, was firmly on the side of Parliament. A few minor reforms towards political democracy in City government procedure were added to those implemented in the first months of the year. But few official ordinances were passed to codify the governmental

13 Fraser, *Cromwell*, 97-98; Gardiner, *Great Civil War* Vol. I, 47 and fn. 2

14 Hexter, *King Pym*, 9

15 Manning, *English People*, 246; Hexter, *King Pym*, 55; Underdown, *Pride's Purge*, 60

16 Fraser, *Cromwell*, 138

17 Fraser, *Cromwell*, 141-145; Hill, *Century*, 108. The Self-Denying Ordinance of 1645 prohibited anyone with a seat in either house of Parliament from being a military officer in the New Model Army. It was passed as a way of removing the compromising and incompetent aristocrats from the army leadership. An exception was subsequently voted for Oliver Cromwell.

18 David Wootton, "From Rebellion to Revolution: The Crisis of the Winter of 1642/3 and the Origins of Civil War Radicalism," *The English Historical Review* 105, no. 416 (July 1990): 654-655, 659, https://www.jstor.org/stable/570756 Accessed November 11, 2018

revolution of early 1642. This was not an oversight, but reflected the generally more moderate attitude of many of the new City rulers, corresponding to Pym's middle group in the House of Commons, rather than its left wing, of which Pennington was a part.[19]

> The overwhelming majority of the members who remained at Westminster after 1642 were Puritans in the broad, undifferentiated moral sense... They took religion seriously, disliked sabbath-breaking, stage plays, church-ales, and long hair, wished to purge the Church of England of the "popish" innovations introduced by the Arminians, and to have no more of episcopacy as practised in the 1630s. They were not necessarily opposed to bishops in principle...[20]

"For the essence of the 'middle group' was that they did not see themselves as revolutionaries. They constantly affirmed their support for the traditional and fundamental law, they staunchly upheld the monarchical system..."[21] While endorsing practical measures to limit or remove royalist intrigues, the influence of the City moderates acted as a brake to limit what Pennington and his "fiery" supporters in the City government and the House of Commons could achieve.[22] The door to reaction was being cracked open.

Program and tactics of the radical Independents

Since the battle at Edgehill, "many hundreds" of London citizens had been furiously working to construct "trenches and ramparts" on the roads into the city, and by order of Parliament on 25 October all shops were closed to maximize the available labor.[23] In mid-November, two of Parliament's regiments of foot, headed by Lord Brooke and Denzil Holles, were "destroyed" by Prince Rupert, leaving London exposed. Cavalier troops pillaged Brentford, a mere eight miles west of London, even as Parliament and the king were exchanging messages on the possibility of negotiations.[24] City radicals, on behalf of "'the most godly and active part of the City'" sent a delegation led by Richard Shute to petition the Commons against any accommodation with the king. To support their demand they offered to raise an immediate 1,000 horse and 3,000 troops under Serjeant Major General Philip Skippon, commander of the London militia, for the army of Essex, whose unpreparedness and weak leadership they strongly criticized.[25] This was an early attack on the earl's half-hearted military policy. Trained Bands from the county of Essex had come to London "but were sent back again because the lord general had

19 Pearl, *London and the Outbreak*, 246, 249-250

20 Underdown, *Pride's Purge*, 15-16

21 Valerie Pearl, "Oliver St. John and the 'Middle Group' in the Long Parliament: August 1643-May 1644," *The English Historical Review* 81, no. 320 (July 1966): 493, http://www.jstor.org/stable/561660 Accessed October 8, 2015

22 Pearl, *London and the Outbreak*, 250

23 Nagel, "The Militia of London," 71-72

24 Nagel, "The Militia of London," 72; Gardiner, *Great Civil War* Vol. I, 65-66; "Brentford & Turnham Green: November 1642," BCW Project, http://bcw-project.org/military/english-civil-war/edgehill-campaign/brentford-turnham-green Accessed June 28, 2016; Pearl, *London and the Outbreak*, 252

25 Pearl, *London and the Outbreak*, 252

no use for them."[26] Skippon, on the other hand, was "close politically to the City's radicals," but well-regarded by nearly all parliamentary factions.[27]

Given the imminent threat, the Commons had little choice but to accept the radicals' offer. The House recommended Skippon to be subordinate to Essex, and designated the Earl of Warwick to oversee the committee to raise volunteers.[28] Among those appointed to the volunteer committee were other radical Independents, such as John Kendricke, soon to be an alderman, and Lord Mayor during the Commonwealth,[29] and the future Leveller leader William Walwyn.[30] This was the first time official recognition had been given to City radicals by the Commons.[31]

The reduced but still sizable army under Lord Essex, with the London Trained Bands and the hastily recruited auxiliary volunteers, faced off against the royalist army at Turnham Green, just west of the City, next day. Charles, outnumbered two to one, chose to withdraw.[32] Following the king's rejection of Parliament's negotiating proposals soon after, both Houses accepted the proposal for regular taxes on London to finance the war. Pennington and the City Sheriffs were authorized to establish a committee at Weavers' Hall "to appoint collectors in each parish…[with] powers to fix individual assessments, levy distresses and call in the assistance of the Trained Bands to deal with recalcitrants."[33] Whereas up to this point contributions in support of the war had been voluntary, they were now made mandatory.

Parliament's negotiations with the king had gone nowhere, but on 1 December a new petition against accommodation was signed by 95 "'godly citizens.'" The leaders included the activist Independent ministers Hugh Peter, John Goodwin and Jeremiah Burroughs, "major architects of the radicals' offensive,"[34] as well as the war party Independents Mayor Pennington, Randall Mainwaring and Richard Shute. The petition demanded the arrests of royalists and malignants and seizure of their estates to pay for the war. It urged an active prosecution of the war by Essex, and offered to raise 6,000 troops. It also asked for the sequestration of pro-royalist, Episcopal church ministers, and their replacement by godly ones.[35]

26 Manning, *English People*, 244

27 Brenner, *Merchants and Revolution*, 436-437

28 Brenner, *Merchants and Revolution*, 436; Pearl, *London and the Outbreak*, 252; "City Forces," House of Commons Journal Volume 2: 15 November 1642, British History Online, https://www.british-history.ac.uk/commons-jrnl/vol2/pp850-852#p46 Accessed 28 February 2021 [Two entries]

29 Pearl, *London and the Outbreak*, 321

30 Brenner, *Merchants and Revolution*, 437-438

31 Brenner, *Merchants and Revolution*, 438. Although Pearl describes the citizens' offer to raise troops, she does not mention this committee.

32 "Brentford & Turnham Green: November 1642," BCW Project

33 Pearl, *London and the Outbreak*, 253; Hexter, *King Pym*, 17-18; "November 1642: An Ordinance for the assessing of all such as have not contributed…," Acts and Ordinances of the Interregnum, 1642-1660, British History Online, https://www.british-history.ac.uk/no-series/acts-ordinances-interregnum/pp38-40 Accessed 14 August 2020

34 Brenner, *Merchants and Revolution*, 439

35 Pearl, *London and the Outbreak*, 253-254

Neither did the radicals hesitate to wield their power over Parliament: "'...if the destructive counsels of accommodation be reassumed they shall think it necessary to look to their own safety and forbear to contribute to their own ruin.'"[36] The godly men were thanked, but since no alderman appeared for the petition, the Commons sent it back to the City, where it was rejected by the Common Council.[37] Parliament had already that day given a warrant to a linen draper to search "for Monies, Plate, and Horse, in the Houses of all Papists and Malignants whatsoever."[38] Two weeks later, however, they also began to extend the Ordinance for assessments and collections to the rest of the country.[39] On the same day, 1 December, Parliament ordered the printing of a justification for its actions provided to it by Jeremiah Burroughs.[40]

> In 1638 Burroughs discussed and supported the Scottish Covenant. Among the earl [of Warwick's] intimates, Burroughs also advocated republican government and armed resistance to the king, singular positions in those pre-revolutionary days.[41]

In a sermon at the end of the December, 1642 Burroughs "went on to defend four basic freedoms to which everyone (and not merely freeholders) should lay claim: the rights to property, to government by consent, to freedom of conscience, and to reliable justice in place of grace and favour."[42] A year after the revolution in London, the universal application of such bourgeois democratic rights was still a very avant-garde idea.

In the late fall of 1642, the 200 remaining members in the House of Commons were very far from one mind.[43] For a time the illusions of the peace party were able to prevail.

> From November [1642] to January [1643] a majority of the members of the House of Commons supported the policy of treating with the King;...Pym gave the members anxious for a treaty their chance, a chance they used to frame the most moderate proposals presented to the King during the whole course of the war...[44]

Many if not most members indulged "the persistent faith that the war would be short, or...that there would not really be a war at all."[45] Indeed, Cromwell's

36 Brenner, *Merchants and Revolution*, 438

37 Pearl, *London and the Outbreak*, 254

38 "Search for Money, &c.," House of Commons Journal Volume 2: 01 December 1642, British History Online, https://www.british-history.ac.uk/commons-jrnl/vol2/pp870-872#p2 Accessed January 31, 2021

39 Pearl, *London and the Outbreak*, 254; "Ordinance of Assessment," House of Commons Journal Volume 2: 17 December 1642, British History Online, https://www.british-history.ac.uk/commons-jrnl/vol2/pp892-893#p39 Accessed 17 February 2021

40 Brenner, *Merchants and Revolution*, 441 fn. 89

41 Shipps, "The 'Political Puritan,'" 204

42 Wootton, "The Crisis of the Winter of 1642/3," 667

43 Hexter, *King Pym*, 67 fn. 5; Porter, "Impact of the Civil War Upon London," 177

44 Hexter, *King Pym*, 49-50; Gardiner, *Great Civil War* Vol. I, 93

45 Hexter, *King Pym*, 7

first commission to raise a troop of horse in August 1642 had read, "that the men should be ready to fight for 'King and Parliament.'"[46]

"The spectre of treason prompted parliament to tread carefully, to react to the actions of the king rather than pre-empt them. This...gave rise to a parliamentarian war effort that was both reactive and defensive."[47] Johnson uses some bad arguments to support this very real aspect. The Militia Ordinance and the initial voluntary collection taken up in London may have been forced on a cautious Parliament by the king's efforts to raise an army, but this does not detract from their transgressive, i.e., revolutionary, nature. The retrograde influence of the House of Lords and the peace party in both Houses, which he also cites, contains much more substance. Here again the contradiction in gentry politics is revealed. While Johnson's observation is generally correct, Parliament nonetheless did react, and did not back down. It slowly took logically needed measures under the pressure of the war party, and prodding by Pym and his co-thinkers.

During the first half of 1643 this cautious approach, however, together with a prevailing belief that a single battle would force the king to negotiate,[48] prevented the Commons from undertaking more serious preparations for a war. Pym's policy was not to oppose negotiations as they proceeded, while building an administrative, fiscal and military machinery that could be used to support Parliament when, as he clearly expected, they failed.[49] Every royalist military and propaganda attack, every arrogant rejection and violent condemnation by Charles, was used as an argument by Pym to push his proposals through Parliament. Supported in each case by the war party in the Commons and the radicals in the City government, he had mostly succeeded by the time negotiations with the king in Oxford for a treaty collapsed in April 1643.[50]

The City divided: royalism strikes back

Charles' propaganda, on the other hand, "strove to detach the urban populace from their radical leaders."[51] "Messengers, scouts and spies, and 'certain adventurous women', concealing secret despatches in their voluminous skirts, passed to and fro..."[52] In mid-December 1642 the Common Council banned the wearing of party colors to suppress open royalist sentiment.[53] Nevertheless, the combination of royalist and acco-

46 Fraser, *Cromwell*, 91

47 Johnson, "Disintegration of the Parliamentarian War Effort," 76. Johnson is clearly on the conservative side politically: while not overtly pro-royalist in this work, he is rather contemptuous of Parliament, and obviously hostile to the London Puritan movement and its leadership.

48 Gardiner, *Great Civil War* Vol. I, 40

49 Hexter, *King Pym*, 14, 49-50; Johnson, "Disintegration of the Parliamentarian War Effort," 82

50 Hexter, *King Pym*, 15-17, 56-57

51 Ian Gentles, "Parliamentary Politics and the Politics of the Street: The London Peace Campaigns of 1642-3," *Parliamentary History* 26, no. 2 (May 2007): 141

52 Ian Roy, "'This Proud Unthankefull City': A Cavalier View of London in the Civil War," in *London and the Civil War*, ed. Stephen Porter (New York: St. Martin's Press, 1996), 157

53 Pearl, *London and the Outbreak*, 255; Gentles, "The London Peace Campaigns," 144

modationist pressure was strong enough that Pennington, as Mayor, was forced to agree to bring a private counter-petition for peace to the House of Commons later in the month. It was signed by 100 of "'the most substantial inhabitants of the citie of London.'"[54] A few days earlier, a group of up to 1,000 antiwar protesters, angry over higher taxes, had seized the Guildhall and beaten up the quartermaster of John Venn's regiment. Only when the Trained Band threatened to blow in the doors with cannon did they surrender, and were arrested.[55] The Common Council obtained permission from Parliament to send a petition to Charles in York asking for peace, and the king agreed to receive it.

As polarization in the City was deepening, the stridency of the radicals was alienating the gentlemen of the House. To undercut these dangers, Pennington brought a second, official City petition with him to the Commons, setting out in conciliatory language London's conditions for peace to be sent to the king. (He also took care to have the originators of the peace petition imprisoned.) The king's reply, by his own request, was read in Common Hall on 13 January 1643. True to form, Charles rejected the terms offered, insulted the municipal delegation which brought them, and demanded that several Independent leaders, including Pennington and Randall Mainwaring, MP John Venn and Alderman John Fowke, be handed over for trial on charges of high treason. The king also went out of his way to indict and denigrate the entire London government, which made it clear that no supporter of the governmental changes the previous January, which included most of the House of Commons, would be safe. Pym addressed Common Hall to great acclaim, supported by the new Earl of Manchester, reunifying the City's adherence to Parliament.[56] No less than Clarendon conceded their speeches were "entertained with all imaginable applause, and…with a general acclamation, 'that they would live and die with the houses…'"[57] The peace party was set back, and two weeks later both Houses agreed on a bill to abolish episcopacy.[58] The radicals resubmitted their petition of 1 December, but again without success.[59]

The City united: London defends itself

Pennington's plan to build extensive and massive fortifications around London and its suburbs was moving forward about this time. Begun in the fall of 1642,[60] it was widely, even wildly, popular, both in and out of gov-

54 Pearl, *London and the Outbreak*, 255; Gentles, "The London Peace Campaigns," 142 and fn. 17

55 Nagel, "The Militia of London," 75-76; Gentles, "The London Peace Campaigns," 142, 145

56 Pearl, *London and the Outbreak*, 255-257; Brenner, *Merchants and Revolution*, 442-443; Gardiner, *Great Civil War* Vol. I, 95-96

57 Edward Earl of Clarendon, *The History of the Great Rebellion and Civil Wars in England* Vol. 3 (Oxford: Clarendon Press, 1826), 400, https://archive.org/details/england03claruoft/page/n8/mode/2up?view=theater Accessed 1 November 2021; Gentles, "The London Peace Campaigns," 147

58 Gardiner, *Great Civil War* Vol. I, 98; "Abolishing Espiscopacy" (sic), House of Commons Journal Volume 2: 30 January 1643, British History Online, https://www.british-history.ac.uk/commons-jrnl/vol2/pp947-949#h3-0007 Accessed November 30, 2019

59 Pearl, *London and the Outbreak*, 257; Brenner, *Merchants and Revolution*, 443

60 Nagel, "The Militia of London," 71-72

ernment. Moderates who favored negotiations with the king saw it as "a way of strengthening the City as an independent force capable of bargaining with either side." It also had the side virtue for them of extending the municipal government's authority to the areas outside the walls, which were often where radical workers lived. For the bourgeois radicals, it provided the parliamentary army with a large and secure source of weapons and supplies, as well as helping to safeguard against royalist activities. Terror inspired by the Cavalier depredations at Brentford in November 1642 fed the citizens' enthusiasm. The fortifications surrounded London, and the suburbs of Southwark and Westminster, with trenches and periodic forts in sight of each other. "Open streets leading out into the suburbs were barricaded and armed, and batteries of ordnance were mounted at strategic points."[61] The walls were built far enough away from residential areas that they would be safe from artillery.[62]

In the spring of 1643 the Common Council ordered ministers to preach for defense of the City. One thousand "fish wives…marched from Billingsgate in martial order headed by a symbolic goddess of war." Each day a different parish neighborhood reported for work, and livery companies "marched out with 'roaring drums, flying colours and girded swords;' over fifty trades were said to have competed in friendly emulation…"[63] Up to 20,000 people a day, whole families including women and children, worked for no pay, only food. Feltmakers and cappers, tailors, watermen, gentlemen vintners with their wives and servants, porters, shoemakers, fishmongers and coopers participated in their thousands.

> …even the "clerks and gentlemen" participated as a profession. Those belonging to Parliament, the Inns of Court, and other public offices, were mustered in the Piazza in Covent Garden at seven o'clock in the morning with "spades, shovels, pickaxes and other necessaries."[64]

The work continued even on Sundays.[65] Completed by the spring of 1643, the forts were built of earth and timber, "the ramparts being 9 feet thick and 18 feet high, and extending for 18 miles,"[66] "the most extensive system of defences in Europe."[67]

This visceral demonstration of the City united in its own defense against the plunder and destruction of the king's army was only made possible by an exceedingly large and solid core of organized support for the program of the revolution in church and state, and its parliamentary Puritan leadership. It came a year or so after the revolutionary days of 1641-42 that had intimi-

61 Pearl, *London and the Outbreak*, 262-263. For a very detailed description, see Victor Smith and Peter Kelsey, "The Lines of Communication: The Civil War Defenses of London," in *London and the Civil War*, ed. Stephen Porter (New York: St. Martin's Press, 1996)

62 Porter, "Impact of the Civil War Upon London," 176

63 Pearl, *London and the Outbreak*, 264-265; Gentles, "The London Peace Campaigns," 140

64 Pearl, *London and the Outbreak*, 264, 265; Manning, *English People*, 216-218

65 Pearl, *London and the Outbreak*, 264

66 Manning, *English People*, 218

67 Nagel, "The Militia of London," 77

dated the king and checkmated his *coup d'ëtat*; and only a few months after the Trained Bands and citizens, with Essex, had stood up to the royalists at Turnham Green. The revolutionary consciousness of the working and middling classes was confirmed to be not only still alive, but only waiting for opportunities to show itself in action.

Parliament and London: The alliance of gentry and merchants

Customs farming was in the hands of the old company merchants who, as staunch royalists, refused to lend money to Parliament. They were dismissed, and replaced by a commission composed of new merchants in January 1643. In particular, the new customs commission was to provide money for the navy, most of whose officers and crews, with their ships, had gone over to Parliament. The customs commissioners included Maurice Thomson, John Fowke, Thomas Andrewes and Richard Chambers. With the exception of Chambers they were all radical parliamentarians, and six of its eight members were also militia commissioners. A few months earlier, Parliament had appointed the leftwing MP Sir Henry Vane to lead a commission of twelve to organize and administer the navy, evenly split between civilians and MPs. Six of these naval commissioners, including Maurice Thomson, were Atlantic merchants or had ties to them. Other members again included John Fowke and Richard Chambers. The commission had the Puritan Earl of Warwick appointed admiral of the fleet.[68]

The new secretary to the admiralty was a close collaborator of Maurice Thomson, and had been a commissioner for the Additional Sea Adventure to Ireland. Charles' importation of arms and money from the Continent was a serious problem at this early stage.[69] In need of more ships to isolate enemy ports and wage war against the king, as well as to protect its commerce abroad, Parliament contracted private armed ships from their supporters in the Atlantic trade. These were manned by "'naval officers of a new type, who had been trained in merchant ships and replaced the old aristocratic commanders in Parliament's navy.'" Sixty such colonial merchant ships were hired during the Civil War years.[70]

Senior aldermen and the wealthiest citizens, unsurprisingly, were strongly resistant to the assessments ordered by Parliament the previous November, which were set at "one-twentieth of real property and one-fifth of personal estate."[71] Reportedly the City's list of malignant persons contained 800 names. Some sitting aldermen had had their homes searched by the sheriffs for arms. During January and early February 1643 at least three royalist aldermen, and another five wealthy citizens were imprisoned for

68 Brenner, *Merchants and Revolution*, 432-433; D. E. Kennedy, *The English Revolution 1642-1649* (Basingstoke, Hampshire: MacMillan Press, 2000), 17-18, https://www.academia.edu/35661079/D_Kennedy_The_English_Revolution_1642_ Accessed 30 June 2021

69 Johnson, "Disintegration of the Parliamentarian War Effort," 85

70 Brenner, *Merchants and Revolution*, 433-434

71 Pearl, *London and the Outbreak*, 253 fn.68

refusing to pay assessments.[72]

Parliament and London: The gentry/merchant alliance opens the way for reaction

Also during late January and February four letters written by Charles, intercepted by Essex and Fairfax, were read in Parliament.

> They proved the prevalence of Popery in the Duke of Newcastle's Royalist army and indicated that Charles wanted nothing done to discourage the enlistment of Papists under the Duke's standard. ... In one the King revealed that he regarded the Oxford treaty less as a means to peace than as a vehicle to show forth his own magnanimity and the stubbornness of the rebel Parliament... The second royal letter proved to Parliament's satisfaction that in Ireland the King had identified his interests with the triumph of the Papists over the Protestants. The letters had a profound effect.[73]

Nevertheless, "...in February 1643 more than a hundred men voted to continue a peace treaty with the King despite his unfavorable answer to Parliament's proposal."[74] On the first of the month, a committee of both Houses left to negotiate a treaty in Oxford.

In the first half of 1643, "parliament's political and administrative preparations for civil war were essentially defensive..."[75] This was a product both of the circumspect program of the middle group, and of obstruction by the Peace party, whom Pym would not risk dividing from. On the same day the negotiators left London, 1 February, the treasurer for the army reported that there was no more money to pay the troops.[76] The voluntary collections and weekly assessments were simply insufficient.

This uncertain situation was left to fester. Despite the City Independents' and war party's many attempts to force the Commons to take the offensive, backed up by implicit threats to mobilize the population, it would not be until the military crisis in July/August that the House would engage to treat the war seriously. Meanwhile, also in February, the queen returned from the Continent with "significant quantities of money and munitions."[77] She also brought "a few hundred mercenaries,"[78] although she failed to persuade any foreign governments to send troops to support Charles. Parliamentary forces were unable to prevent her reaching the king.

From 18-21 February 1643, the Common Council debated three new sets of proposals, similar to the program in the 1 December petition, for submission to Parliament "purged of radical phrases." One list came from

72 Pearl, *London and the Outbreak*, 254-255 and fn. 74, 257

73 Hexter, *King Pym*, 20, 23

74 Hexter, *King Pym*, 35

75 Johnson, "Disintegration of the Parliamentarian War Effort," 70

76 Johnson, "Disintegration of the Parliamentarian War Effort," 83, 152; Hexter, *King Pym*, 21

77 Johnson, "Disintegration of the Parliamentarian War Effort," 11; Gardiner, *Great Civil War* Vol. I, 109

78 Malcolm, "A King in Search of Soldiers," 272

the peace party. The other two were designed to attract broad support for the political strategy of Pym and the middle group in the Commons. In return for passage of a new assessment bill by the House of Lords authorizing stricter enforcement,[79] Pym had agreed to continue negotiations with Charles. The new proposals from the Council therefore no longer called for breaking off negotiations with the king, but for practical steps to enhance the Parliamentary army: seizure of delinquents' rents, revenues and estates; distribution of the Ordinance for assessments throughout the country; and for a religious covenant "to bind together the 'well-affected' of the kingdom." The final petition, presented to the Commons on 20 February, did not include support for the assessments, but rather the moderates' appeal for a reduction in the size of the City's contribution. Nor did it contain the demands regarding delinquents' estates or a covenant, but these were added back the next day by the Council after further debate, along with an indirect attack on the Earl of Essex. The petition also asked the House to consider only official government communications to represent the "'sense'" of the City,[80] another slap to the radicals.

The conflicts over competing petitions in the first months of 1643 formalized the division in the City government between the factions, reflecting those in the House of Commons, but even more intensely. MPs and peers inclined toward the king had removed themselves from Westminster, either to the court at York or their estates. Most remaining members of the Commons belonged to neither extreme: like Pym, they supported an efficient and vigorous prosecution of the war, but only to put the democratic reforms of 1641 into effect.[81] While most in the London government were willing to protect the City from openly royalist influence there was little attempt to *systematically* suppress it. The radicals were hamstrung by the House of Commons, and City moderates would never have countenanced it.

Whereas in Paris 1793 the Jacobins followed the Gironde to power, here it was the other way around. The necessity of a civil war resulted from the lack of a Terror against the feudal aristocracy as a whole. There do not seem to have been any organized revolutionary or neighborhood committees, although some alert citizens may have informally monitored the situation, as during the Army Plots. In Paris such plebeian committees were vital to keep watch over and suppress royalist conspiracies and counter-revolutionaries. The House of Lords continued to sit until 1649: "almost every peer associated with Pym in 1643 had by 1648 become an advocate of peace with the King."[82] Any idea of removing the king, much less executing him, would have been viewed with abhorrence by the gentlemen at Westminster (as indeed it still was in 1649 when it came to pass). Henry Marten was virtually alone

79 "Order for assessing divers Persons in London, according to the Ordinance of 29 November," House of Lords Journal Volume 5: 8 February 1643, British History Online, https://www.british-history.ac.uk/lords-jrnl/vol5/pp592-596#p40 Accessed August 14, 2020

80 Pearl, *London and the Outbreak*, 257-259

81 Brenner, *Merchants and Revolution*, 393; Pearl, "Oliver St. John," 494

82 Hexter, *King Pym*, 58 fn. 49

in favoring a republic.[83] The deep, hard split to come in 1793 between the bourgeois and the aristocrat did not occur in 1642 because the bourgeois leaders, both the Atlantic merchants and the mostly moderate businessmen of the livery companies, were *politically allied* with a substantial wing of the aristocracy. As a result, the members of the Commons were able to make use of the people's support through their Puritan and merchant partners, while deterring their more revolutionary programmatic demands.

Despite the radical Independents' attempts to push the Commons toward their more republican program, it was utopian to think the landowners would embrace it. As the traditional counterweight to the crown, and the champions of a freer economy and individual rights, the middling/working people had reason to accord the Commons the primary role in the struggle. Parliament's political leadership was thus for the most part willingly accepted by the urban masses in these early years. The MPs were not, after all, *their* landlords. The association was overtly reinforced by the support of the leftwing City leaders, first and foremost the popular and devout Isaac Pennington who, instrumental in both arenas, was the glue cementing the London citizenry to the ruling gentry. The road to counter-revolution in the city was the direct result of the London leadership's dependence on, and its political subservience to, Parliament, in spite of all its energetic activity.

The question of sovereignty

In January 1643 an anonymous, highly radical pamphlet had appeared, *Plaine English*, most probably by the Presbyterian minister Edward Bowles. He

> spoke the mind of many when he scoffed at the pretense, carefully maintained by Parliament, that the King was not personally responsible for the deeds which made peace impossible, that in such matters he was misled by evil councillors. ... The King himself denied that anyone misled him... All Parliament's talk about evil councillors was patently a silly fiction.[84]

In an attempt to break through aristocratic obstruction, the London Independents at the end of March presented a citizens' Petition and Remonstrance, a statement of their program, to the Common Council, really intended for Parliament's notice. It explicitly linked "their strategic aim of harnessing the people's power to the parliamentary cause." For the first time, however, it was asserted, "'That originally the supreme power being in the whole people... in the Parliaments of England, acting for the same doth the supreme power reside...'"[85] If sovereignty did not reside in the person of the king, but in Parliament acting on behalf of the people, then the king was without question

83 Hexter, *King Pym*, 9, 199; C. M. Williams, "The Anatomy of a Radical Gentleman: Henry Marten," in *Puritans and Revolutionaries*, eds. Donald Pennington and Keith Thomas (Oxford: Oxford University Press, 1978), 120

84 Hexter, *King Pym*, 106

85 Brenner, *Merchants and Revolution*, 446

subject to its laws. The petition reiterated the radicals' call for "'trustworthy'" public officials, for strict conditions of settlement with the king, and for a national religious covenant. William Walwyn supported it,[86] and Hugh Peter was said to have lobbied for it at the door. Despite being "committed" to four of the most radical aldermen, John Towse, John Warner, John Fowke and Thomas Andrewes, there is no evidence that it passed the Council.[87]

It was nonetheless the first formal assertion in England of the fundamental bourgeois tenet that sovereignty derived from the people. The idea would be elaborated by John Locke some 50 years on, and become the theoretical basis for the American and French Revolutions 80-100 years after that. That power lay with the people had already been propounded in New England by the Puritan clerics Thomas Hooker in 1638, and John Cotton in 1640.[88] For all that it reinforced the ties between the people and Parliament, this was a revolutionary conception quite unlike the balance of power between king and Parliament that Pym and the middle group used to justify their program. Yet it only logically extended the implications of Parliament's Militia Ordinance being declared law one year earlier, and the citizens' armed defense against the king previous to that. Like many others, the question of the relationship between the people and the parliament would be revisited after the Civil War.

It was not until April 1643 that the negotiations in Oxford finally collapsed. The Commons' rightwing opposition to Pym's proposals now began to give ground, as the growing inevitability of a serious war and the need for defense became ever more glaring.[89] But still

> the Lords announced that "in the general combustion of the kingdom" the Weekly Assessment barely met the operational needs of the counties in which it was levied. In addition the City was so hard pressed that "it can hardly support the Lord General's army, unto which a great arrears remains unpaid, both for pay and supplies of the magazine."[90]

This was true, but to the Lords it justified continuing to seek an as-yet–unspecified settlement with the king on whatever terms he would agree to. This appeal to fear, nurtured by the peace party in the Commons as well, had its effects.

Repeated failures to negotiate with the king, and Cavalier military successes around the country, resulted in sharpening polarization in London. The "sentiment for peace in London concealed a good deal of clandestine activity subversive of the parliamentary war effort…"[91] Relations between the London radicals and the war party in Parliament, on the other hand, grew

86 Lindley, *Civil War London*, 307; Brenner, *Merchants and Revolution*, 448

87 Pearl, *London and the Outbreak*, 260-261; Lindley, *Civil War London*, 308; Brenner, *Merchants and Revolution*, 445-448

88 Tyacke, "Revolutionary Puritanism," 759

89 Hexter, *King Pym*, 31-32; Johnson, "Disintegration of the Parliamentarian War Effort," 88

90 Johnson, "Disintegration of the Parliamentarian War Effort," 159

91 Roy, "A Cavalier View of London in the Civil War," 161

closer in this period. New measures had to be taken to defend Parliament. City radicals, led by Randall Mainwaring,

> would constitute a whole series of commissions, organized by Parliament, that had as their purpose either the collection by force of money or supplies required for the military effort or the repression or surveillance of groups of citizens thought to be hostile to Parliament.[92]

Such activity by the London leadership, however, could not hope to substitute for mass involvement in stamping out the threat of royalism.

The political struggle intensifies

The ordinances expanding weekly assessments and for sequestration of delinquents' estates in early 1643[93] also established a parliamentary committee for each county. These acted as "the standard and universal organ of central control over local administration until the Restoration."[94] The regional county associations designated by Parliament were denounced by the king as traitorous, and he simultaneously turned down a truce proposal from the House of Lords. Pym's request for additional men and money from the City government in March received the answer that no more could be raised.[95] Money from a subscribed loan was coming in slowly, and the City government had no authority to enforce it.[96] Moreover an earlier loan had not yet been repaid. The auxiliary volunteers raised the previous November had been made part of Essex's army, and men were needed as guards on the City's new fortifications and could not be spared.[97]

> But the City radicals, in a petition originally presented to Common Council by Alderman Fowke, made up for the lack of response by offering to raise at their own charge three regiments of horse and seven of foot. Parliament and the municipality accepted their offer and by an Ordinance of April 12th [1643], a Sub-Committee, subordinate to the Militia Committee, was established at Salters' Hall for this purpose. Now the radicals had an organization of their own, with an official status in the City.[98]

Many Subcommittee members had been revolutionary militants during 1641-1642, and later became left-Independents or Levellers. Their aim was to establish a new, independent force of auxiliaries that would bypass City officials as well as the Earl of Essex. They sought to "place it in the hands of the militant citizens themselves" just as the Additional Sea Adventure to

92 Brenner, *Merchants and Revolution*, 443

93 "January 1643: Instructions for the Lords Lieutenants...," Acts and Ordinances of the Interregnum, 1642-1660, British History Online, http://www.british-history.ac.uk/no-series/acts-ordinances-interregnum/pp55-58 Accessed May 23, 2017

94 Hexter, *King Pym*, 24

95 Brenner, *Merchants and Revolution*, 444; Hexter, *King Pym*, 23

96 Pearl, *London and the Outbreak*, 260

97 Nagel, "The Militia of London," 79

98 Pearl, *London and the Outbreak*, 260; "Ordinance for raising Forces in and about London," House of Lords Journal Volume 5: 12 April 1643, British History Online, https://www.british-history.ac.uk/lords-jrnl/vol5/pp714-716#p31 Accessed 17 March 2020

Ireland had done,[99] and they were particularly intent on putting only "godly" officers in charge. Of the seven regiments raised, five godly men are known to have been appointed colonels, who were also captains in the Trained Bands. Two became Presbyterians, the other three would support the New Model Army. In the main they seem to have recruited apprentices.[100] Pym, however, continued to back the prickly Essex, whose prestige and position on the right flank of the middle group made him indispensable to keeping these centrists somewhat stable and unified.[101] The question of whether this new force could be used for fighting outside of London was apparently never made explicit, but Pym knew that the Subcommittee was telling volunteers that they would not be. It was a reasonable inference from Parliament's 12 April ordinance, which stated the "Auxiliaries to the Trained Bands" were "for Safeguarding the said City, Parliament, and Parts adjacent," but it did not prohibit the possibility.[102]

With the wind apparently in the radicals' sails, religious Independent leaders now began to create new gathered congregations, openly contravening the parish principle for the first time.[103] As the king's army was winning victories around the country, religious passions again broke out in London. "Catholic embassies whose chapels were open for worship to English Catholics were targeted in April and May 1641. On Easter Sunday, crowds of apprentices and others beset the Spanish and Portuguese embassies."[104] Both the Common Council and the House of Commons now authorized demolition of public structures considered to be superstitious or idolatrous.[105]

At the same time some further democratizing measures were introduced into the City government. The most important change was the wholesale removal of aldermen's deputies by the Common Council, an additional blow to the power of City royalists; the deputies were now required to be elected councilmen. Additionally, in an attempt to smooth the way for loans from the City to Parliament, two Acts dating back to Henry VII were repealed. One transferred elections for two City posts from the Court of Aldermen to Common Hall. As a result, the royalist City Chamberlain was immediately replaced.[106] But such relatively minor matters clearly indicated that democratization had all but come to a halt.

In May, five royalist aldermen were removed from their positions, one of whom had already left the city to join Charles. These were in addition to five aldermen, among many other wealthy men, then in jail for refusing

99 Brenner, *Merchants and Revolution*, 398

100 Nagel, "The Militia of London," 81-82

101 Hexter, *King Pym*, 113-114, 115-116

102 Nagel, "The Militia of London," 80; "Ordinance for raising Forces in and about London," British History Online

103 Brenner, *Merchants and Revolution*, 450

104 Lindley, *Civil War London*, 75

105 Brenner, *Merchants and Revolution*, 450-451

106 Pearl, *London and the Outbreak*, 247-248; Brenner, *Merchants and Revolution*, 451

to pay assessments. "'I have no more authority in the City than a Porter,'" Alderman Garway, one of those removed, reportedly complained.[107] At the end of the month, a royalist conspiracy led by MP Edmund Waller, authorized by Charles,[108] and involving some of the wealthiest citizens and former Common Councilors, was exposed.[109] (Suspicious MPs had engaged the royalists' servants as spies.)[110] It depended on royalists in the trained bands seizing arms and positions, as well as Pennington, Pym and their supporters, and opening the City gates to a force of 3,000 to be sent by the king.[111] Close after Waller's treachery had been spiked came news of Charles' negotiations to enlist the Catholic rebels in Ireland on his side.[112]

Together, these events changed the political situation in London. The king had very nearly struck a devastating blow from within the city itself. Parliament overwhelmingly passed a new Vow and Covenant it had previously rejected: "to support the forces raised in defence of Parliament against those raised by the King, 'so long as the Papists now in open war against the Parliament shall by force of arms be protected from the justice thereof.'"[113] No longer was there any mention of "'defence of the king's person and authority.'" "Liberty of the Subject" was thereby given more prominence by being solely linked with "Preservation of the true Protestant Religion." A more stringent censorship law was also enacted.[114] In the renewed militantly religious atmosphere, the House of Lords finally approved the creation of an Assembly of Divines to begin work on a new national church.[115] Aside from the suppression of the conspirators, these measures by themselves were hardly sufficient against what was shortly to become "the greatest military emergency of the war..."[116] But the seriousness of the situation was beginning to be felt in Parliament, and also London. Fanned by Puritan clergy, anti-monarchism was becoming ever more overt in the summer of 1643.[117]

And yet, a dangerous pro-royalist minority still existed in the City. During the spring and summer, the East India Company outright refused

107 Pearl, *London and the Outbreak*, 265-266 and fn. 120; Roy, "A Cavalier View of London in the Civil War," 157

108 Johnson, "Disintegration of the Parliamentarian War Effort," 90; Roy, "A Cavalier View of London in the Civil War," 160; Gardiner, *Great Civil War* Vol. I, 172-173

109 Pearl, *London and the Outbreak*, 265-266; Johnson, "Disintegration of the Parliamentarian War Effort," 90. His name is incorrectly given as "Edward" Waller in Pearl's text, but not the Index.

110 Roy, "A Cavalier View of London," 161

111 Gardiner, *Great Civil War* Vol. I, 171-172

112 Gardiner, *Great Civil War* Vol. I, 173; Johnson, "Disintegration of the Parliamentarian War Effort," 90-91

113 Gardiner, *Great Civil War* Vol. I, 173-174; "June 1643: The Covenant to be taken by the whole Kingdom," Acts and Ordinances of the Interregnum, 1642-1660, British History Online, https://www.british-history.ac.uk/no-series/acts-ordinances-interregnum/pp175-176 Accessed September 12, 2019

114 Johnson, "Disintegration of the Parliamentarian War Effort," 91; Gardiner, *Great Civil War* Vol. I, 174

115 Gardiner, *Great Civil War* Vol. I, 174

116 Brenner, *Merchants and Revolution*, 450

117 Hexter, *King Pym*, 105-106; Brenner, *Merchants and Revolution*, 444-445

"Parliament's direct order to lend ordnance to the City militia committee..."[118] Before fleeing to Oxford early in 1643, the Company's Master, Sir Nicholas Crispe, "courtier-merchant, customs farmer, African slaver... continued active in London politics even while he helped organise [royalist] cavalry recruitment..."[119] Resistance to Pennington's regime was increased by the high taxes and the proliferation of fees charged. As a security measure, passes into and out of the City now cost two shillings. His attacks on such Puritan fixations as idolatry and sport did not help the regime's popularity,[120] as would also be the case during Cromwell's Protectorate. Since the previous September stage plays had been banned by Parliament.[121]

Conservative power in the London government was strong enough to block any more loans to Parliament or provide money to pay for additional troops. It was pro-peace and anti-tax, and drew its support in the first instance from the monopoly trading companies. Able to rally support from London's population around these issues the counter-revolutionary royalist opposition remained a grave threat to the new regime. In addition there was the unpredictable possibility that the king might return. These factors caused many on the Common Council to remain cautious in their pronouncements and actions, and to favor an accommodation with the king if at all possible.[122]

As reaction grew, Pennington was increasingly unable to represent the policies of radical Independency as the position of the municipal government. Instead, he and his supporters were forced to create *ad hoc* nongovernmental organizations such as the Subcommittee of Volunteers, meeting in Salters' Hall, and the Committee for the General Rising, created in July.[123] Despite their apparent strength, power was slipping away from the Independents.

The leading London radicals, Independents and Atlantic merchants of the war party, were in a delicate political position. Unlike Pym and the middle group, they were republican or semi-republican in outlook, and demanded abolition of episcopacy. They realized that achievement of these goals meant continuation of the revolution by the London citizens' movement against those moderates who looked for some kind of vague compromise with the king. But as they themselves were wealthy men they understood the risk of the lower classes getting out of hand. To maintain control over the people while engaging them against the enemy was the tricky task, to a greater or lesser degree, of the entire parliamentary London leadership, Independent or Presbyterian, but especially the former. Pym and the moderates had, in a

118 Brenner, *Merchants and Revolution*, 451, 688; Pearl, *London and the Outbreak*, 265-267, 273-274

119 Roy, "A Cavalier View of London in the Civil War," 155

120 Pearl, *London and the Outbreak*, 261-262

121 "Order for Stage-plays to cease," House of Lords Journal Volume 5: 2 September 1642, British History Online, https://www.british-history.ac.uk/lords-jrnl/vol5/pp334-337#p59 Accessed August 30, 2020

122 Brenner, *Merchants and Revolution*, 435-436

123 Pearl, *London and the Outbreak*, 250-251

sense, solved this problem for themselves by seeking only a reduction in the monarchy's powers, however utopian that proved to be; they had no desire to further stir up the people.

The Atlantic merchants were among the most politically radical (outside of the religious sectaries) of Parliament's supporters, and they were prepared to take the greatest risks because they stood to make the greatest gains, economically and politically.[124] Thus their attempts to implement, first the Irish expedition, and then their own army to fight the king with their own resources, and largely on their own authority. Their day would come with the establishment of the Commonwealth in 1649. Meanwhile, they lacked the clarity or the strength, or both, to implement a revolutionary dictatorship of the bourgeoisie of the Jacobin type; or were not prepared to risk putting the people into power. Democracy had definite limits for these men as would soon be shown. As a result, most of them "would end up in the less-radical wing of political independency..."[125] thereby betraying their middling class followers. Their failure to politically mobilize the citizens to fully suppress royalism, or to neutralize conciliationist sentiment, undermined the revolutionary forces in the City. Only once, when compelled by circumstances at the most critical point, would they do so.

Differences in the London leadership

The political difficulties caused by the City merchant leaders' adherence to the gentry in Parliament contributed to a dispute that broke out between radical activists on the officially sanctioned Subcommittee of Volunteers at Salters' Hall and the Militia Committee. The Subcommittee proposed a voluntary collection to support the new regiments, and the members expected to appoint the officers themselves. "They not only impugned the management of the war, but claimed powers to levy men to fight on their sole authority, without reference to the Committee of the Militia."[126] These claims were denied by the Committee, "a body that could hardly be accused of wavering in its support of Pym and the middle group of the Commons."[127] Despite Independent leaders of the City and Militia Committee having secured Parliament's authorization for the Subcommittee, men like Pennington, Mainwaring, Fowke, John Warner, Towse and Andrewes were not going to allow activists, probably of lesser status and even more radical than themselves, to control an armed force on their own.[128]

The argument was referred to the Common Council, a more conservative body, whose middle group and peace party members were both opposed to the idea of a separate radical military force. The Council must have also been aghast at the Subcommittee's intention to extend their scope to the suburbs

124 Brenner, *Merchants and Revolution*, 454-455

125 Brenner, *Merchants and Revolution*, 400

126 Pearl, *London and the Outbreak*, 268; Nagel, "The Militia of London," 82

127 Pearl, *London and the Outbreak*, 267

128 Brenner, *Merchants and Revolution*, 453

where some of the most radical artisan and poorest manufacturing workers lived.[129] The April Ordinance creating the Subcommittee had explicitly stated that men could be raised "within the said City and Liberties thereof, as also within the Parishes and Places adjacent...," but the moderate parliamentarians evidently blocked with the peace party in the Council to successfully back the Militia Committee. As something of a sop, they offered to elect seven radical members of the Subcommittee to it. This would tend to fuse the two committees together. The addition of six more members, including Mayor Pennington, added simultaneously, would further dilute the radicals' vote. The total membership of the Militia Committee was thus brought to thirty. This solution was then presented to Parliament by a peace party alderman on behalf of the official City government, with all of the implied criticisms stripped out, and with a demand to control the suburban militias added in.[130] This victory for the City moderates, enabled by leading London Independents, exposed the limits of the latter's political tolerance,[131] and thereby curbed the House of Commons' own militant left wing. Reaction was hitting its stride.

129 Pearl, *London and the Outbreak*, 40-41

130 Pearl, *London and the Outbreak*, 267-269; Brenner, *Merchants and Revolution*, 455; Nagel, "The Militia of London," 82-83

131 Brenner, *Merchants and Revolution*, 455-456

16) THE CRISIS OF THE REVOLUTION (Summer, 1643)

> *The parliamentarian party which had gone to war against the King in 1642 was in essence a coalition...the majority of the parliamentarian gentry [believed] that the war was fought for limited goals, mainly political and constitutional, but also including a further moderate reformation of the Church, leaving the essential framework of government and society intact. That of the minority for whom Pride was the obedient agent was that it was fought for a total and complete reconstruction of Church and State, in the interest of "Godly Reformation" and (for some) social justice, to achieve which all measures, even revolution, were justified.*
>
> ~David Underdown[1]

One of the greatest political crises of the entire war was now rapidly approaching. Due to the deteriorating military situation, the cause of Parliament, and with it the revolution, suddenly appeared all but doomed. This not only brought the conflict between the war and peace parties to a head, but severely strained the merchants' war party alliance with the gentry middle group.

The July Crisis

In early July, Fairfax's army suffered a crushing defeat against a far superior enemy in the north. Two weeks later, despite some earlier victories in the west, Sir William Waller's army suffered the same fate. Parliamentary losses included "the populace counties of Devon, Dorset, Gloucester, Somerset, and Wiltshire, with large parts of Hampshire and Berkshire..." Also lost were the West Riding of Yorkshire, Derbyshire and Lincoln, and Hull was under siege.[2] While conflicting authorities in the parliamentary command structure,[3] and in particular some outright betrayals,[4] contributed to the situation, the fault for this chiefly lay with the House of Commons. During the first half of 1643 Parliament failed to provide its armies with pay and supplies that it needed to be effective, despite repeated pleas from its generals.[5] The military crisis gave the Peace party new life, and increased the polarization within and between Parliament and the City, straining it to the breaking point.

> Following a series of disastrous defeats of the parliamentary army under the earl of Essex and some spectacular revelations concerning Essex's own equivocal attitude toward the Civil War struggle, war-party elements in both Parliament and the City began openly to advocate Essex's dismissal

1 *Pride's Purge*, 7

2 Hexter, *King Pym*, 128

3 Johnson, "Disintegration of the Parliamentarian War Effort," 137-138, 165-168; Gardiner, *Great Civil War* Vol. I, 156-157

4 Johnson, "Disintegration of the Parliamentarian War Effort," 11-12, 54, 97, 131; Gardiner, *Great Civil War* Vol. I, 122, 164-165, 186-188

5 Hexter, *King Pym*, 108-109 fn. 18; Johnson, "Disintegration of the Parliamentarian War Effort," 87-89, 141, 157-160; Kennedy, *The English Revolution*, 23

> from the supreme command and his replacement by the godly general Sir William Waller.[6]

Fearful for the safety of London, moderates joined the radicals in an official City government petition to Parliament on 18 July 1643 to put all forces in the greater London area under the command of its own Militia Committee, overseen by the two Houses. According to Hexter,

> This apparently innocuous request concealed an implied threat: that unless the Houses removed the Earl of Essex from all part in control of the London forces they could not hope for support from the City in this hour of adversity.[7]

This is surely an overstatement. Although Parliament was dependent on the City for financial support, the Lord Mayor and Common Council were no more anxious for a break with Parliament than it was with them. In the military and political crisis, radical elements in and out of London's government were both willing and able to leverage the revolution's extraordinary power to *pressure* the House of Commons for its demands, but this was the most it could do. All factions in the Common Council were constrained by their political support for Parliament; it was hardly about to abandon Parliament now.

One of the radicals' demands was to create an independent military force to provide for an aggressive military crusade against the king. An unofficial petition with 20,000 signatures was presented to the Commons two days after the official City petition, calling for an independent "committee for a general rising." It was to be made up of MPs to organize a 10,000-man volunteer citizen army not responsible to Essex, who would appoint a commander-in-chief, all officers and local subcommittees on their own authority. The motivation provided was "'so the fullness of their Commission may encourage the whole nation as one man...with all cheerfulness and vigour to join themselves with us for the speedy ending of this destructive war.'"[8] A public notice advertising the petition's availability for signatures had quite a different tone: "'...for raising the whole people of the land as one man, against those Popish blood-thirsty forces raised, to enslave and destroy us, and our posterity.'"[9] In this can be seen the necessary pandering to the gentry by the Puritan leadership. War party radicals in the Commons, including Isaac Pennington and Sir Henry Marten, were specifically named as candidates for the new committee.[10] Those specified included "ten future Commonwealth-men [Independents], seven future nominees to the High Court of Justice that tried the King, and two future regicides."[11] Pym "had to tread carefully in handling any offers from the city, for the lord general's army depended for

6 Brenner, *Merchants and Revolution*, 456; Hexter, *King Pym*, 117-121

7 Hexter, *King Pym*, 122-123

8 Pearl, *London and the Outbreak*, 269-270

9 Pearl, *London and the Outbreak*, 270 fn. 138

10 Pearl, *London and the Outbreak*, 270

11 Hexter, *King Pym*, 123; Brenner, *Merchants and Revolution*, 457

its pay and supplies on the wholehearted support of the citizens."[12] Given the military crisis, the Commons overlooked the effrontery of being told whom to assign, and agreed to the formation of the new committee.

Near the end of July, Sir William Waller returned to London to be greeted by masses of people as a hero. The same day, at a meeting organized by Pennington with Henry Marten's participation, the Presbyterian general was elected Commander-in-Chief of the new committee's yet-to-be-acquired army. But Parliament, at the behest of the Militia Committee which now had authority over all City forces, instead only appointed Waller to command of those forces.[13] He and the Committee for the General Rising were thereby kept under the Militia Committee's control, although outside of Essex's military chain of command.[14] Parliament also transferred responsibility for the Tower to the Lord Mayor and sheriffs of London.[15] Added to its own 19 regiments of infantry and two of cavalry, the City government was now a substantial power unto itself.[16]

Caught between the pressures of the king's victorious armies, the London government's demands, and the radicals' confrontational agitation, Parliament, led by Pym, finally began to take action to reinforce and supply Essex's army with men and money.[17] In late July the Commons approved the Excise (sales tax) Ordinance, which had failed to pass the previous April.[18] In early August they easily renewed the weekly assessment.[19]

Although the Committee for the General Rising was completely filled by war-party MPs, including Pennington, in close coordination with the Militia Committee, the effort proved a dead end.[20] Pym and company, busy building up Essex and his army,[21] gave lip service to it, while they actively worked to undermine it.[22] The middle group in Parliament, as well as its

12 Glow, "The Methods of Moderation," 376

13 "London Forces," House of Commons Journal Volume 3: 29 July 1643, British History Online, https://www.british-history.ac.uk/commons-jrnl/vol3/pp186-187#h3-0016 Accessed 10 October 2021

14 Pearl, *London and the Outbreak*, 271; Glow, "The Methods of Moderation," 379-380

15 Gardiner, *Great Civil War* Vol. I, 212; Johnson, "Disintegration of the Parliamentarian War Effort," 125. Johnson misconstrues the impact of the Committee for a General Rising by failing to mention William Waller's subordination to the Militia Committee.

16 Nagel, "The Militia of London," 114

17 "Army Affairs," House of Commons Journal Volume 3: 24 July 1643, British History Online, https://www.british-history.ac.uk/commons-jrnl/vol3/pp179-181#p23 Accessed February 27, 2020

18 Hexter, *King Pym*, 25 and fn. 61; "Raising Money," House of Commons Journal Volume 3: 16 May 1643, British History Online, https://www.british-history.ac.uk/commons-jrnl/vol3/pp87-88#p14 Accessed February 27, 2020; "Ordinance for [Printing] the Excise," House of Lords Journal Volume 6: 22 July 1643, British History Online, https://www.british-history.ac.uk/lords-jrnl/vol6/pp144-146#p64 Accessed February 27, 2020

19 Hexter, *King Pym*, 134; "Ordinance for raising Money for the Army, by a Weekly Assessment," House of Lords Journal Volume 6: 3 August 1643, British History Online, https://www.british-history.ac.uk/lords-jrnl/vol6/pp163-170#h3-0014 Accessed September 12, 2019

20 Pearl, *London and the Outbreak*, 272-273; Brenner, *Merchants and Revolution*, 457-459; Glow, "The Methods of Moderation," 379

21 Hexter, *King Pym*, 147

22 Glow, "The Methods of Moderation," 380; Manning, *English People*, 243

supporters in the City, did not trust the radicals on the new committee, and would have preferred to see the two committees merged.[23] Both competed for recruits, but because the Militia Committee had the financial backing of the City government it could offer more attractive terms. Forced to depend on purely voluntary contributions, the Committee for a General Rising was only able to offer promises of future pay. Partly for this reason, in its first week the Committee made only a small number of enlistments to the new army.[24]

Pym meanwhile worked diligently to reconcile the London government and General Essex. He was instrumental in getting the Common Council to send a politically mixed delegation to visit Essex on 1 August, to assure the earl of their support.[25] With such regressive opposition to the radicals' efforts nothing could be accomplished *unless there had been a new upsurge by the populace.* The radicals themselves had pointed to "'the affections of the people...from all quarters to rise and appear in considerable bodies'" for Parliament in their Petition and Remonstrance the previous March.[26] Except for the public reception of Sir William Waller and the General Rising petition however, the radicals appear to have done little or nothing to organize or prepare for any such mass political mobilization. Their failure to do so substantially undermined their recruiting efforts.[27] Before the end of the month, Pym managed to broker a compromise agreement wherein the City's forces joined Essex to relieve the siege of Gloucester, but under the command of their own Militia Committee officers.[28]

Whatever its merits might have been, the City bourgeois radicals' attempts to form a separate military force under their own command stood in contradiction to their *political* unity with the gentry in Parliament. Their July petition to the Commons had once again implicitly acknowledged Parliament's leadership, and their inability to recruit in the summer of 1643 was in stark contrast to the outpouring of volunteers a year earlier. Without doubt, the lack of action by Essex's army; the confusion sown by Parliament's increasingly desperate attempts to keep negotiations alive; the slow pace of its war preparations; the military successes of the royalists; as well as the imposition of new taxes and other unpopular measures, all contributed to an uncertainty and disorientation on the part of the "well-affected" in the London population. The Scottish commissioner Robert Baillie wrote of the "'horrible fears and confusion in the city; the king everywhere victorious.'"[29]

23 Pearl, *London and the Outbreak*, 271-272

24 Hexter, *King Pym*, 126-127; Glow, "The Methods of Moderation," 379; Pearl, *London and the Outbreak*, 272-273

25 Glow, "The Methods of Moderation," 379; Pearl, *London and the Outbreak*, 272

26 Brenner, *Merchants and Revolution*, 446-447

27 Brenner, *Merchants and Revolution*, 447

28 Johnson, "Disintegration of the Parliamentarian War Effort," 190; "Ordinance for Relief of Gloucester," House of Lords Journal Volume 6: 23 August 1643, British History Online, https://www.british-history.ac.uk/lords-jrnl/vol6/p194#p21 Accessed January 16, 2020. Johnson is appalled by the autonomy given to London's revolutionary militia.

29 Johnson, "Disintegration of the Parliamentarian War Effort," 173

The reticence of the people to enlist in the summer of 1643 was in good part a consequence of their tight political attachment to the vacillating Parliament, an attachment cemented by the radicals themselves. A godly army on Parliament's behalf under these conditions, without Parliament's active support, was not going to succeed.

To counteract these influences, the radical leadership would have had to politically break with Parliament. They would have had to independently prepare their "more humble followers in the City and the suburbs"[30] to mobilize against *both* the centrists and peace party as obstacles to a serious fight against the royalists — that is, to counterpose their own leadership to Parliament's. Such a step might plausibly have succeeded given the military crisis in July, but would of course have risked unleashing the people in a far more thoroughgoing revolution.

London saves the Commons from itself

Such a prospect threatened to be forced on London's leaders as the situation continued to deteriorate. News received on 1 August that Bristol, a major port in western England, had fallen after heavy fighting to the royalists, increased the mood of pessimism. On 4 August, the Lords passed a series of propositions to be put to the king in hopes of forestalling a vengeful conquest of London by the Cavalier army. The proposals amounted to an abject surrender: among other concessions, all forts, ports and armories were to be returned to Charles' control. "Hull and Plymouth, Portsmouth, and the Tower of London itself would be his without striking a blow..."[31] Sent to the Commons next day, a Saturday, hot debate immediately erupted as the war party argued strenuously to reject the propositions out of hand. But by 29 votes the House elected to consider them, and when it got late, to continue the debate on the following Monday.

The Lords' propositions posed the question of the revolution's survival point-blank. For if the House of Commons voted *not* to preserve its own cause, how was the revolution to go forward? It was Parliament that had provided the legal cover and authority for the revolution in 1641-1642 that drove out the king. If the Commons pulled out now, the alliance of the gentry and City merchants would be shattered. London would be left on its own, politically and militarily.

The situation very nearly prefigured the split to come in December, 1648. The Independent leadership of the victorious New Model Army, along with the minority of Independent MPs, under extreme pressure from the Army ranks, purged the bulk of the gentry from the Commons.[32] The Rump Parliament then abolished the monarchy and House of Lords, establishing the Commonwealth, a republic by another name.

30 Pearl, *London and the Outbreak*, 274

31 Gardiner, *Great Civil War* Vol. I, 215; Hexter, *King Pym*, 143

32 Known as "Pride's Purge," for Colonel Thomas Pride who was in charge of carrying it out.

Following the vote in the Commons, Mayor Isaac Pennington immediately called an emergency Common Council meeting. The middle group joined with the radicals to petition the Commons to reject the peace propositions to the king.[33] They attached a draft ordinance for impressing men to the petition, whose "speedy passing" they urged "for our and your Defence…"[34]

The demand for new troops had been first raised by Pennington and "'divers citizens'" in May, and had been part of the general rising petition in July.[35] As originally conceived by the radicals, it was to be a voluntary enterprise in order to keep it independent and under their own control. Only when they failed to recruit in the short period before the critical vote in the Commons did they encourage Parliament to pass an ordinance which had the force of law. Already, on 1 August, the Commons had ordered an ordinance for compulsory enlistment be prepared for debate.[36] The impressment measure was akin to the Jacobin *levé en masse* for the defense of the French Republic.

Whereas up to this point it was the Commons gentry who had been the senior partner in the alliance with London's Puritan merchants and clergy, at this watershed moment it was the City leaders who were propelled to the forefront. That same Sunday, Puritan "pulpits rang"[37] with exhortations against the peace propositions, and leaflets were posted calling on citizens to arrive at Parliament first thing Monday morning. For the first and only time since February 1642, the Puritan merchant leadership mobilized their base of supporters for direct agitation at Parliament.

On Monday, 7 August, five thousand unarmed men showed up at Parliament demanding rejection of the propositions for peace. Mayor Pennington took his seat in the House of Commons, and the London government's petition was presented by a group of aldermen and councilmen. The House of Lords was outraged by the presence of the citizens creating a ruckus in Parliament Yard. They immediately voted to condemn the demonstration and adjourn.[38] They informed the Commons that they would not reconvene until the tumult was ended. The Lords were jeered, but the demonstrators made no attempt to prevent them from leaving.[39]

33 Johnson, "Disintegration of the Parliamentarian War Effort," 119; Pearl, London and the Outbreak, 272 and fn. 145

34 "A Petition of the City of London against Propositions Kent from the Lords, Aug. 7," Rushworth Historical Collections: July-December 1643, British History Online, https://www.british-history.ac.uk/rushworth-papers/vol5/pp341-387#h2-0007 Accessed September 9, 2019; Johnson, "Disintegration of the Parliamentarian War Effort," 121

35 Pearl, *London and the Outbreak*, 269, 270

36 Glow, "The Methods of Moderation," 379; "Raising Soldiers," House of Commons Journal Volume 3: 1 August 1643, British History Online, https://www.british-history.ac.uk/commons-jrnl/vol3/pp189-190#p34 Accessed March 4, 2020

37 Gardiner, *Great Civil War* Vol. I, 217

38 "Multitudes coming down to the House, the Lords resolve to adjourn," House of Lords Journal Volume 6: 7 August 1643, British History Online, https://www.british-history.ac.uk/lords-jrnl/vol6/p172#h3-0006 Accessed December 26, 2019

39 Gardiner, *Great Civil War* Vol. 1, 218; Hexter, *King Pym*, 145

The threat by the Lords was a minor nuisance, since it technically meant no legislation could be passed until they again took their seats. Far more important was the difficult political situation at this precarious instant. Pym was firmly opposed to the peace proposals, but he was also opposed to putting the more radical war party into power, which the people's appearance threatened to do. He obviously could not condemn them, but neither could he openly condone action by the masses to impose their program on Parliament, even if he wished to. To side with the people *against* Parliament would be to split with the Lords and half the remaining MPs; all his work toward unity would be ruined. This left him without any method of affecting the outcome, forcing him to *de facto* rely on Pennington and the City radicals to influence events.

Pennington was also in an odd, and dangerous, situation. As the foremost Puritan leader in and out of the Commons since 1640, he was quite familiar with the men he was dealing with there. Like Pym, he was determined to prevent a surrender to the king, and to preserve the cause of Parliament. But what if he couldn't? There were rumors that he intended to arrest the leaders of the peace party, but opted first to try to pressure the House of Commons (with, some thought, Pym's covert support).[40] The diary of Sir Simonds D'Ewes is the sole source for this allegation, but as D'Ewes himself was now for peace his bias was obvious.[41]

Nonetheless it may have been true. For if Parliament gave up on the war, the only way to continue it would be for the London Puritan government itself to assume leadership of the national war effort. The question which then loomed was whether the City leadership was, in fact, prepared to lead if the House of Commons defaulted. It would doubtless require a more stringent, revolutionary dictatorship in the City, one that might well carry out a purge of the Commons and/or the London government, and likely require a more intense political mobilization of the citizenry as well: in short, a Jacobin type of regime.

How far men like Pennington, John Venn, Randall Mainwaring, Maurice Thomson, Richard Shute, Henry Marten and Oliver Cromwell, among others, were prepared to go in this direction is, of course, unknown. But it is not beyond the realm of possibility that they, leading figures of the City revolution and war party, representing the free-trade merchant interest, along with other allies, could have attempted to lead a revolutionary regime, however reluctant they may have been to have such a role thrust upon them. The mere fact of the demonstration at Parliament on 7 August; the subsequent suppression of demonstrators for peace; and the substantial and politically dedicated forces at the London Militia Committee's disposal; show that this

40 Pearl, *London and the Outbreak*, 272 and fn. 145; Johnson, "Disintegration of the Parliamentarian War Effort," 122

41 Gardiner, *Great Civil War* Vol. I, 217; Johnson, "Disintegration of the Parliamentarian War Effort," 2, 119-120. Gardiner hedges his statement: "Unless D'Ewes was misinformed…," and Johnson appends a consideration titled "Sir Simonds D'Ewes — Can We Believe Him?"

was not a fantasy, despite the many uncertainties in the adverse situation.[42]

To appease the Lords and peace party the Commons voted a mild resolution that Mayor Pennington should endeavor to prevent tumults at Parliament; this he promised to do. On a motion by the war party they then proceeded to a direct vote on the peace proposals without any more debate. In spite of all their efforts, the proposals to the king were passed by the narrowest of margins, 81-79. But an opposing member objected that the vote was not accurate, and "the House not being satisfied with the Report of the Tellers" agreed to take a second vote. This time the peace proposals were defeated 88-81.[43] The London Puritan merchant leadership had rescued the revolution, and preserved its partnership with the Commons gentry, though it took the risky step of marshaling the people to do so. This placed Pym and the middle group in control of events once more, and he immediately began pushing the House to make good on its promises to reinforce the army under Essex.[44]

The vote "raised the alarming possibility that the house of peers might abandon the cause altogether."[45] The MPs passed a resolution to the Lords, urging them not to abandon the struggle, and promising that "this House will do their utmost for their Defence, as well as for their own."[46] Even the fig leaf of a much-reduced House of Lords was considered preferable to their absence by the reluctant revolutionaries in the House of Commons. Despite this effort, "Seven Lords quickly left the capital, five of whom made their way to the king at Oxford."[47]

On 9 August a violent demonstration by women demanding peace, wearing white silk ribbons in their hats, took place in Westminster. There were 6,000 women, led by "a well-known royalist," Lady Brouncker, whose husband was a former gentleman of the privy chamber to Charles.[48] Some men "(including several disguised in women's clothes) were said to have been spotted inciting the women."[49] According to the testimony of participants, the demonstration had clearly been organized out of one or another Lord's house.[50]

42 Johnson claims the London government's petition "constituted a thinly veiled threat to take control of the war effort unless parliament rejected the Lords' propositions." "Disintegration of the Parliamentarian War Effort," 124. He describes the House of Commons as "menaced by the threat of a City backed political coup…" 172. More hysterically, that "mob rule prevailed." 231

43 "Propositions to the King," House of Commons Journal Volume 3: 7 August 1643, British History Online, https://www.british-history.ac.uk/commons-jrnl/vol3/pp196-198#h3-0013 Accessed November 6, 2019; Johnson, "Disintegration of the Parliamentarian War Effort," 129

44 Hexter, *King Pym*, 147

45 Johnson, "Disintegration of the Parliamentarian War Effort," 174

46 "Defence of the Kingdom," House of Commons Journal Volume 3: 7 August 1643, British History Online, https://www.british-history.ac.uk/commons-jrnl/vol3/pp196-198#p38 Accessed November 6, 2019

47 Johnson, "Disintegration of the Parliamentarian War Effort," 174-175; Gentles, "The London Peace Campaigns," 149-150, 158

48 Gentles, "The London Peace Campaigns," 155

49 Lindley, *Civil War London*, 351

50 Gentles, "The London Peace Campaigns," 156

The women presented a petition for peace,[51] but then refused to disperse. They attacked any passing man with short hair to pull it,[52] and beat on the door to the House of Commons for two hours, "vociferously demanding…'Give us those traitors who were against peace, that we may tear them to pieces! Give us that dog Pym!'"[53] and "crying out 'we will have peace presently and our King.'"[54]

The guards at Parliament shot blanks at the women, but the women responded by throwing stones and brickbats at the guards. When they had almost broken down the outer door to the Commons, Pym and other MPs sent for a troop of Waller's cavalry to disperse them, and the guards opened fire with live ammunition, killing two men. "The women at once rushed" at the horsemen, "calling them Waller's dogs, and attempted to tear the ribbons from their hats."[55] The troopers used the flats of their swords, but when the women persisted, they used their blades. The confrontation resulted in a few deaths, including a woman passerby, an unknown number of wounded, and hundreds of arrests.[56]

In the wake of their suppression, demonstrating the London government's control of the city, the House of Lords approved the impressment bill on 10 August;[57] Pym used it to supply men to the army of Essex. "…in spite of the great hardships suffered by much of the population, the decisive response of the parliament and City had the support of the majority of the citizens."[58] The war party Independents who had just saved the Commons from collapse were sidelined, solving Pym's problem of how to exclude the leftwing radicals from power. Thanks to the London leadership's undying support to Parliament, Pym had in effect broken with the war party by withholding open support from them, while retaining the allegiance of the peace party. Waller was removed from his command over the militia, and leadership of the war was consolidated under Essex and the House of Commons.[59]

London itself again came under threat later that month when Essex's army and the Trained Bands had gone to relieve the siege of Gloucester and were cut off from the city by the Cavaliers. They had to fight their way back, and it was not until after the day-long First Battle of Newbury in September

51 "The Womens [p]etition presented, Aug 9," Rushworth Historical Collections: July-December 1643, British History Online, https://www.british-history.ac.uk/rushworth-papers/vol5/pp341-387#p106 Accessed January 12, 2020

52 Gentles, "The London Peace Campaigns," 155

53 Gardiner, *Great Civil War* Vol. I, 218-219; Lindley, *Civil War London*, 351

54 Gentles, "The London Peace Campaigns," 155

55 Gardiner, *Great Civil War* Vol. I, 219

56 "The Womens Tumult at the House of Commons, Aug.7" [possibly misdated], Rushworth Historical Collections: July-December 1643, British History Online, https://www.british-history.ac.uk/rushworth-papers/vol5/pp341-387#p111 Accessed January 12, 2020; Gardiner, *Great Civil War* Vol. I, 219; Lindley, *Civil War London*, 352; Gentles, "The London Peace Campaigns," 155

57 Gentles, "The London Peace Campaigns," 156

58 Roy, "A Cavalier View of London in the Civil War," 170

59 Hexter, *King Pym*, 147

that they were able to return. "The royalists strained every sinew to deliver a knockout blow, one that would enable Charles to return to his capital in triumph."[60] The contemporary royalist historian Lord Clarendon credited the Trained Bands' infantry with standing their ground and forcing Prince Rupert's cavalry charge to "wheel about" before their pikes, saving the day.[61] The army was cheered by crowds on its return, and the victories refurbished the reputation of Essex as the savior of the cause.

Reaction conquers the City

But pessimism and defeatism grew.

> The peace party and the moderates were increasingly powerful on the aldermanic Bench and by August 1643 were beginning to win support even from a few members of the Militia Committee. Penington's radical associates included a number of the Militia Committee, a handful of Common Councilmen, a few Captains of the Trained Bands and some prominent City clergymen...[62]

These men were the heart of the Independent leadership in the City, though some nonofficial Atlantic merchants and London radicals were active as well.

The Committee for the General Rising was subverted by its failure to recruit, and finished when the Commons removed its funding. With Pym leading the charge against his long-time *bête noir*, Sir Henry Marten was sent to the Tower "ostensibly for insulting the King."[63]

> City radicalism never again (before the victory of the army in 1647) brought pressure to bear on Parliament and the City government with as much success as during the summer months of 1643. The failure of the Sub-Committee to achieve independent status and the election of Alderman Wollaston as Lord Mayor in the place of Penington removed the main props of the radical party. A Sub-Committee at Salters' Hall, Bread street, was still sitting in 1644, and still organizing radical petitions to Parliament, but the radicals were not able to make it independent of the Militia Committee; nor were they able to secure any foothold in the City government.[64]

As the military crisis receded so did the influence of the radicals and Atlantic merchants.[65] The Common Council, which the revolution had put into a dominant position with its own independent military force, ("...jesting Royalists called it the third House of Parliament"),[66] became more politically moderate as time went on. The Council got the better of the expanded Mi-

60 Johnson, "Disintegration of the Parliamentarian War Effort," 195

61 Manning, *English People*, 216; Nagel, "The Militia of London," 125-129; Hill, *Century*, 104; Firth, "London During the Civil War," 29

62 Pearl, *London and the Outbreak*, 250

63 Pearl, *London and the Outbreak*, 272-273; Hexter, *King Pym*, 148

64 Pearl, *London and the Outbreak*, 273

65 Brenner, *Merchants and Revolution*, 459

66 Hexter, *King Pym*, 107

litia Committee whose members were taken up with military and financial matters. The moderates who came to take over the City government, "would be likely to oppose at all costs a restitution of the *ancien régime*, for their personal fortunes were involved with those of Parliament; but they were unlikely to be the initiators of social revolution."[67]

> ...except in one critical respect: they wanted to complete the Puritan reformation of religious institutions. They were the primary beneficiaries of London's constitutional revolution of 1641-1642, although they were not, by and large, its chief creators.[68]

In the House of Commons, with the end of the First Civil War in mid-1646, the bulk of the middle group would now mostly bloc with the peace party.

Reaction conquered the London government a few years before it took hold in the Commons. The London Puritans elected in support of Parliament in January 1642 did not share a unified program or a single ideology, but rather a spectrum of Puritan thought on matters religious and political. And a substantial and wealthy royalist minority continued to exist in the City, which remained very incompletely suppressed. It was centrally entrenched in and supported by the pro-feudal merchants in the monopoly overseas trading companies, which Parliament had sanctioned if shaken down, and high livery company officers.[69] The most organized and radical Puritans, the Independents (and the even smaller Anabaptists), were themselves a minority, only episodically able to influence events. Compelled by their electoral orientation, they had to continuously struggle for their program in the City government as they did in the House of Commons; but the strong moderate and conservative presence in both was an insuperable obstacle. Not until 1647, when the radical troops of the New Model Army elected their own class representatives, known as Agitators, were these obstacles overcome, and the revolution carried through.

Isaac Pennington, the chief Independent leader in both arenas, also assumed the Lieutenancy of the Tower in July 1643 (which he held until the Self-Denying Ordinance of 1645). His replacement as Lord Mayor by a moderate in October 1643, however, consolidated a shift that led to a long rightward political slide in the City.[70] This reversal was due in no small part to the difficulties and dislocations caused by the war, which were left without remedy by the House of Commons' inability or refusal to act. Thus isolated, the Independents were slowly but steadily purged from municipal government posts, opening the way towards an eventual rapprochement between moderates, peace party and royalists.[71]

67 Pearl, *London and the Outbreak*, 273

68 Brenner, *Merchants and Revolution*, 461

69 Pearl, *London and the Outbreak*, 273-274

70 Pearl, *London and the Outbreak*, 274

71 Pearl, *London and the Outbreak*, 275

17) CONCLUSIONS

The historians who grabbed my teenage attention were serious academics confident that the stories they told and vehemently disputed mattered to the present. According to these stories, the English Revolution was an event of seismic proportions, at the epicentre of powerful social, economic and cultural forces which transformed the country from a medieval backwater into 'the first modern society.' ... But few historians denied that political revolution was one dimension of a larger set of historical changes which made us what we are today. ... In the 1980s this consensus position came under severe pressure...[which] was especially violent and decisive. ... What all revisionists agreed, however, was that there were no 'deeper' causes of the English Revolution (if indeed it could be called a 'revolution'): just contingencies and events which, almost by accident, disrupted a prevailing political consensus.

~Phil Withington[1]

M. Guizot deems it superfluous to mention that the subordination of the kingship to Parliament was its subordination to the rule of a class. ... He has just as little to say about Charles I's direct interference in free competition, which made England's trade and industry more and more impossible; or about his dependence upon Parliament, which because of his constant financial straits became the greater the more he sought to defy Parliament.

~Karl Marx[2]

Historical summary

Because of the long rule by the absolute monarchy, intensified by Louis XIV in the 17th century, the French Revolution of 1789 was an all-the-more explosive social reverse, with consequently sharp and distinct class lines. In England under the early Stuarts, however, the monarchs, dominant within the ruling feudal class thanks to their Tudor predecessors, were only able to aspire to such power as their French and Spanish counterparts possessed. The imposition of a parliamentary council by the Norman-derived nobility in the 13th century, and the effective abolition of serfdom in the first part of the 15th, blocked a true absolutism from developing, which allowed for the growth of domestic market relations, in part stimulated by the wool trade.

The century and a half between 1490 and 1640, when there was no large-scale warfare on English soil, provided the time needed for these relations to expand and capital to accumulate. Reactionary as he was, James I and VI was politically calculating, maintaining a certain stability based on this thriving economic sector and a state policy of peace. In the last few years of his reign economic depression hit England; serious opposition to his rule begins at

1 "Past v. Present," *London Review of Books*

2 "A Review of Guizot's Book 'Why Has the English Revolution Been Successful?,'" in *Marx and Engels On Britain*, 347

this time. Ideologically devoted to feudal tradition, Charles I succeeded his father in the middle of this muddle. Confronted with an unprecedented transformation in English (and European) history, Charles refused to recognize that the ground had shifted under his feet; the money interest was now infinitely more important to, indeed, dominated the national economy, as the economic depressions of the 1620s and '30s demonstrated all too well. Only the traditional *forms* of feudal political relations remained, hollowed out of any real social content. When the central contradiction between a capitalist economy and a feudal political system had spawned the twin crises in state and church, the king was left with only his courtiers, the bishops, and monopolists to support him.[3]

After a relatively brief struggle during the late 1620s, the majority of overseas company merchants abandoned any pretense of opposition, and became the most slavish supporters of the king.[4] This is hardly surprising as this social grouping benefited most from the protection of the old order, and stood to lose a great deal in a more open and competitive economy. They had learned the lesson of their impotent strike of 1628-1629 against the monarchy all too well (although a few became firm supporters of Parliament). But the hatred of domestic manufacturers for the companies' regulatory role, and the obstacle they presented to less exalted traders anxious to share in their outsize profits, created a deep antagonism that would break out in revolt at the first opportunity. That opportunity came with the opening of the colonial trade to the Americas.

The new Atlantic merchants, *arrivistes* from the middling class, wasted no time in seeking their fortunes, and making political alliances with Puritan holy men and aristocrats. As open opposition to Charles' reign grew, they were increasingly in the forefront, the most dedicated supporters and influencers of the House of Commons, boldly transgressing feudal social and political relations. Their vanguard role in commerce and military adventure abroad, and politics and religion at home, provided the English Revolution with the bourgeois leadership which Christopher Hill appears to have had such trouble identifying. By so doing they drew the bourgeois businessmen in the middle layers of the livery companies to active service in the new, revolutionary regime. The division between the monopoly and free-trade merchant groups, most thoroughly documented by Robert Brenner, explains the paradox posed by Tawney that the bourgeoisie was on both sides, even if the latter's conception was somewhat different.

Puritanism vs. Catholicism

The virulent antipathy to Catholicism by Puritans and active Protestants of all stripes must not be seen as equivalent to the dead-end interethnic and religious wars so prevalent in our contemporary, decaying era, particularly since the collapse of the Soviet Union. In 17th-century England,

3 Brenner, *Merchants and Revolution*, 691

4 Brenner, *Merchants and Revolution*, 314, 686-688

thoroughgoing Protestants were the heirs of the revolutionary Reformation of Luther and Calvin, and the target of the reactionary Counter-Reformation spearheaded by Rome. The import of the Vatican's crusade had been forcefully exemplified during Queen Mary's horrific time, and Elizabeth herself had been excommunicated, not once, but twice by the popes after coming to the throne. Forced to sit on the sidelines, English Protestants could only watch in fear as the Thirty Years' War ground on.[5]

Whereas Catholicism laid all the burden on the individual as a sinner with a constant need to repent, Calvin's doctrine of predestination relieved individuals from responsibility for their salvation, since "Only God knows his elect." Those whom God appeared to favor were the frugal, but assiduous, rich, "a spiritual aristocracy."[6] Calvin's audacious new discipline for the reform of society influenced the early Tudor Archbishop, Thomas Cranmer, author of the Book of Common Prayer, prompting much theological debate in the century between 1550 and 1650. This was the period when capitalism began its rapid ascendancy, particularly in Holland and England. The bourgeois frontal assault on the feudal order, integrated with and overlorded by the Catholic Church for the previous millennium, necessarily failed to distinguish between these because they were in fact indistinguishable. Only once feudalism had decisively given way to capitalism, and the landowners had been reconciled to the political rule of the bourgeoisie, could any form of equal tolerance for Catholics be envisaged.

The Protestant attack was a major advance for the liberation of the masses despite itself being expressed and justified in religious terms. A more flexible theology than Catholic dogma, it grew up along with the development of urban society.[7] For some Puritans in the early 17th century, such as John Corbet, "The puritan was responsible for his own salvation,"[8] an argument that went beyond Calvin's ideology of predestination. The topic was thus subjected to extensive, often tortured, disputes, along with other religious issues. Puritanism was especially popular with the petty and middle bourgeoisie because it preached the freedom to individually pursue their economic betterment and religious beliefs. This enormously extended the measure of control they had over their own lives, freeing them from the tyranny of the priest and the terrors of hell. "...this insistence that a well-considered strong conviction overrode everything else had a great liberating force,"[9] and "elevated the self-respect of his congregation."[10] This is likely why Calvinism did not hold sway very long after the revolution: freedom for the lower classes included freedom of conscience; and once it was accepted that free-trade merchants or capitalist manufacturers could become rich through their own

5 Hibbard, "Early Stuart Catholicism," 31; Clifton, "The Popular Fear of Catholics during the English Revolution," 43

6 Hill, *World*, 153

7 Hill, "Protestantism and the Rise of Capitalism," 35-36

8 Manning, "The Godly People," 106

9 Hill, "Protestantism and the Rise of Capitalism," 23, 27; *World*, 154

10 Hill, "Henrician Reformation," 44

efforts, what need was there for God's blessing? But for a time it suited them to say their gaining wealth was God's work.[11] The complete stripping away of religious domination and obfuscation, resulting in the triumph of bourgeois secularism, would first be attempted by the Leveller party in the latter 1640s. Eventually, after the setback of the Restoration of Charles II, secularism would be confirmed in its essentials by the Revolution of 1688.

A bourgeois revolution from below

Without London there would have been no civil war and no eventual parliamentarian victory."[12] The events in London from 1640 to 1643 expose the empty claims of rightwing Revisionist historians as absurd frauds. They demonstrate beyond any doubt the existence of a pro-democratic social movement composed of tens of thousands who were neither rich nor poor, though some portion of the poor also followed it some of the time. The petty bourgeois citizens' movement was at least partially organized by, and closely responsive to, the new City leaders, colonial merchants and guild members, along with Puritan clergy.

> ...although there was a large element of spontaneous protest and social revolt, it was not the upsurge of a desperate population. Its day to day tactics (but not its long-term strategy) bore all the signs of careful planning and resolute leadership...[13]

This movement intervened at decisive moments to pressure the House of Commons or, at moments of greatest threat, to protect its members with arms in hand. (From this comes the second amendment to the U.S. Constitution: both Alexander Hamilton and James Madison argued that the militias — "citizens with arms" — were the guarantee of the people's liberties, *even from* the federal government if necessary.)[14] Without the armed support of the London masses, along with the Trained Bands who went over to them, under Puritan (Presbyterian, Independent, Anabaptist) and sectarian leadership, the Commons did not have the power to overcome the king.

Thus it was "the awakened petty-bourgeois masses, who had become the most important force of the revolution."[15] The power and revolutionary nature of the London citizens' movement had been badly underestimated, or simply ignored, by Whig and even Marxian historians in large part due to their singular focus on the admittedly novel role of the House of Commons. The fact that the gentry, as represented by the MPs in the Long Parliament, was seriously divided was used to attack the Marxist position by claiming that the Civil War was nothing more than an intra-ruling class squabble, not unlike the earlier War of the Roses, if perhaps with loftier phrases. "...Revi-

11 Hill, "Protestantism and the Rise of Capitalism," 32-33

12 Lindley, *Civil War London*, 404

13 Pearl, *London and the Outbreak*, 279

14 *The Federalist Papers* #29, #46 (New York: Mentor Books, 1962), 185, 299

15 Trotsky, "Two Traditions: The Great Rebellion and Chartism," 112

sionists insisted that most actors in the period 1603 to 1640 were not seeking fundamentally to change the system."[16] In reference to the consciousness of the gentry this was true enough; but a large number of them *were* seeking to make changes which they did not consider revolutionary, to say nothing of the urban Puritan masses which did. The weakness in Hill's and Tawney's gentry argument was thereby exploited by conservative and Revisionist historians, who were able to gain credence for their attacks on what *they* claimed was the orthodox Marxist view.

In place of any sort of class struggle or progressive trajectory, many if not most Revisionists came to embrace either a theory of tensions between local and central government authorities,[17] or alternatively, a war of religion,[18] as adequate explanations. A number were eventually forced to come to grips with such issues as "Court Catholicism, ecclesiastical Arminianism, and popular fear of popery," though they mainly strained to misinterpret these in various ways.[19] While perhaps providing useful research via local or regional studies, the Revisionist onslaught was squarely aimed at denying, indeed burying, the revolutionary history of England.

The petty-bourgeois artisan and working class combination here played the same revolutionary role as its later historical analogue, the Sansculottes. It also had the active support of the sailors, who were military men. It was precisely reliance on the lower classes that caused large sections of the gentry and nobility to withdraw from the anti-absolutist struggle in favor of either the king or neutrality. The extraordinary breadth of anti-royalist sentiment, which united to build fortifications to protect London in 1642-1643, stretched across nearly all but the uppermost classes of the city. Likewise the enormous response of volunteers and money for the Parliamentary army in 1642; the London Trained Bands' heroism under competent leadership at Edgehill in 1642 and Newbury in 1643; and defense of the City at Turnham Green by Army troops, Bandsmen, and ordinary citizens; all demonstrated a *political* consciousness that was revolutionary in scope, however weighted down with religious notions it may seem to us today.

> To thousands of Englishmen, Puritanism was the very Gospel itself, the voice of God speaking to a careless generation. Those who believed this were ready to die rather than allow God's voice upon earth to be silenced. If the existing law was against it, let the law be broken. If Parliamentary majorities were against it, let them be silenced.[20]

16 Harris, "Revisiting the Causes of the English Civil War," 620

17 Zaller, "The Concept of Opposition," 215-216, 227, 228-229; "What Does the English Revolution Mean?," 626. This theory, known as "court vs. country," is most closely associated with Perez Zagorin. See, for example, his "The Court and the Country: A Note on Political Terminology in the Earlier Seventeenth Century," *The English Historical Review* 77, no. 303 (April 1962), https://www.jstor.org/stable/561547 Accessed July 15, 2019

18 Baskerville, "Puritans, Revisionists, and the English Revolution," 152-153; Zaller, "What Does the English Revolution Mean?," 628-629; Hirst, "Revisionisms and Early Stuart Studies," 611-612

19 Zaller, "What Does the English Revolution Mean?," 629-630

20 Gardiner, *Great Civil War* Vol. I, 31

"Godliness" was the rallying cry of the anti-feudal, anti-Catholic Church movement. Two hundred years later, John Brown among others was moved by no less an imperative.

Following the revolution in London the widespread disaffection of the peasantry broke out. Enclosures and manor records were destroyed, especially in the southeast. Yeoman farmers and tenants joined townsmen, occasionally led by a local gentleman, in seizing weapons caches all over the country for Parliament. The peasant uprisings in the countryside were only surface manifestations of the deep antipathy to the feudal state and church, upheld by so many of their landlords. While peasant opposition was certainly not uniform throughout the country, it helped to batter down feudal tradition, making recruitment to the king's army more difficult.

Revisionism: fabrications in service to counter-revolution

From the 1970s through the 1990s, Revisionist historians all strove to provide yeoman service to the capitalist ruling classes, which were hurriedly charging toward an intensified immiseration of the working populations in Britain and America. If they could discredit revolution as exaggerated or insignificant, it would reinforce an ideological justification for social reaction. "...nearly all the major positions were in place by the early 1980s, and as Tom Cogswell has pointed out, they achieved a rapid takeover of what one might term the commanding heights of textbook orthodoxy."[21]

The Revisionists' reactionary intent is revealed whereby

> The developments highlighted by Marxists are regarded as illusory, ambiguous or irrelevant, and at best as unproven assertions. Their efforts to trace long-term causes for the Civil War, rooted in economic and social shifts, have generally been rejected as deterministic or based on hindsight. And the designation of the resistance to the monarchy as "progressive" by both Whigs and Marxists is also discarded. In some versions it is the monarchy which is innovative... It was the Crown's opponents, especially in the House of Commons, who were "conservative," stubbornly clinging to outmoded customs and rights.[22]

These sorts of anti-Marxist, anti-democratic aspersions are hardly new, as Hill noted in 1950:

> A school of Roman Catholic propagandists, headed by Hilaire Belloc, has attempted a synthesis of a kind. They depict Charles I as trying to defend the people of England from the aggressive greed of a gang of wicked capitalists.[23]

Cust and Hughes continue:

21 Lake, "From Revisionist to Royalist History," 659

22 Richard Cust and Ann Hughes, "Introduction: after Revisionism," in *Conflict in Early Stuart England*, eds. Richard Cust and Ann Hughes (London: Longman Group, 1989), 3

23 Hill, "Historians on the Rise of British Capitalism," 309

> There is a particular tendency [by Revisionists] to take as true some of the more favourable perceptions of Charles and Laud. ... If revisionist historiography has attacked Whig interpretations as parliamentarian, we have come increasingly to regard revisionist accounts as echoes of seventeenth-century royalist views. ... Royalist accounts are also echoed in the emphasis on high politics and the relationships of great men at court as a sufficient explanation of events..."[24]

Revisionist dismissals of social analysis as "hindsight" — as if nothing new had been learnt in the ensuing four centuries — were merely a cover to rewrite history. At bottom, they were an attempt to refurbish the moral image of the feudal monarchy.

A mainstream centrist historian reviewing a 1977 collection of Revisionist essays by multiple authors found their claims false to the point of absurdity.[25]

> They dismiss, either overtly or covertly, all long-term social or sociopolitical developments and leave in their place what looks like a Clarendonian vision. ... Writing of the years following the Self-denying Ordinance, no less, he [Farnell] feels able to assert that "a group of peers organized and led the campaign against Charles I."[26]
>
> ...he [Christianson] maintains that, "for the purposes of this article, it suffices to extend those electoral ties...into the sitting of Parliament" and so proceeds to construct his thesis. With a methodology like that, who needs methodologies?[27]

The right-leaning, maverick American historian J. H. Hexter further deflated the Revisionists' "purely political" offerings:

> Now it is possible that in the early seventeenth century the men who opposed some of their king's actions were Livian republicans. It is also possible that they were defenders of an imaginary ancient English constitution. And it is even possible that they were Mahayana Buddhists. Unfortunately, on the evidence provided by Farnell it is not possible to tell which, if any, of the three they were. It is perhaps unnecessary here to chase further after the ephemeral phantasms of Farnell's overheated historical imagination.[28]
>
> It is surely significant that despite this abundance of the printed record none

24 Cust and Hughes, "Introduction: after Revisionism," 14-15

25 The essays in *The Journal of Modern History* 49, no. 4 (December 1977) included: James E. Farnell, "The Social and Intellectual Basis of London's Role in the English Civil Wars," http://www.jstor.org/stable/1875624 Accessed November 30, 2016; Paul Christianson, "The Peers, the People, and Parliamentary Management in the First Six Months of the Long Parliament," https://www.jstor.org/stable/1875621 Accessed February 25, 2019; Mark Kishlansky, "The Emergence of Adversary Politics in the Long Parliament," http://www.jstor.org/stable/1875623 Accessed November 18, 2016; John K. Gruenfelder, "The Electoral Patronage of Sir Thomas Wentworth, Earl of Strafford, 1614-1640," https://www.jstor.org/stable/1875620 Accessed March 30, 2019; Clayton Roberts, "The Earl of Bedford and the Coming of the English Revolution," https://www.jstor.org/stable/1875622 Accessed March 30, 2019

26 Hirst, "Unanimity in the Commons," 52

27 Hirst, "Unanimity in the Commons," 62

28 Hexter, "Power Struggle, Parliament, and Liberty in Early Stuart England," 24. On Farnell, see also Hill, "Parliament and People in 17th-Century England," 105-107

of our writers directly confronts the question of the nature of the troubles between king and Parliament. Kishlansky drowns out the noises of conflict by pulling out the stops on consensus, thus producing an improbably loud sound of dovelike cooing. Russell rather cavalierly evades the question by arguing that the apparent conflict between king and Commons was really a conflict between court and country. Farnell's essay and Christianson's on "The Causes of the English Revolution,"...manage to avoid any citation of the rich record of the House of Commons. They appear to regard that record as a matter of no importance, except as it reflects the control exercised by the peers over the Commons. Which, since the peers didn't, it doesn't.[29]

Revisionist attempts to propound new "theories" were thus built on sand, when not simply invented wholesale. Their real purpose was not to improve the historical understanding of the revolutionary period, but to deny or smother any hint of revolution, and at any cost, as an historian described in 1980:

> Unfortunately, the new revisionists...proceed to minimize to the point of nonexistence any substantive conflict between Crown and Parliament before 1640, and finally to deny that an "English Revolution" took place at all. What happened, in the new exegesis, was simply a breakdown of administrative order which, confessedly, got a little out of hand.[30]

A 1981 presentation on Revisionism posed a central question:

> ...one begins to wonder why parliament was summoned at all. If its demands were self-defeating, its proceedings disorderly, its subsidies not worth the fuss, and its initiatives and influence minimal, why did anyone bother with it? Why did not the crown dismiss subsidies as not worth the effort? A crucial element is missing...[31]

> The startling programme of the early 1640s did not spring new-born from the minds of a few parliamentary leaders. The abolition of Star Chamber and High Commission, the assault on [anti-Calvinist] ministers, the Triennial Act, and the Grand Remonstrance may have been revolutionary, but the criticisms on which they were based...had been voiced long before. Why else did the Grand Remonstrance begin with a rehearsal of the principal grievances of the 1620s?[32] ... The progression, slow and drawn out, was not inevitable, but it *was* a progression. ... Unless there is an understanding of how events relate to one another, the accumulation of details will lead nowhere.[33] [Emphasis in original]

In 1983 Jack Goldstone, while against Marxist interpretation, credited Manning, Fletcher, Pearl, and even Hill for their work demonstrating "rural

29 Hexter, "Power Struggle, Parliament, and Liberty in Early Stuart England," 29-30. Hexter is here referring to a similar essay by Paul Christianson, "The Causes of the English Revolution: A Reappraisal," *Journal of British Studies* 15, no. 2 (Spring 1976), https://www.jstor.org/stable/175132 Accessed May 2, 2019

30 Zaller, "The Concept of Opposition," 220

31 Rabb, "The Role of the Commons," 62

32 Rabb, "The Role of the Commons," 71

33 Rabb, "The Role of the Commons," 75, 76

riots and tumults in London" to have been "key" to the conflict,[34] and criticized the Revisionists' short-sightedness:

> Was the virtual simultaneity of the English Revolution, the *Fronde*, the rebellions in Catalonia, Naples, and Sicily, and the Ukranian revolt of Khmelnitsky merely a concatenation of coincidences? Was the whole "crisis of the 17th century" mere happenstance? If the English Revolution was simply a product of Charles's bad choice of policies and advisors, rather than part of a larger, more encompassing set of social changes, then its concurrence with similar political crises throughout Europe is baffling to say the least.[35]

Nine years after the critiques by Hirst and Hexter an historian could still observe, "If a revolution was not what took place in England between 1640 and 1660, at least in any strong sense of the term, then what did? This is a question to which revisionists by and large are not yet willing to commit themselves."[36]

In 1990, David Wootton detailed the debate, between Puritan ministers and royalists, over the issues of parliamentary sovereignty and the people's right to overthrow their leaders, in the pamphlet war of the time. Despite some of their later views, in these early years Puritans like Edward Bowles, Jeremiah Burroughs and William Prynne were espousing radical political ideas about government and society that did much to justify and extend the ground for revolution.[37] In *Plaine English*, Bowles (the almost certain author)

> proposed to form a bond or association of those willing to fight on should Parliament come to terms with the King, committed "To the maintainance of our establish'd Religion and Law *with all possible improvement.*" ... Here was a clear threat of a war not for constitutional but revolutionary ends, and of a settlement finally imposed against the wishes not only of King, but also of Parliament. ... Perhaps there was no "high road to civil war;" but there evidently was one from rebellion to revolution...long before the Leveller movement came into existence.[38] [Emphasis in original]

This evidence was greatly reinforced in 2007 by David Como, who established the existence of a clandestine pamphlet (one of many) advocating resistance to the king, printed in 1640 London before the convening of the Long Parliament:

> ...if a *King* maintaine a Faction about him, which goe about to oppresse his whole *Kingdome*, and *People* in their *Laws* and *Liberties*, and most of all in the true Religion...but seeks to make all his *Subjects, Slaves*, by bringing their *soules, Bodies, estates* under a miserable bondage: is it not now high

34 "Since the appearance of Manning's work [*The English People and the English Revolution*], even historians like Fletcher, committed to a largely elite perspective on the origins of the English Revolution, have been compelled to find a place for the people in the Revolution." Sharp, "The Place of the People in the English Revolution," 96

35 Jack A. Goldstone, "Capitalist Origins of the English Revolution: Chasing a Chimera," *Theory and Society* 12, no. 2 (March 1983): 145, https://www.jstor.org/stable/657429 Accessed 4 April 2020

36 Zaller, "What Does the English Revolution Mean?," 621

37 For Burroughs, see the section in Chapter 15, "Program and tactics of the radical Independents."

38 Wootton, "The Crisis of the Winter of 1642/3," 664, 668; Manning, *English People*, 242-243

> time...to stand up as one man to defend themselves and their Countrey, untill the Faction shalbe utterly cashered, and so the King reforme himselfe, and renew the *Covenant* and *Conditions* of the Kingdome to the good and just Satisfaction of the People.[39] [Italics in original]

This early propaganda came from an underground press operated by Richard Overton, the future Leveller leader.[40] That they were produced from such an early date proved that

> ...there existed, at least in London, an aggressive and organized confederation of activists, who were willing to engage in overtly treasonable behaviour...promoting parliamentary governance, upending the tyrannical style of prerogative rule that had evolved under Charles, and most significantly, abolishing the Church of England and replacing it with a purified order of gathered voluntary Churches.[41]

The Revisionists' "...presumed absence of radical political and religious ideas in the England of 1640"[42] is thus shown to be wishful thinking.

Looking back in 2015, Peter Lake described how Revisionism casually wrote off any inconvenient views to the contrary:

> ...there could be no ideological causes for the breakdown; Charles's failure had to be sought in his personality rather than his beliefs, ideology, or program. Hence Conrad Russell's otherwise rather eccentric insistence that Charles's "arbitrariness" was "temperamental" rather than "constitutional." Religion did not count as an ideology because it was something that just happened to people... Moreover, the more extreme manifestations of religious belief or affiliation like anti-popery could be categorized under the sign of the "irrational" and thus rendered even less capable of being rationally explained. Attempts at such explanation in terms of wider social or ideological contexts or forces could be dismissed as irredeemably reductionist.[43]

Thus, on the one hand, Revisionist academics blithely ignored the ideas in people's heads which they believed and argued about, and fought and killed for, while on the other, focusing at great length on the personality of the king.[44]

Contemporaries were far more cognizant of the real magnitude of what was occurring. A royalist tract of 1643 ended by declaring that if posterity asked

> "who would have pulled the crown from the king's head, taken the government off the hinges, dissolved monarchy, inslaved the lawes, and

39 "Englands Complaint to Jesus Christ against the Bishops Canons," quoted in Como, "Secret Printing," 65

40 Como, "Secret Printing," 38, 54, 69-70, 74, 82

41 Como, "Secret Printing," 75

42 Como, "Secret Printing," 78

43 Lake, "From Revisionist to Royalist History," 660. Lake's essay traces contradictions between the earlier and later writings of prominent Revisionists.

44 Lake, "From Revisionist to Royalist History," 661

ruined their countrey, — say, 'twas the proud, unthankefull, schismaticall, rebellious, bloody city of London..."[45]

In the first decade of the new century, Mark Kishlansky and Kevin Sharpe were still defending the actions of King Charles against his opponents.[46] In 2015, David Cressy cited their cold-blooded indifference to human suffering under Charles:

> While claiming, erroneously, that there was little public support for Burton, Bastwick, and Prynne, Sharpe at least acknowledged that their punishment in 1637 was a public relations disaster for Charles I's government... From the point of view of [Sharpe's] *The Personal Rule*,[47] however, it was not the degradation, mutilation, and perpetual imprisonment of a lawyer, a cleric, and a physician that mattered, or the heavy-handed overreach of the state, but rather the damage done to the image and authority of the king. Kishlansky, by contrast, stressed that the "martyrs" were not executed, as if this exhibits the tolerance of the Caroline regime.[48]

The construction of academic careers by Revisionists was founded merely on the basis of anti-communism. Given the purpose and frailty of their own positions, it was not enough to question Marxist interpretation; Revisionism had to malign its entire ideology, even if it took a denial of reality to do so. Any useful local research they performed, or analytical weaknesses they pointed to, were in service to their counter-revolutionary agenda. In the rampant conservative milieu of the 1980s their doctrinal posture was welcome, and treated seriously by capitalist academia, politicians, and media; it often still is.

To have a reasonably accurate and encompassing theoretical model does not mean social reality will conform to it in every last instance or detail.

> The history of society is thus a collaboration between general models of social structure and change and the specific set of phenomena which actually occurred. This is true whatever the geographical or chronological scale of our enquiries.[49]

Historians therefore need to understand the developments in society over time as a *process*, and be able to clearly evaluate the relative importance and consequences of different factors, events, and patterns by organized study and honest discussion; to be able to distinguish what is *qualitative* from what is *quantitative*; to appreciate phenomena that are often contradictory as part of a complex social *whole*. This however was never the Revisionists' goal. Their aversion to analysis *per se*, a kind of know-nothing–ism; their at-

45 Quoted in Roy, "A Cavalier View of London," 168-169

46 Mark Kishlansky, "Charles I: A Case of Mistaken Identity," *Past & Present*, no. 189 (November 2005), http://www.jstor.org/stable/3600749 Accessed 8 November 2016; Kevin Sharpe, *Image Wars: Kings and Commonwealths in England, 1603-1660* (New Haven: Yale University Press, 2010), https://www.jstor.org/stable/j.ctt1nq151.1 Accessed May 14, 2020

47 Kevin Sharpe, *The Personal Rule of Charles I* (New Haven: Yale University Press, 1992)

48 Cressy, "The Blindness of Charles I," 655

49 Hobsbawm, "From Social History to the History of Society," 29

tempts to narrow the arenas for research, and declare any others illegitimate; their hunt for superficial gloss masquerading as proof; or their attempts to simply void issues through willful blindness; are the methods of intellectual bankrupts. But such methods have a madness: a deliberate, reactionary defense of the minority class of exploiters and oppressors of the majority in the here and now.

Revolution vs. reform

The enlistment of the London mass movement on the side of Parliament was responsible for the early victories over the king. Whether the people could have actually repulsed a force of the king's men in January 1642 may be open to question, but neither their purpose, background nor determination to do so are. The French ambassador was "astonished" at the lack of bloodshed due to the discipline of the people occupying the streets at the very end of 1641.[50] That the test never came was all to the good; it undoubtedly saved many lives and much agony. Both materially and politically, the king was unlikely to win. Deprived of control over the militia, obstructed by the aristocracy from creating a standing royal army (the pivotal weakness of the English monarchy), Charles was left with few resources.[51] An open military attack of a few hundred so-called "gentlemen"[52] on the 140,000 aroused people of London[53] would have forfeited whatever shreds of legitimacy were left to him after his ham-handed and futile attempt to arrest the Five Members. The urban middling people of 1641 were not the peasants of 1381: they had higher status and more money, were better educated and more skilled, less easy to intimidate, and had God, Parliament, and numbers on their side. Not liking his odds, Charles chose not to chance it and fled. As it was, his constant duplicity would in the end do him in.

It cannot be denied that thorough-going Protestantism, i.e., militant Puritanism, provided a broad ideological justification for revolution. The struggle over church governance for control of religious practices was a major political issue in promoting the conflict. The lower classes' (unsuccessful) attack on tithes was an instrumental part of their rejection of the established church under the bishops. The deep resentments of the royal monopolists by the middling class, who regarded them as oppressors in multiple ways, gave them every reason to fight the feudal monarchy and its highly undemocratic lackeys in the London government. Their revolutionary demand to abolish episcopacy (and also monopoly) implicitly meant, and was intended to achieve, the end of the feudal political system as it then existed. In Puritanism, the small and middle bourgeoisie found the expression for its all-sided opposition to a society in which religion had always oppressively

50 Pearl, *London and the Outbreak*, 279

51 "He [Charles] arrived at York with only thirty-nine gentlemen and seventeen guards." Cressy, "Revolutionary England 1640-1642," 35

52 Stephen Porter, "Introduction," in *London and the Civil War*, ed. Stephen Porter (New York: St. Martin's Press, 1996), 2-3

53 Hill, *Century*, 103; Cressy, *England on Edge*, 394; Lindley, *Civil War London*, 123

saturated social life. "These new ideas, therefore, were unavoidably colored by religion."[54] Although the kingdom of Jesus was a chimera, belief in it was not, and reflected a burning desire for a different kind of society, one which seemed newly within reach.

Radical religion's prominence as an issue was due to the urban workers and manufacturers, domestic traders and small retailers, who actually powered the revolution, and not to the hesitant rural gentlemen trembling in their seats in the House of Commons. What they shared was an acute sense of Protestantism under siege that made both classes diehard opponents of Laud and Arminianism, thus enabling their early unity to be more easily achieved. "...in their hatred of Roman Catholicism the most moderate members [of the House of Commons] did not yield to the most violent."[55] Pym knew what he was doing in his constant appeals for the defense of Protestantism.

The aristocrats' participation in capitalist markets, financial investment and early industry explains their general opposition to the monarchy's moves toward absolutism, and their willingness to ally with the anti-monopoly colonial merchant bourgeoisie. But with very few exceptions they were not themselves conscious revolutionaries, or even anti-feudalists.

"The contortions into which M.P.s got themselves while arguing passionately against abuses...and simultaneously trumpeting their eternal loyalty to the king, shows they were really pushed into a corner."[56] More plainly, it displays the untenability of their position. In 1648 most of Pym's middle group members would be excluded or arrested during the Army's purge of the Commons.[57] Even Russell, referring to the 1620s, makes a salient point, described by Hirst:

> ...when the parliament-men went home and donned their other hats as JPs or deputy-lieutenants, they often had to contribute to the implementation of privy council directives which had come under criticism in parliament.[58]

This highlights tensions within the ruling class, tensions which existed long before the outbreak of war. There is no reason historians, least of all Marxists, should shy away from acknowledging this manifest contradiction. On the contrary, it is essential to a dynamic understanding of the English Revolution. "The idea that the civil war was made by a 'revolutionary party in the House of Commons' has, one hoped, gone forever," Christopher Hill wrote in 1981.[59]

The stress laid on this point is necessary to spotlight the skew it introduced as the revolutionary process played out. The gentry's actions

54 Trinterud, "William Haller," 35

55 Hexter, *King Pym*, 20

56 Hill, "Parliament and People in 17th-Century England," 110

57 Underdown, *Pride's Purge*, 231

58 Hirst, "Parliament, Law and War in the 1620s," 456

59 Hill, "Parliament and People in 17th-Century England," 106

from 1640 on were at almost every step driven, as we have seen, by the people in the streets of the capital, or by their leaders with their explicit or implicit support. Hill was retreating under the blows of Revisionists who opportunistically exploited the weakness in his argument for their own purposes; but the largely neglected or disparaged work of Pearl, Manning, and Brenner, as well as Hill himself, provide much of the detail for a wholly consistent social class analysis.

"Anyhow, had it not been for that yeomanry and for the *plebeian* element in the towns, the bourgeoisie alone would never have fought the matter out to the bitter end, and would never have brought Charles I to the scaffold."[60] Most certainly neither would have the gentry. As traditional, paternalistic landowners they continued to dominate local political affairs, and the peasantry who were obliged to them for their copyhold leases. As such they were still, socially and legally, a feudal stratum *within* the ruling class, the untitled nobility, a role they continued to occupy even after the king's military defeat. Sequestration, and later composition, were designed to keep large estates more or less intact, and therefore beyond the peasants' ability to purchase them. The desire of many aristocrats to grow rich through capitalist investment required eliminating their obligatory feudalistic tenures to both the king and the copyholders. They did not hesitate to use the latter's subordination to violate their welfare through enclosure and other methods, any more than they did to use their newly-won power after the war to free themselves in law from the throne.[61]

Emergence of the bourgeois class

In this way they were able to clear the ground of the feudal overgrowth, to free capitalist production, and let the non-monopoly bourgeois class emerge. The moderate reform program of 1640-1641 espoused by the Commons' leadership, and codified in the Nineteen Propositions, quite transparently sacrificed the monarchy's power to their own. But trapped between the hostility of the monarchy and the unrelenting pressure of the London mass movement, the aristocrats were forced to go further than they had envisioned if they were to achieve their goals, and remain true to their principles. Their anti-absolutist program was progressive precisely because it dovetailed with the bourgeoisie's need to smash feudalism: the removal of government interference in the economy, religion, personal liberty, and above all, property. The alliance provided a portion of them confidence to act. Nonetheless, the gentry's dualistic social position made them irresolute, causing them to hold the door open for the king's return. The Commons repeatedly tried to negotiate a new governmental arrangement with Charles, right up through 1648; the only differences were over how much to concede. In the summer of 1643 they very nearly voted to throw in the towel, and once again, it was intervention by the Puritan populace and their bourgeois leaders that saved the outcome for the men now in power. Unsurprisingly

60 Engels, Introduction to *Socialism: Utopian and Scientific*, 389

61 Hill, *Reformation*, 146-148; "Land in the English Revolution," 28-29

then, when civil war became inevitable in 1642, a large minority of MPs deserted to neutrality or outright royalism.

Had Parliament not existed, or had it failed to win a measure of power independent of the crown, the events of 1640 to 1643 would undoubtedly have looked quite different. Recall that the Third Estate was forced to break with its assigned role in the *États-Généraux* of 1789 in order to transform themselves into the National Assembly. But the English gentry were quite content to keep their "house" as it was, only expanding its functions through the prolific use of committees. The purge of bishops from the House of Lords on the other hand required a mammoth struggle. The English Revolution might well have occurred rather later, and even more powerfully, had the Stuarts had as much rein as the Bourbon kings did.

The financial bankruptcy of the French feudal state was brought on by long and repeated military campaigns, including the American War of Independence. In 1788, 50% of French state expenditure was going to interest payments.[62] Bankruptcy however was not the main issue in 1640 England, although the king's government was heavily mortgaged. Money could be raised had Parliament been willing to do so,[63] and it repeatedly (and self-servingly) offered to take over the king's finances to, they claimed, "stabilize" them. But under the disruptive conditions of economic depression and class struggle the king was unable to obtain loans for his war against the Scots. Legally blocked from the usual sources of income, Charles' authority to raise new revenues was continuously challenged, calling into question his ability to rule. Had Ship money been successfully collected it "would have made the government independent of the will of Parliament and the tax-payers."[64] This was the crux of the political program by those leaders in the feudal government who wanted to reform it: in a money economy, control of taxation is crucial. Without it, armies cannot be paid, and control of armed forces means control of state power. "For many years during and after the Civil War, in their eagerness to defeat the old order, the moneyed classes willingly accepted taxes three and four times as heavy as those they had refused to pay to Charles I."[65] The revolutionary divide was deep, principled, and programmatic: a clash between social classes.

Even the king instinctively understood this essential, which is why he refused to compromise his powers: to give in would mean the end of any serious monarchy, and therefore the feudal order as a whole. "As Charles explained, 'Kingly Power is but a shadow' without command of the militia."[66] The feudal state was destroyed by the armed citizens of London in January 1642, and the more perceptive members of Parliament were happy to make use of this expedient. The absolutist aspirations of the crown were

62 Anderson, *Absolutist State*, 102, 104-106, 111.

63 Zaller, "The Concept of Opposition," 226

64 Hill, *Reformation*, 107-108

65 Hill, *1640*, 56-57

66 Schwoerer, "the Militia Controversy," 45

defeated. But just as the presence of Parliament had attenuated the power of the monarchy, it also attenuated the power of the Revolution. "[Parliament] was able for the most part — although not at all points — to hold the City movement within bounds."[67] By providing a reformist source of opposition to the monarchy it absorbed into itself a good portion of the people's fury. This did not leave the House of Commons itself unaffected. Rather, its resistance to the king and its reliance on the citizens transformed it from the feudal "great council" into a bourgeois legislature, a process codified after the fact by the Militia Ordinance.

Ultimately the parliamentarians were able to win the civil war only because they held London and its environs, which importantly gave them access to loans and tax revenue the king could not obtain. The pockets of bourgeois businessmen were deeper than those of rural landlords.[68]

Leadership and program

A *tactical* policy of support to the Commons' reform program by the middling/working class movement would have been more than appropriate. Its eventual betrayal was set up by its *strategic* reliance on Parliament, however much it tried to bring pressure on it. The failure to counterpose a democratic program *independent* of the gentry/merchant alliance left the middling people with no political alternative. Not until the Levellers later in the decade would this be provided. But in the first half of the 1640s, it was the House of Commons that benefited by acting in part as a political safety valve, dissipating the people's steam, thereby creating an opening for royalist counterrevolution.

This function, and danger, is most clearly seen in the governmental revolution that occurred in the midst of the democratic uprising that shattered the fabulously wealthy oligarchs' power in London. "From then on the City, indeed all London, was controlled by a new ruling group."[69] The new leadership, with the Commons' now eager sanction, rapidly undertook military measures to reform the militia and secure the City. But Parliament continued to treat with the king, codifying its reform program for control of the state in the Nineteen Propositions of June 1642. Only after the king's almost immediate rejection of these conditions did recruitment of an army truly begin.

This effort was successful, but the new leaders did not further mobilize the population in any extensive action except the building of the fortifications around London during 1642-1643. Eager volunteers, whose conscious identification with the revolution made them pick up and leave their more remote homes for London or other towns, were turned away rather than

67 Brenner, *Merchants and Revolution*, 394

68 Johnson, "Disintegration of the Parliamentarian War Effort," 160-161; Porter, "Impact of the Civil War Upon London," 175

69 G. E. Aylmer, "London's Revolution," *The Guardian*, 28 April 1961, https://www.proquest.com/historical-newspapers/londons-revolution/docview/184772837/se-2? Accessed August 25, 2020

made use of. The more militant Puritans and merchants complained of this,[70] but the sober business men on the Common Council, like the centrist gentry in the Commons, had no inclination to whip up the population any further than minimally necessary. They understood the political challenge to their own positions that could ensue from a maelstrom of unmediated activity by the oppressed people of England. Meanwhile, the official armies were for many months left unpaid and un-supplied, resulting in numerous military fiascos. When Parliament's noble commanders eventually got around to placing troops in the field, they mostly played at combatting the king's army. This unnecessarily prolonged the war, risked defeat, and stoked reaction.

The subsuming of the revolution under Parliamentary leadership, both in London and nationally, explains the absence of any Terror directed against the feudal ruling class as a whole. While the power of royalists in the City was curtailed, and some were jailed, no moves were made to arrest or remove the bulk of them, leaving them free to fester and undermine the revolution as they could. (Prominent royalists were arrested when the king's army was threatening London in October 1642.)[71] In particular, despite a great deal of talk, the alliance of the *haute* bourgeois monopoly company merchants with the crown was barely touched, let alone broken, as they were effectively able to buy off the Commons.

The Puritan leadership's failure to organize the people in arms against the aristocracy, as the Jacobins later did, was a direct consequence of the political unity between bourgeois moderates *and* radicals in the City government with the majority of the gentry in the House of Commons. The businessmen of the livery companies were chiefly concerned with maintaining stable conditions in which to conduct their commerce, and MPs were obviously not going to sponsor a campaign against themselves. Despite being less conservative, the Independent leadership was not prepared to break with parliamentarianism. As republicans or semi-republicans, the ascendant bourgeois legislative councils were their natural homes and arenas of struggle. This commitment condemned them to being displaced and made irrelevant until the Army interventions of 1647 and 1648. By that time, however, they were being challenged from the left by the more active and courageous Levellers.

The single exception to mobilizing the citizenry against Parliament came when it appeared the Commons was about to give up the struggle in August 1643. The implicit threat the bourgeois City leaders held over the gentry MPs, of independent popular action, was made manifest for the first and last time, and only in an unarmed demonstration at that. In this manner, they used it to recommit the Commons gentry to a resolute war against the king, thereby preserving the alliance between them, and cementing Parliament's leading role in it. Had the Commons voted to accept the peace proposals, dissolving the alliance, the London government would have faced the issue of leading the civil war itself. It is not possible to say what might have happened in this

70 Manning, *English People*, 244-245

71 Nagel, "The Militia of London," 72

hypothetical situation, but it was a clear crisis point for all the parliamentary factions, foreshadowing events after the war.

The Marxist class analysis summarized

The comparison with the French Revolution, only cursorily addressed here, illustrates the qualitative transformation of England during the revolutionary years. This transformation is explained by Marxist social class analysis, and Marx was well aware of the specifics of the English situation:

> The only explanation M. Guizot is able to offer of...the puzzle of why the English Revolution was conservative in character, is that it was due to the superior intelligence of the English, whereas its conservatism *is to be attributed to the permanent alliance between the bourgeoisie and the greater part of the big landlords*, an alliance which essentially differentiates the English Revolution from the French — the revolution that abolished big landownership by parcellation. Unlike the French feudal landowners of 1789, this class of big landed proprietors, which...incidentally, had arisen already under Henry VIII, was not antagonistic to but rather in complete accord with the conditions of life of the bourgeoisie. In actual fact their landed estates were not feudal but bourgeois property. On the one hand, the landed proprietors placed at the disposal of the industrial bourgeoisie the people necessary to operate its manufactories and, on the other, were in a position to develop agriculture in accordance with the state of industry and trade. Hence their common interests with the bourgeoisie; hence their alliance with it.[72] [Emphasis added]

The alliance of the Atlantic merchants and Puritan preachers with a section of the aristocracy brought the revolutionary part of the bourgeois class — colonial merchants and middle layers of the livery companies — to power in London. Only later, with the Independents' seizure of power via the New Model Army in 1648, were the radical pro-capitalist forces able to go further. They created a republic, without and against the bulk of the landowners and by-then hostile Presbyterians in London. In both instances they had decisive support from a mass of the petty bourgeois middling class.

The disregard of abundant material on unwelcome historical episodes by state powers or their apologists is not unusual. It is not for lack of research or published work that propagandists and pundits can and do disseminate the most outlandish and frivolous theories. The actual events shown here support the orthodox Marxist viewpoint of a social conflict that abolished the feudal political system, and brought major sections of the capitalist class to power, however much conservative historians tried to wriggle around it.[73] A resolutely non-Marxist historian wrote in 1970:

> Puritanism, constitutional opposition and business opposition were all assaulting the same citadel. ... It would be absurd to suggest that constitu-

72 Marx, "A Review of Guizot's Book," 348-349

73 George, "The Making of the English Bourgeoisie," 385-391

> tional ideas *per se* could have attracted such wide support if they had not been intimately connected with men's material interests.[74]

The paramount weight of the capitalist economy by 1600 affected every social class in England. Aristocrats ramped up their participation in agricultural markets servicing the urban areas. Economic growth allowed, and inflation compelled, them to rationalize their country holdings and/or make investments in manufacture or trade, to maintain their idle livings. Enclosures were the most direct method to improve estates. Displaced peasants became urban or rural wage workers to the extent they could find work at all. More well-off and adventurous members of the petty-bourgeois middling class, from families of minor gentry and yeomen, or urban business, spilled into the opening of colonial free trade, breaking the stranglehold of the joint-stock companies. Having made fortunes, they used their money and connections to assume leading roles in the democratic movement that smashed the feudal monarchy, church hierarchy, and monopolist oligarchy.

This put mainly radical Independent colonial merchants and moderate Presbyterian businessmen of the livery companies into power in London, in alliance with the bourgeoisified aristocratic investors in Parliament. The pro-capitalist gentry were dedicated to security of property, persons and even reformed religion as long as these were under their own control. Despite all of the leftover trappings of feudal society, neither the divisions within the bourgeois class in this early revolutionary period, nor the strains on its alliance with the reforming landowners, change the fact that the royal court, established church, and London oligarchs — in short, the feudal state — had been overthrown and replaced.[75] A simple fact Revisionist historians, and not only them, did their mightiest not to acknowledge.

The divisions within the bourgeois/aristocratic alliance and its component parts, leading up to the Commonwealth and Cromwell's Protectorate, are subjects for another work. That the new ruling class' insecure hold on power would be interrupted by the Restoration in 1660 (the real Interregnum) changes nothing. "...the Stuart monarchy came back in 1660. The old regime, however, was not restored along with it."[76] The gains of the revolution meant that English society could no more return to its pre-1640 condition than Mary Tudor could reverse her father's Reformation. The bourgeois revolution, supported by and building on the mid-century events, would be completed in 1688-1689, triumphing over absolutism once and for all.

But that is down the road. As the Civil War dragged on and conditions worsened, disappointment and reaction would grow and take over the city. The locus of revolutionary action would shift to the soldiery of the New Model Army. The same worker-craftsmen and rural yeomen constituted the main repository of revolutionary cadre, driven by their highly radical, more

74 Ashton, "The Civil War and the Class Struggle," 105

75 Brenner, *Merchants and Revolution*, 373

76 Tyacke, "Revolutionary Puritanism," 767

egalitarian Puritan principles. Pro-revolutionary forces remained in London and other towns as well. But during the long pause in the war (1646-1647), it was the Army troops, disciplined and battle-hardened, and influenced by the Levellers, who had developed a new view of themselves as a collective social group of consequence. And they would not just stand idly by and let go of all they had so painfully won.

APPENDIX

English Rulers 1485-1714

Tudors

Henry VII	1485-1509
Henry VIII	1509-1547
Edward VI	1547-1553
Mary I	1553-1558
Elizabeth I	1558-1603

Stuart Era

James I and VI	1603-1625 (England and Scotland respectively)
Charles I	1625-1649 (Civil War 1642-1648)
Commonwealth	1649-1653
Protectorate	1653-1659 (Richard Cromwell 1658-1659)
Charles II	1660-1685
James II and VII	1685-1688
William III & Mary II	1689-1702
Anne Stuart	1702-1714

Timeline of Events

1618

- Depression in English textile export trade.
- Thirty Years' War begins on the Continent.

1625

- Death of James I and VI. Charles I becomes king.
- Charles appoints a royal governor to Virginia colony.

1626

- Charles bans Calvinist teaching.

1627

- Charles orders forced loan.
- Five Knights case.

1628

- For the first time, London Common Hall nominates and elects all four MPs to the House of Commons.
- Parliament passes the Petition of Right.
- Anti-enclosure riots by peasants break out in the west of England. Disturbances continue for the next three years.

1629

- Beginning of Charles I's Personal Rule without Parliament.

1633

- William Laud appointed Archbishop of Canterbury by Charles.

1635

- First annual collection of Ship Money extended to inland areas.

1637

- Rebellion in Scotland over imposition of Episcopal Book of Common Prayer;
- Puritan religious martyrs of Star Chamber maimed and imprisoned.

1638

- Scots raise army to defend the National Covenant.

1639

- First Bishops' War.
- London Common Council votes petition of grievances.

1640

JANUARY

- Earl of Strafford raises Catholic army in Ireland to fight the Scots.

APRIL-MAY

- Short Parliament.
- Charles imprisons four Aldermen for refusing to provide lists of wealthy men in their parishes.
- Rowdy demonstration at Archbishop Laud's palace.

JUNE

- Common Council refuses king's request for 4,000 troops.
- King seizes Mint in the Tower.

JUNE/JULY

- Mutinies and disorders of conscripted English soldiers marching north to Scotland.

AUGUST

- Scots' army invades England — Second Bishops' War.
- Twelve peers petition king for new Parliament.

SEPTEMBER

- Popular London petition of grievances with 10,000 signatures presented to king in York.
- London Common Hall rejects oligarchic candidate for Mayor, elects four Puritan merchants as MPs.

OCTOBER

- High Commission session at St. Paul's Cathedral disrupted by large throng.

NOVEMBER

- Long Parliament opens.
- Puritan martyrs of the Star Chamber freed and enter London in triumph with demonstration of 10,000 people.

DECEMBER

- "Root and Branch" mass petition for abolition of episcopacy presented to House of Commons.
- Archbishop Laud and Earl of Strafford impeached by House of Commons.

1641

JANUARY

- Commons investigates monopoly overseas companies, reverses many previous actions by magistrates who are penalized.

MARCH

- Archbishop Laud attempts to flee London, committed to Tower.
- Commons votes to exclude bishops from House of Lords and clergy from government offices.

APRIL

- Mass petition and demonstrations against Strafford.
- House of Commons passes Bill of Attainder condemning Strafford to death.
- Commons passes bill against dissolution of Parliament without its consent.
- John Pym and Earl of Bedford negotiate with Charles to join government.

MAY

- Mass demonstrations against Strafford at Parliament.
- First Army Plot — Armed men sent by Charles to rescue Strafford from the Tower are refused entrance. Plans for *coup d'etat* by the king and royalists discovered.
- Protestation passed in Commons.
- House of Lords passes the Bill of Attainder and bill against dissolution of Parliament without its consent.
- Strafford executed.

JUNE

- London Common Hall demands the right to elect both sheriffs.
- House of Lords rejects exclusion of bishops.

JULY

- Star Chamber and High Commission abolished.
- House of Lords rejects exclusion of Catholics from government

offices.
- Modified Root and Branch bill introduced in Commons.

AUGUST

- Charles leaves London for Scotland.
- Commons votes to abolish superstition and idolatry.

SEPTEMBER

- King signs treaty with Scots whose army returns to Scotland.
- Commons and Lords issue conflicting orders on religion.
- Attacks on churches and ministers by radical Puritans increase.
- Peasants attack royal deer park for food.

OCTOBER

- Charles conspires against Covenanter leaders in Scotland — "The Incident" sparks fears of popish plots in England.
- At request of both Houses Trained Bands are posted by Earl of Essex to guard Parliament.

NOVEMBER

- Irish rebellion and massacre of colonial Protestants.
- Commons votes requirement for Parliamentary approval of all military officers appointed by the king.
- Grand Remonstrance passed by Commons.
- Motion to quash first Militia Bill fails in Commons.
- King returns to London. Against Parliament's wishes, he replaces Earl of Essex with Earl of Dorset over Trained Bands.
- Dorset orders Trained Bands to shoot at hundreds of demonstrators with swords and staves chanting "No bishops!" at House of Lords.

DECEMBER

- Grand Remonstrance presented to king.
- Mass petition presented to Commons for expulsion of bishops and papists from House of Lords, and parliamentary control of militia.
- House of Lords again reaffirms episcopacy as state church.
- Commons votes to publish Grand Remonstrance.
- Elections give Puritan radicals majority in London Common Council.
- Charles rejects the Grand Remonstrance, and replaces Lieutenant of the Tower with Colonel Lunsford, a royalist.
- Commons passes Declaration against Lunsford.
- Disturbances in London against Lunsford, shops close.
- King dismisses Lunsford, but authorizes Trained Bands to shoot to kill demonstrators.

- Large crowds at House of Lords chanting "No bishops!".
- Seven Cavaliers, including Lunsford, attack demonstrators inside Parliament with swords. John Lilburne leads crowd in defense.
- Demonstrators prevent bishops from entering House of Lords.
- Armed men assemble at Westminster Abbey and Whitehall.
- Cavalier guards twice attack demonstrators.
- Lords defeat motion "this is no free parliament".
- Twelve bishops protest their exclusion to Charles who declares laws passed without them null and void. They are impeached by Commons and imprisoned by Lords.
- King appoints new royalist to Tower, and again authorizes use of force against demonstrators. Common Council threatens anyone failing to report for duty in Trained Bands.

1642

JANUARY

- King attempts to arrest Five Members in House of Commons for treason.
- House of Commons takes refuge in London.
- Puritan opposition takes control in Common Council and elects London Committee of Safety (Militia Committee).
- Armed populace occupies the streets overnight in support of the Five Members, and against any *coup* attempt by the king.
- Charles appears at Common Council and demands Five Members be turned over to him.
- Armed people again guard the City overnight on 6 January, along with Trained Bands who join them without Mayor's authorization.
- House of Commons takes away the Lord Mayor's sole authority over the Trained Bands.
- Charles flees London.
- MPs return to Westminster accompanied by huge crowds, seamen and Trained Bands.
- Thousands of people from surrounding counties bring petitions of support with grievances to Parliament.
- Militia Committee reorganizes and expands Trained Bands.

FEBRUARY

- Mass petitions and demonstrations force Lords to pass bills to exclude bishops from their House, and to require Parliament's approval of military officers.

MARCH

- Militia Ordinance is declared law without royal approval.

APRIL

- Hull refuses to open gates to Charles.

MAY

- Royalists from both Houses leave Westminster to join King at York.
- Anti-enclosure riots and attacks on manors and deer parks occur in counties north of London.

JUNE-JULY

- Parliament sends its demands to Charles in the Nineteen Propositions. The king rejects them.
- Parliament recruits army in London headed by Earl of Essex.
- Parliament puts Lord Mayor on trial.
- House of Commons begins collection of voluntary contributions from London.
- Weapons caches are seized for Parliament around the country by yeomen and townsmen over the next months.
- Additional Sea Adventure to Ireland is authorized.

AUGUST

- Royalist Lord Mayor convicted and imprisoned by Parliament;
- Charles raises standard in Nottingham.
- Anti-royalist riots occur in East Anglia.

SETEMBER

- MP Isaac Pennington elected Lord Mayor.
- Charles disarms county Trained Bands, and accepts armed Catholics into his army.

OCTOBER

- Inconclusive Battle of Edgehill.
- London population builds initial fortifications against the king's army, completed the following spring.

NOVEMBER

- Essex's army, Trained Bands and Auxiliaries muster at Turnham Green, preventing a Cavalier attack on London.
- Weekly assessment on London is instituted by Parliament to pay for the war.

1643

JANUARY

- Three aldermen and other wealthy men imprisoned for refusing to pay assessment.
- Ordinance expanding weekly assessment outside London and establishing parliamentary county committees.
- Charles rejects London government's peace proposals, and demands City leaders be turned over as traitors.
- Parliament agrees on bill to abolish episcopacy.

FEBRUARY

- Charles' intercepted letters read in Parliament.

MARCH

- Radicals' Petition and Remonstrance asserts sovereignty derives from people and resides in Parliament.
- Ordinance for sequestration of delinquent's estates.

APRIL

- Negotiations in Oxford for treaty collapse.
- Subcommittee of Volunteers established at Salters Hall.

MAY

- Five royalist aldermen removed from office.
- Royalist conspiracy of Edmund Waller exposed.

JUNE

- Parliament passes new Vow and Covenant pledging defense of its forces against those of the king.
- Assembly of Divines authorized by Parliament.

JULY

- Parliament's three armies defeated.
- London government petitions Parliament for control over its armed forces.
- Petition with 20,000 signatures submitted to House of Commons for a "committee for a general rising".
- Meeting organized by Isaac Pennington and Henry Marten elects Puritan Sir William Waller military commander of Committee for a General Rising. Appointed by Parliament to head London forces under Militia Committee instead.
- Ordinance for Excise tax passed.

AUGUST

- Bristol falls to Royalists.
- Commons narrowly rejects Lords' peace propositions after 5,000 men demonstrate at Parliament in favor of war.
- Violent demonstration in London by women led by royalists against the war broken up.
- Impressment Ordinance passed.
- Essex's army and Trained Bands relieve siege of Gloucester, but are cut off from London.

SEPTEMBER

- First Battle of Newbury — army returns to London.

OCTOBER

- Isaac Pennington replaced as Lord Mayor by a moderate.

INDEX

Michael Sturza has been a life-long socialist political activist. A native New Yorker who grew up in Brooklyn, he learned about radical politics from his father who had been active in the labor movement of the 1930s. In 1966, at the age of 14, he attended his first mass anti-Vietnam War rally with other students from his high school. In college, while actively involved in working class struggles, he studied Marxism, and, in 1974, graduated cum laude from the State University of New York at Buffalo.

In the following decades, while continuing to study Marxism and the history of labor and liberation movements, he remained a labor activist. Throughout the '80s and '90s, Sturza also helped mobilize workers and minorities against Klan and Nazi terror in major cities across the country, demonstrating that the integrated labor movement was the main force that could defend all of their intended victims.

Read the full bio,
or contact the author,
on thmaduco.org:

For any related live events or collaborations, please contact The Mad Duck Coalition through its contact form.

Author Recommendations

Christopher Hill
The English Revolution 1640
The Century of Revolution 1603–1714
The World Turned Upside Down
Reformation to Industrial Revolution 1530–1780
Society and Puritanism in Pre-Revolutionary England

Valerie Pearl
London and the Outbreak of the Puritan Revolution

Brian Manning
The English People and the English Revolution

Robert Brenner
Merchants and Revolution

Mark O'Brien
When Adam Delved and Eve Span

Perry Anderson
Lineages of the Absolutist State

Karl Marx and Frederick Engels
The Communist Manifesto

And the special works of his fellow mad ducks.

Publisher's Concluding Note

Thank you so much for purchasing this work! Your support allows us to continue to avoid resorting to anti-consumer DRM practices and encourages our authors, not just this one, to continue following their passions and producing intellectually stimulating works. It also enables us to provide special programs for supporters like you!

One of our programs is a special discount for reviews, positive and negative! We believe that even negative feedback is vital feedback, so you should say what you really think. For more information about our review program, contact us through our contact form and select the appropriate category. In short, if the thought of supporting the authors and our jolly little coalition isn't enough to move you, we offer 5% off your next order for each review you post, with limitations obviously. So send us a message!

Information about our other programs and offers can be found on our website, including but not limited to: complimentary copies, contests, and collaborations.

Please reach out for further information. If you couldn't tell, we like to...*quack!!!*

The Mad Duck Coalition

The Mad Duck Coalition publishing house is a group of innovative intellectuals who want to publish what they are passionate about without compromising themselves or their work solely in the hopes of being published.

As such, The MDC publishes quality works that intellectually stimulate the mind, not necessarily the pockets. We wholeheartedly believe that quality and commerciality are two different things and that quality is far more important.

Check us out at thmaduco.org:

www.ingramcontent.com/pod-product-compliance
Lightning Source LLC
LaVergne TN
LVHW010649110826
845149LV00014B/2998
* 9 7 8 1 9 5 6 3 8 9 0 3 6 *